PHILIP'S

SUPERPLANNER
ROAD ATLAS
BRITAIN
& IRELAND

CONTENTS

III-VIII — ROUTE PLANNING

III	Key to Map Symbols
IV-VII	Route Planner
VIII	Distance Table

1-40 — ROAD MAPS

1	Key Map
2-31	Great Britain at 12 miles to 1 inch
32-40	Ireland at 12 miles to 1 inch

41-72 — TOWN AND CITY PLANS

41	Town Plan Locator
42-43	London Approaches map
44-45	London city plan
46-72	Town Plan section

73-88 — INDEX TO ROAD MAPS

Second edition published 1997
First edition published in 1996

Published by George Philip Ltd
an imprint of Reed Books
Michelin House, 81 Fulham Road, London SW3 6RB
and Auckland, Melbourne, Singapore and Toronto

To the best of the Publisher's knowledge, the information in
this atlas was correct at the time of going to press.
No responsibility can be accepted for any errors or their
consequences.

The representation in this atlas of any road, drive or track is
no evidence of the existence of a right of way.

The mapping on pages 42-43 is based upon the Ordnance
Survey 1:250 000 Digital Database with the permission of the
Controller of Her Majesty's Stationery Office © Crown
copyright.

The mapping on page 47 is based upon the Ordnance Survey
map with the permission of the Controller of Her Majesty's
Stationery Office © Crown Copyright. Permit No.976

The mapping on page 54 is based upon the Ordnance Survey
Map by permission of the Government of the Republic of
Ireland. Permit No. 6347

The other town plans are based upon the Ordnance Survey
maps with the permission of the Controller of Her Majesty's
Stationery Office © Crown Copyright.

Cartography by Philip's
Copyright © 1996 George Philip Ltd
Printed and bound in Spain by Cayfosa

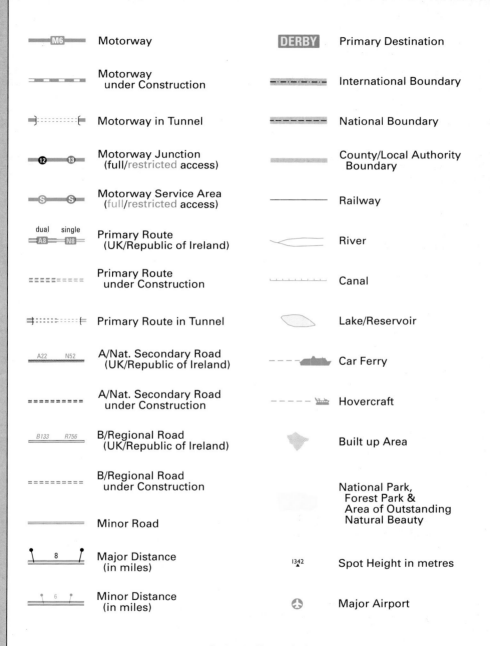

M6	Motorway
	Motorway under Construction
	Motorway in Tunnel
12 13	Motorway Junction (full/restricted access)
S S	Motorway Service Area (full/restricted access)
dual A8 single N8	Primary Route (UK/Republic of Ireland)
	Primary Route under Construction
	Primary Route in Tunnel
A22 N52	A/Nat. Secondary Road (UK/Republic of Ireland)
	A/Nat. Secondary Road under Construction
B133 R756	B/Regional Road (UK/Republic of Ireland)
	B/Regional Road under Construction
	Minor Road
8	Major Distance (in miles)
6	Minor Distance (in miles)

DERBY	Primary Destination
	International Boundary
	National Boundary
	County/Local Authority Boundary
	Railway
	River
	Canal
	Lake/Reservoir
	Car Ferry
	Hovercraft
	Built up Area
	National Park, Forest Park & Area of Outstanding Natural Beauty
1342	Spot Height in metres
✈	Major Airport

Scale: 12 miles to 1 inch

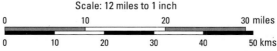

0 10 20 30 miles
0 10 20 30 40 50 kms

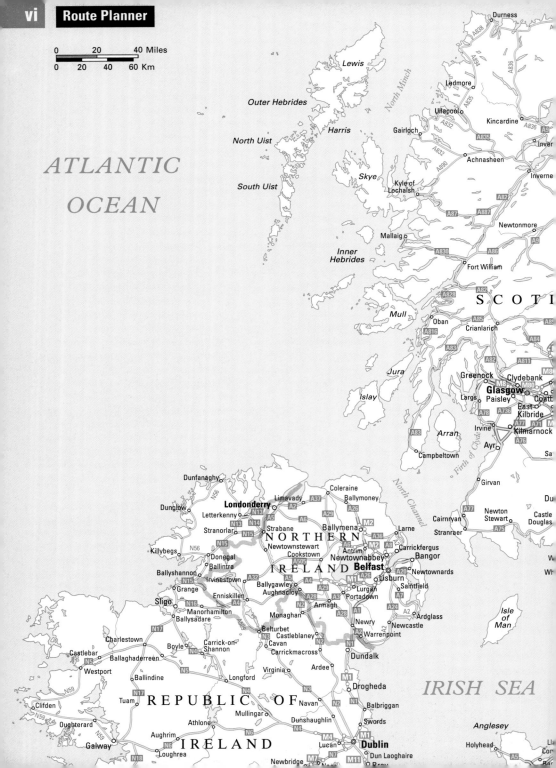

0   20   40 Miles
0   20   40   60 Km

ATLANTIC

OCEAN

Durness

A838

Lewis

Outer Hebrides

Ledmore

Ullapool
A832

Kincardine
A836

Inver

Harris

Gairloch
Achnasheen
A832

Inverne

North Uist

A890

Kyle of
Lochalsh

A87

Newtonmore

South Uist

Skye

A830

A86

Mallaig

Fort William

*Inner
Hebrides*

A828   A82

S C O T I

Mull

A85
Oban

A816
Crianlarich

A82

A83

A811

Jura

A82

M8
Greenock   Clydebank
M80
Glasgow   Coat

Islay

Largs   Paisley   East
Kilbride
A78   A736
A77   A71
Irvine   Kilmarnock
A83   *Arran*
A76

Ayr   Sa

Campbeltown

Girvan

A77
Newton
Stewart

Cairnryan
Stranraer   A75

Castle
Douglas

Du

Dunfanaghy

Coleraine
Ballymoney

North Channel

Larne

Dunglow   **Londonderry**   Limavady
A37
Letterkenny   N13   A2
A6   A29   A26   M2

*Isle
of
Man*

Stranorlar   N15   N14
N13
Strabane   **NORTHERN**
Ballymena
A36

Carrickfergus

Killybegs   N56   N15   Newtownstewart   A505   M2   A8
Cookstown   Antrim   Bangor

Donegal   Ballintra   **IRELAND**   A6
Newtownabbey
Newtownards

Ballyshannon   A32   Irvinestown   **Belfast**
A4   Ballygawley   A26   M1   Lisburn   A20
Grange   Aughnacloy   A28   Lurgan   Saintfield
N15   Enniskillen   A4   N2   Portadown   A7

Sligo   N16   Monaghan   Armagh   A1   A24   A2   Ardglass
Manorhamilton   A28   Newcastle
Ballysadare   Newry

Charlestown   N17   Belturbet   N2   Warrenpoint

IRISH   SEA

Castlebar   N5   Boyle   N4   Carrick-on-   Castleblaney
Ballaghaderreen   Shannon   Cavan   Dundalk

Westport   N5   Carrickmacross

Ballindine   Longford   Virginia   Ardee   M1
Drogheda

Clifden   N59   Tuam   N4   Navan   Balbriggan

REPUBLIC   OF   Mullingar   Dunshaughlin   Swords

Oughterard   Athlone   N6   *Anglesey*

Galway   N18   Aughrim   M4   M50   **Dublin**
Loughrea   Lucan   Dun Laoghaire
Holyhead   A5

IRELAND   Newbridge   Bray

0   20   40 Miles
0   20   40   60 Km

Thurso
Wick
A882
A895
A9

Moray Firth

Fraserburgh
Elgin
Peterhead
ardon
A96
A98
A952
A96
A95

Aberdeen
A93
Braemar

NORTH

SEA

A90 Montrose
A93 Forfar
A92 Arbroath
AND
A90 **Dundee**
Perth
A914 St. Andrews
M90 Glenrothes
A91 A915
Firth of Forth
tirling A92 Kirkcaldy
Falkirk Dunfermline
M9 **Edinburgh** A1
mbernauld
M8 Livingston A68
irdrie A71
dge A702 A703 A7 Berwick-upon-Tweed
otherwell A721 A72 Peebles Coldstream
A702 Galashiels
Jedburgh
A68
uhar Hawick Alnwick
Moffat A697
A76 A7
A74(M) Ashington
fries A75 Morpeth
A696 Tynemouth
Newcastle-upon-Tyne South Shields
Gretna A69 Hexham Gateshead **Sunderland**
Carlisle A692 Washington
A596 Durham A19
A68 Hartlepool
A6 A1(M)
kington Penrith Redcar
A66 Keswick A66 **Stockton-on-Tees**
haven A591 Brough **Middlesbrough**
A595 A685 A66 Darlington Whitby
Ambleside A171
Windermere A19
Kendal Scarborough
ENGLAND
A590 Thirsk
A170
rrow-in-Furness Ripon A165
A61 A1(M) A64 Bridlington
Morecambe Harrogate York A166
Lancaster A59 Wetherby
Fleetwood Clitheroe Keighley A19
Blackpool M6 Selby A614 **Kingston upon Hull**
M55 **Bradford** **Leeds**
Preston Burnley Goole
Southport M61 Blackburn Halifax Dewsbury A15 Immingham
Crosby Rochdale Wakefield A19 M180 Scunthorpe Grimsby
Wigan **Bolton** Bury **Huddersfield** Barnsley Doncaster A46 A16
St. Helens M58 Salford Oldham M62 Rotherham Gainsborough
Wallasey **Liverpool** Sale **Manchester** A628 A16
Birkenhead A561 **Stockport** **Sheffield** Lincoln A158
A55 Ellesmere Port Runcorn **Warrington** A6 Macclesfield Worksop A57 Skegness
udno Northwich M6 Chesterfield A614 A15
Queensferry Buxton M1 A16
Mansfield

HOW TO USE THIS TABLE

Distances are shown in miles

Example: the distance from Cambridge to Dover is 125 miles

	London	Cambridge	Cardiff	Dover
Cambridge	169			
Cardiff	190	45		
Carlisle	289	264	277	
Dover	389	238	125	202
Dundee	523	152	441	406	430

Map of Great Britain showing: John o' Groats, Inverness, Fort William, Oban, Aberdeen, Dundee, Glasgow, Edinburgh, Stranraer, Carlisle, Newcastle upon Tyne, York, Leeds, Kingston upon Hull, Manchester, Liverpool, Sheffield, Lincoln, Holyhead, Shrewsbury, Aberystwyth, Birmingham, Norwich, Cambridge, Fishguard, Gloucester, Harwich, Swansea, Oxford, London, Cardiff, Bristol, Dover, Southampton, Brighton, Bournemouth, Land's End, Plymouth

Distance table (distances in miles)

Each row lists distances to the cities named in the diagonal above it, in the order:
London, Aberdeen, Aberystwyth, Birmingham, Bournemouth, Brighton, Bristol, Cambridge, Cardiff, Carlisle, Dover, Dundee, Edinburgh, Fishguard, Fort William, Glasgow, Gloucester, Harwich, Holyhead, Inverness, John o' Groats, Kingston upon Hull, Land's End, Leeds, Lincoln, Liverpool, Manchester, Newcastle upon Tyne, Norwich, Oban, Oxford, Plymouth, Sheffield, Shrewsbury, Southampton, Stranraer, Swansea.

- **London**
- **Aberdeen** — 517
- **Aberystwyth** — 445 211
- **Birmingham** — 114 420 117
- **Bournemouth** — 147 207 564 107
- **Brighton** — 92 163 253 573 52
- **Bristol** — 147 82 81 125 493 122
- **Cambridge** — 169 116 154 100 214 471 54
- **Cardiff** — 190 45 182 117 103 105 505 157
- **Carlisle** — 289 264 277 370 343 196 224 221 301
- **Dover** — 389 238 125 202 82 174 194 292 588 71
- **Dundee** — 523 152 441 406 430 517 495 349 376 67 448
- **Edinburgh** — 56 462 96 385 345 373 456 439 292 320 125 390
- **Fishguard** — 399 460 331 297 112 270 154 291 222 170 56 504 260
- **Fort William** — 486 144 127 596 206 485 479 486 575 539 392 430 149 510
- **Glasgow** — 101 376 44 83 488 96 385 372 373 468 439 292 320 145 397
- **Gloucester** — 346 454 153 349 410 191 247 56 123 35 159 99 56 102 468 109
- **Harwich** — 196 432 543 337 413 469 125 336 246 67 217 128 187 167 281 535 76
- **Holyhead** — 349 191 330 438 167 333 394 360 231 216 270 206 334 288 148 111 439 269
- **Inverness** — 474 569 504 166 66 542 158 132 622 262 549 505 539 617 597 458 486 105 550
- **John o' Groats** — 129 603 693 628 295 195 671 285 259 747 391 680 630 668 741 724 574 601 232 663
- **Kingston upon Hull** — 518 394 231 196 198 254 369 280 234 295 256 158 244 139 233 245 264 134 223 364 184
- **Land's End** — 421 868 741 405 390 235 573 686 353 574 642 381 477 245 374 200 308 205 281 313 692 297
- **Leeds** — 405 55 487 360 176 223 174 215 329 237 202 258 260 119 232 145 194 260 255 113 169 327 189
- **Lincoln** — 68 371 44 554 427 216 155 159 291 399 272 258 314 202 191 208 85 183 197 209 90 199 383 131
- **Liverpool** — 129 75 361 130 511 382 102 265 140 216 329 160 216 286 299 120 165 194 161 272 234 93 104 341 202
- **Manchester** — 35 84 40 361 95 500 373 124 228 126 215 329 197 215 285 276 119 183 165 161 257 227 80 129 340 185
- **Newcastle upon Tyne** — 132 168 159 92 498 132 395 268 272 308 266 148 253 329 110 166 358 57 325 241 299 352 347 207 257 235 286
- **Norwich** — 264 185 220 105 176 421 149 654 529 311 73 204 385 504 343 366 422 174 289 262 62 252 175 214 166 276 496 114
- **Oban** — 492 233 307 308 387 307 665 346 244 117 427 524 441 92 49 481 123 117 585 188 477 468 465 565 530 384 412 178 499
- **Oxford** — 462 145 260 144 172 137 168 274 192 656 532 238 145 52 356 472 205 372 433 141 260 108 83 74 108 90 64 154 483 57
- **Plymouth** — 199 587 343 410 283 283 293 316 89 355 790 664 328 309 157 495 595 264 496 552 300 399 167 293 122 224 128 203 237 615 218
- **Sheffield** — 283 135 339 146 125 38 72 46 33 361 65 520 393 168 187 126 248 348 215 235 291 245 152 194 120 161 226 216 76 159 360 194
- **Shrewsbury** — 82 225 106 364 205 201 69 58 133 109 303 169 567 438 113 240 77 272 382 145 274 330 251 176 111 103 226 185 45 77 399 160
- **Southampton** — 185 199 151 64 530 206 324 221 239 204 232 228 256 723 598 293 166 105 433 541 233 438 500 143 324 121 148 76 61 31 128 201 547 71
- **Stranraer** — 445 277 263 500 379 148 403 158 220 221 298 220 585 259 379 262 338 435 343 84 195 392 124 167 496 101 390 379 378 475 444 297 325 228 402
- **Swansea** — 417 161 118 217 206 141 506 301 347 187 195 233 248 285 264 696 572 184 267 89 409 496 67 412 473 274 309 41 227 85 222 167 119 73 507 194
- **York** — 272 222 258 133 52 333 181 309 181 84 64 99 75 24 411 37 479 352 204 228 189 217 330 261 194 250 282 121 244 165 222 275 269 130 195 319 207

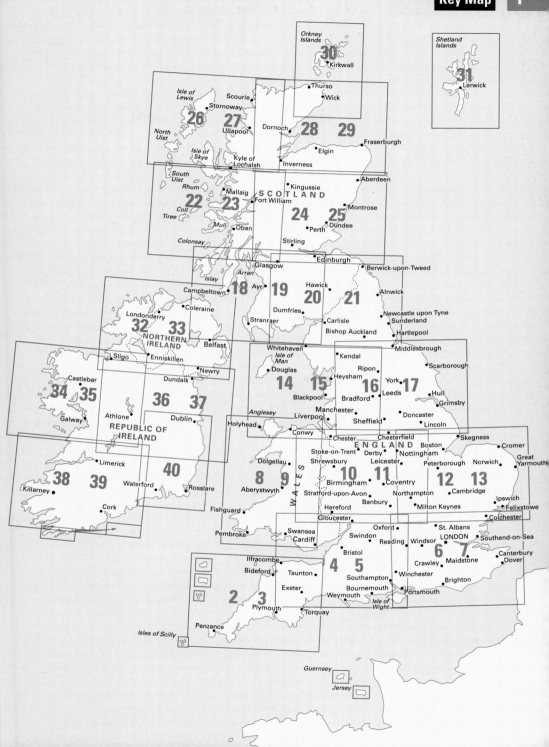

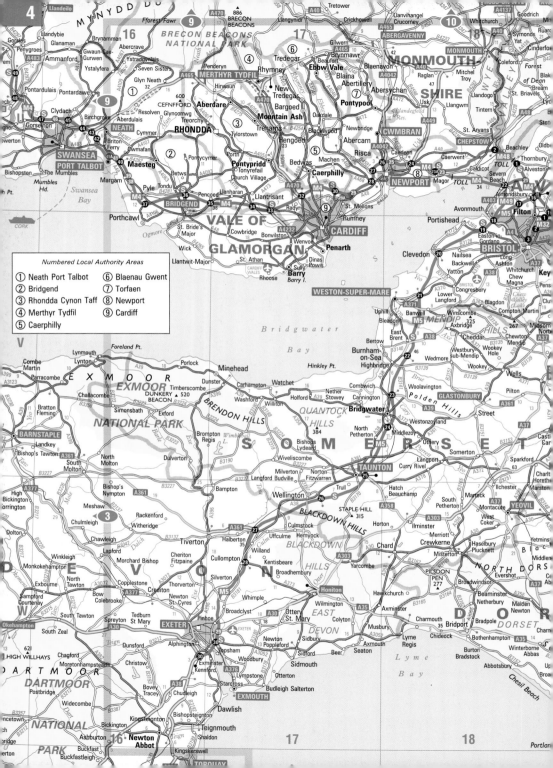

Numbered Local Authority Areas

① Neath Port Talbot
② Bridgend
③ Rhondda Cynon Taff
④ Merthyr Tydfil
⑤ Caerphilly
⑥ Blaenau Gwent
⑦ Torfaen
⑧ Newport
⑨ Cardiff

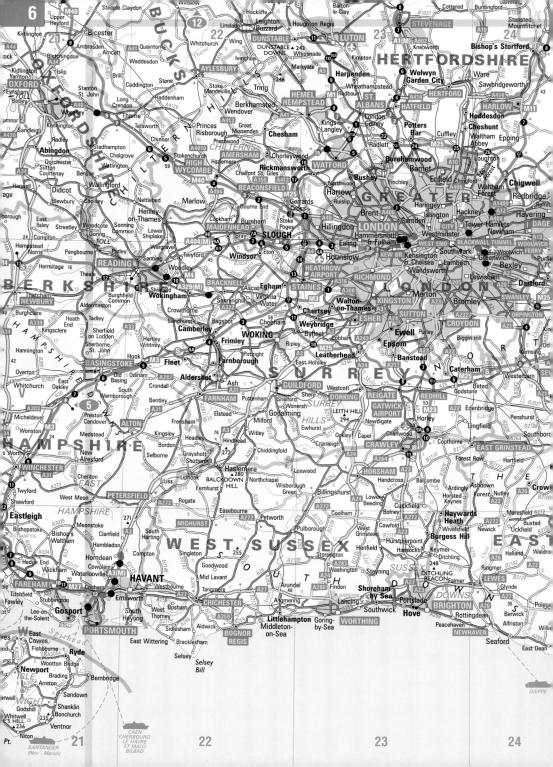

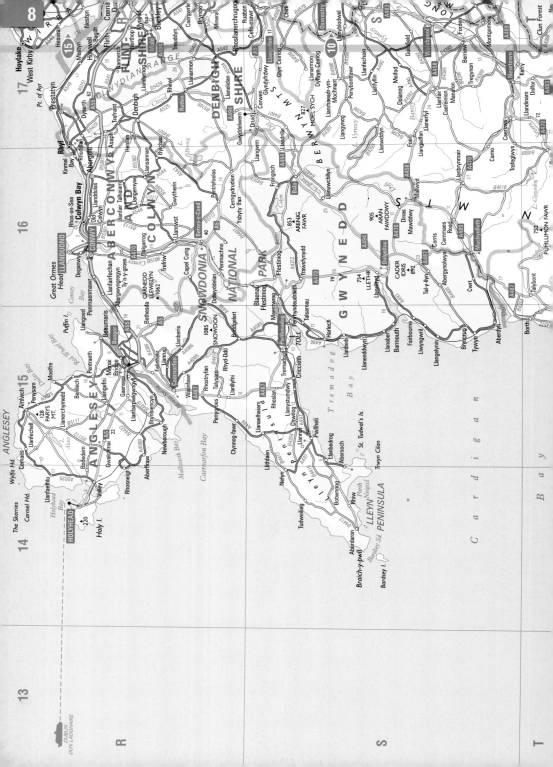

Numbered Local Authority Areas
① Neath Port Talbot
② Bridgend
③ Rhondda Cynon Taff
④ Merthyr Tydfil
⑤ Caerphilly
⑥ Blaenau Gwent

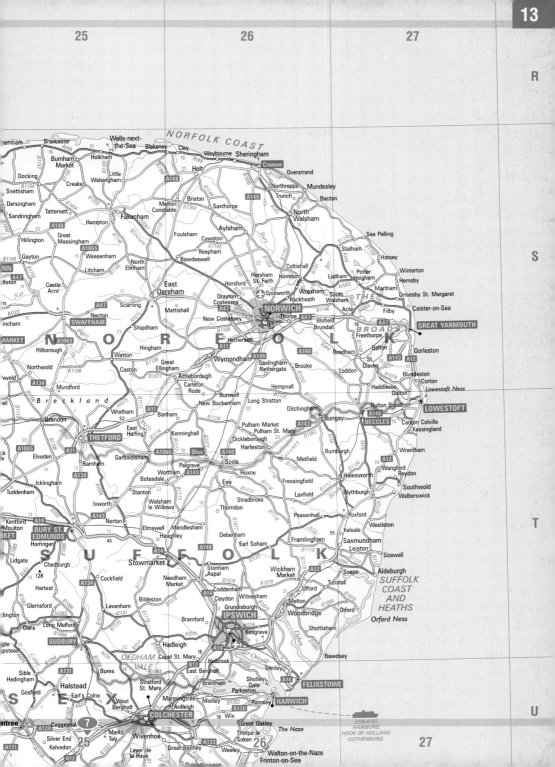

WHITEHAVEN
St. Bee's Hd.
St. Bees
Frizington
Cleator Moor
Egremont
20
LA

Beckermet
Sellafield
Seascale
Gosforth
Drigg
Ravenglass

Calder Bridge
A595
DIST
SC
NAT
PA

Pt. of Ayre

ISLE OF MAN

Bride
Andreas
A9
A10
Sulby
Ramsey
Ramsey Bay
Ballaugh
A3
Maughold
Maughold Hd.
Kirk Michael
SNAEFELL
620
16
A10
A18
A2
ARDROSSAN
(Summer Only)

P

Laxey
Peel
A1
A5
St. John's
9
A3
Onchan
Glenmaye
SOUTH
BARRULE
483
Foxdale
9
Douglas
Bradda Hd.
15
Port Erin
Colby
Ballasalla
RONALDSWAY
Port
St. Mary
Castletown
Calf of Man
Langness

Bootle
BLACK
COMBE
600
A595
Whicham
Haverigg
Dalton-in-
BARROW-IN-FURNESS
Vickerstown
I. of Walne
Hilps

BELFAST
(Summer Only)

DUBLIN
(Summer Only)

Q

I R I S H   S E A

BELFAST

Liver

ME

ANGLESEY
The Skerries
Wylfa Hd.
Cemaes
Amlwch
Carmel Hd.
Llanfechell
Penysarn
Dulas Bay
Llanfaethlu
128
PARYS
MT.
Moelfre
Holyhead
Bay
A5025
Llanerchymedd
A5
A5
Llanddyfnan
Benllech
Red Wharf Bay
Puffin I.
Great Ormes
Head
LLANDUDNO
Pt. of Ayr
Prestatyn
DUBLIN
DUN LAOGHAIRE
HOLYHEAD
A5
220
ANGLESEY
Bodedern
Pentraeth
Llangoed
Conwy
Bay
Rhos-on-Sea
Colwyn Bay
Kinmel
Bay
Rhyl
Rhuddlan
Dyserth
Abergele
R
Holy I.
Valley
Gwalchmai
A5
22
Llangefni
Llanfairpwllgwyngyll
Beaumaris
Deganwy
Old
Colwyn
CONWY
B5381
Llanddulas
Llanfair
Talhaiarn
St. Asaph
Trefnant
Rhosneigr
A4080
Menai
Bridge
Gaerwen
Bangor
A55
Llanfairfechan
Abergwyngregyn
Ty'n-y-groes
Llangernyw
Henllan
Denbigh
Aberffraw
Newborough
Brynsiencyn
Felinheli
Llanrug
A5
Bethesda
8
CARNEDD
LLEWELYN
1062
Dolgarrog
Trefriw
Llansannan
Bylchau
Caernarfon
Llanberis
Llanrwst
Gwytherin
Rhewl

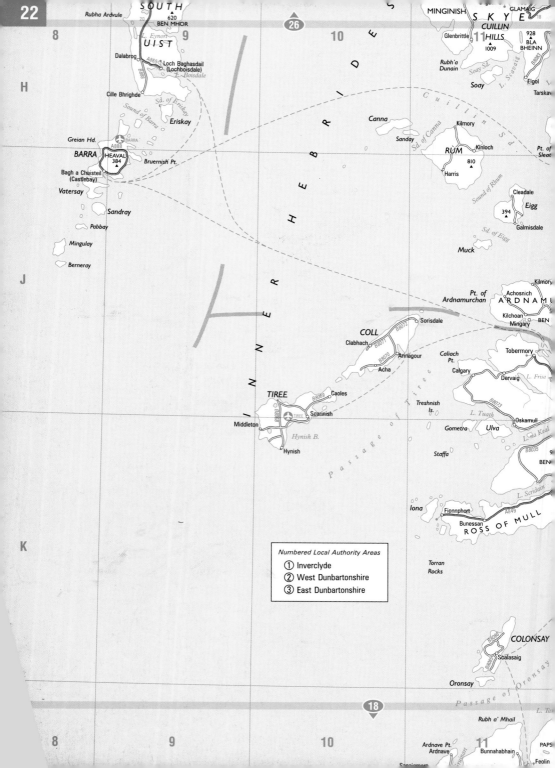

SOUTH
Rubha Ardvule
620
BEN MHOR

8   9   △ 26   10

SKYE
MINGINISH   GLAMAIG

CUILLIN
Glenbrittle   11 HILLS
928
BLA
1009   BHEINN

H

Dalabrog
Loch Baghasdail
(Lochboisdale)
L. Eynort
Sd. of Eriskay
L. Boisdale

U I S T

Rubh'a
Dunain

Soay   *L. Scavaig*
Elgol
Tarskav
Pt. of
Sleat

Cille Bhrighde

Canna
Kilmory

Eriskay   Sanday   *Sd. of Canna*

Sound of Barra   RÙM   Kinloch
810
Harris
Sound of Rhum

Greian Hd.   BARRA   Cleadale
HEAVAL
BARRA   384
384   Bruernish Pt.   394   Eigg
Galmisdale
Sd. of Eigg

Bagh a Chaisteil
(Castlebay)

Vatersay   Muck

Sandray

Pabbay

J

Mingulay

Berneray

Kilmory
Pt. of   Achosnich
Ardnamurchan   ARDNAM
Kilchoan   BEN
Mingary

Sorisdale
B8072

COLL
Clabhach   B8071   Caliach   Tobermory
Pt.
B8070   Arinagour   Calgary   Dervaig   *L. Frisa*

Acha

TIREE   B8069   Caoles   Treshnish
Is.   *L. Tuath*   Oskamull
TIREE   Scarinish   Gometra   Ulva   *L. na Keal*
Middleton
Hynish B.   Staffa   BEN
Hynish

L. Scridain

Iona
Fionnphort
Bunessan   A849
ROSS OF MULL

K

Numbered Local Authority Areas
① Inverclyde
② West Dunbartonshire
③ East Dunbartonshire

Torran
Rocks

COLONSAY

Scalasaig

Oronsay   *Passage of Oronsay*

△ 18

L. Tar

Rubh a' Mhail

8   9   10   11   PAPS

Ardnave Pt.   Bunnahabhain   Feolin
Ardnave

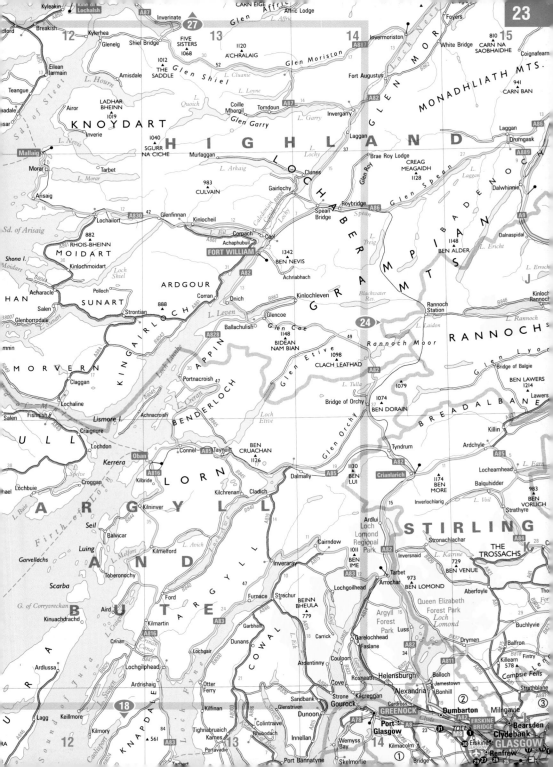

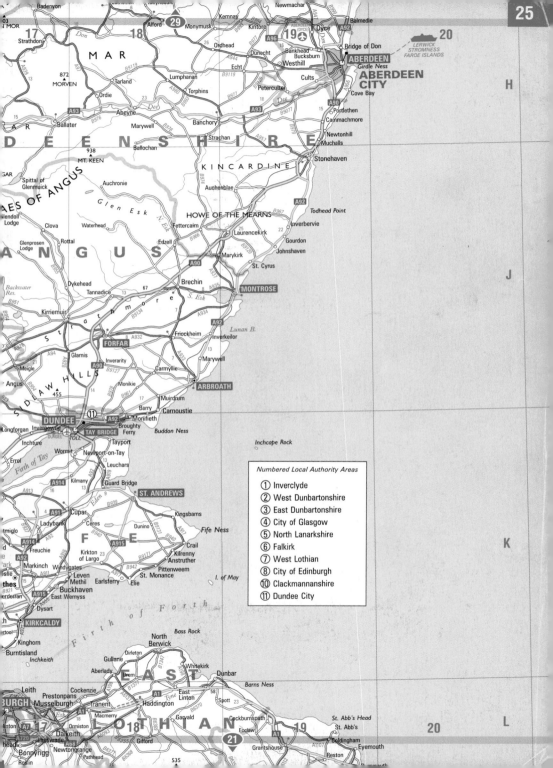

Numbered Local Authority Areas

① Inverclyde
② West Dunbartonshire
③ East Dunbartonshire
④ City of Glasgow
⑤ North Lanarkshire
⑥ Falkirk
⑦ West Lothian
⑧ City of Edinburgh
⑩ Clackmannanshire
⑪ Dundee City

E

F

G

H

John o'Groats
Canisbay
Duncansby Head
Duncansby
17
Freswick
Nybster
Sortat
15
Keiss
Sinclair's B.
Reiss
Noss Hd.
WICK
Staxigoe
A882
A9
Wick
Thrumster
Ulbster
16
Halberry Head

18

19

20

iemouth
Spey B.
Findochty
Portknockie
Cullen
Troup Hd.
Garmouth
Buckie
Portsoy
Macduff
Gardenstown
Rosehearty
Kinnairds Hd.
FRASERBURGH
Lhanbryde
Portgordon
Fordyce
Banff
B9031
Inverallochy
A98
New Aberdour
A98
St. Combs
Fochabers
Craibstone
B9031
Pennan
A92
Rathen
A96
Weachyburn
50
45
New Pitsligo
Strichen
Crimond
Rattray Hd.
Newmill
Aberchirder
B9025
Newbyth
New Pitsligo
B9093
St. Fergus
Mulben
Keith
39
Turriff
Cuminestown
Mintlaw
Longside
PETERHEAD
A Y
Craigellachie
Charlestown of Aberlour
Dufftown
A B E R D E E N S H I R E
Fortrie
New Deer
Maud
Old Deer
A950
Buchan Ness
Boddam
Laggan
Huntly
27
A92
26
Hatton
16
Cruden Bay
A952
49
STRATHBOGIE
A96
Badenscoth
Methlick
A948
NES
Ardwell
Kennethmont
Colpy
Rothienorman
Fyvie
Tarves
Ellon
Hackley Head
Cabrach
Rhynie
53
Oldmeldrum
A920
B9000
Newburgh
Badenyon
722 THE BUCK
B9002
Tullynessle
GARIOCH
FORMARTINE
25
Inverurie
Newmachar
17
18
19
20
Lumsden
Kemnay
Balmedie

B U C H A N

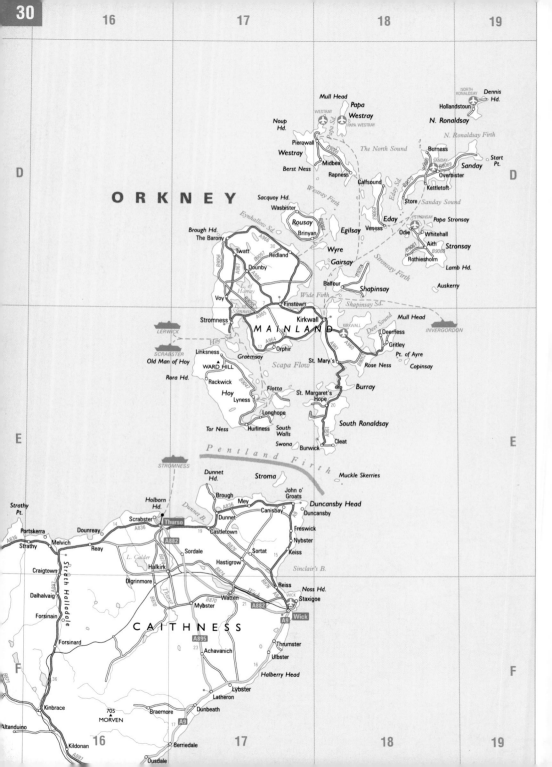

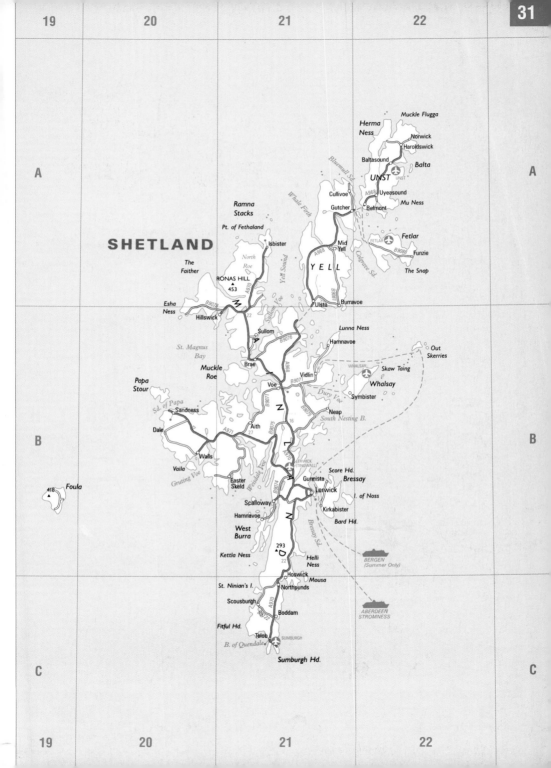

SHETLAND

Muckle Flugga

Herma
Ness

Norwick
Haroldswick
Baltasound
Balta
UNST
Cullivoe
A968 Uyeasound
Gutcher
Belmont
Mu Ness

Fetlar
FETLAR B9088 Funzie

Mid
Yell
The Snap

Bluemull Sd.

Whale Firth

Colgrave Sd.

Ramna
Stacks
Pt. of Fethaland
Isbister

YELL

The
Faither
North
Roe
RONAS HILL
453
Burravoe
Esha
Ness
Ulsta
Hillswick
22

Lunna Ness
Sullom
Hamnavoe
Out
Skerries

St. Magnus
Bay
Muckle
Roe
Brae
Vidlin
WHALSAY
Skaw Taing
Voe
Whalsay
Symbister

Papa
Stour
Sandness
Neap
Sd. of Papa
Aith
South Nesting B.

Dale
Walls
Vaila
Easter
Skeld
Gunnista
Score Hd.
Bressay
Gruting Voe
LERWICK
(TINGWALL)
Lerwick
Foula
418
Scalloway
Kirkabister
I. of Noss
Bard Hd.
Hamnavoe
West
Burra
293
Kettla Ness
Helli
Ness
BERGEN
(Summer Only)
Hoswick
Mousa
St. Ninian's I.
Northpunds
Scousburgh
ABERDEEN
STROMNESS
Boddam
Fitful Hd.
Toab
SUMBURGH
B. of Quendale
Sumburgh Hd.

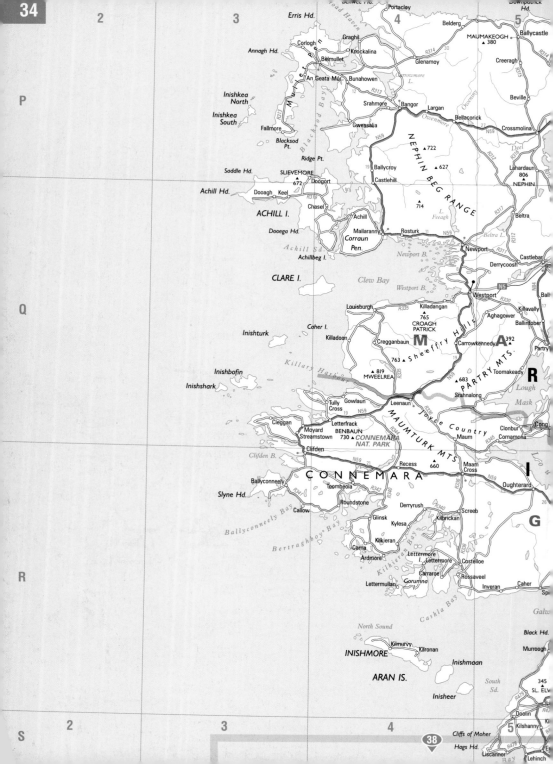

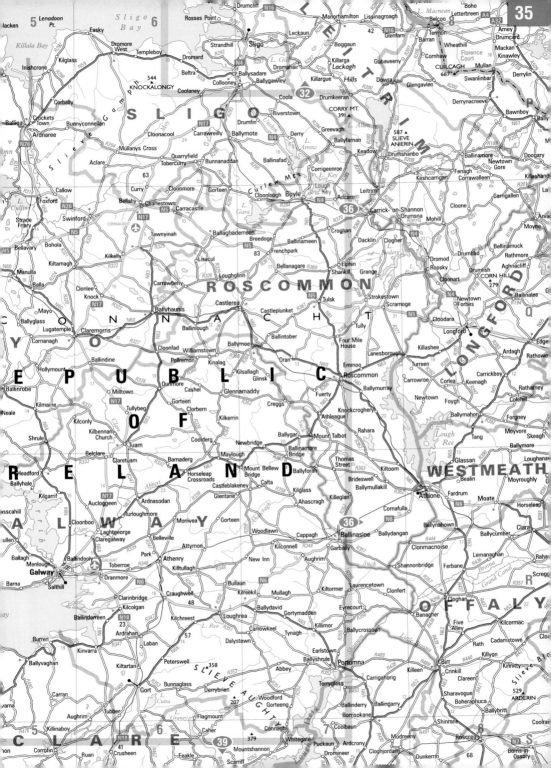

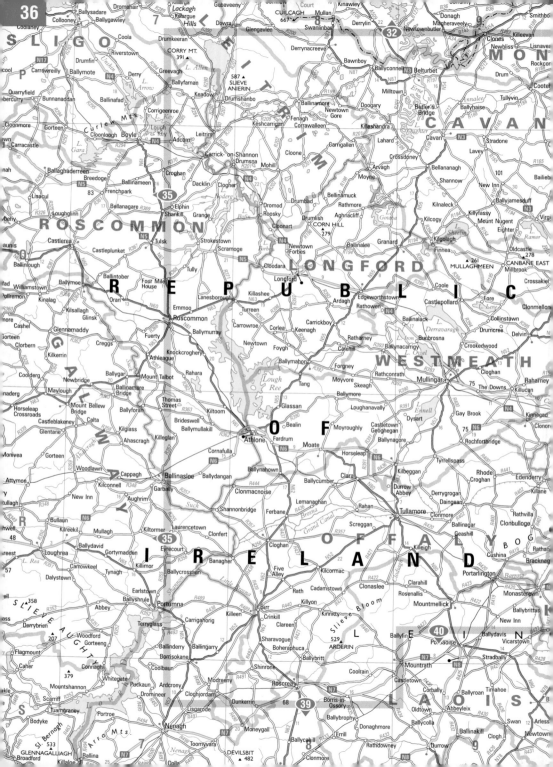

Key to Town Plan Symbols

	Through Route(dual/single)
	Secondary Road(dual/single)
	Minor Road
	Pedestrian Roads
	Restricted Access Roads
	Shopping Streets
	Railway
	Railway/Bus Station
	Shopping Precinct
	Park

✝	Abbey/Cathedral
	Ancient Monument
	Aquarium
	Art Gallery
	Bird Garden
	Building of Public Interest
	Castle
	Church of Interest
	Cinema

	Garden
	Historic Ship
	House
	House & Garden
	Museum
	Preserved Railway
	Railway Station
	Roman Antiquity
	Theatre

i	Tourist Information Centre open all year
i	summer only
	Zoo
	Other Place of Interest
H	Hospital
P	Parking
	Police Station
PO	Post Office
▲	Youth Hostel

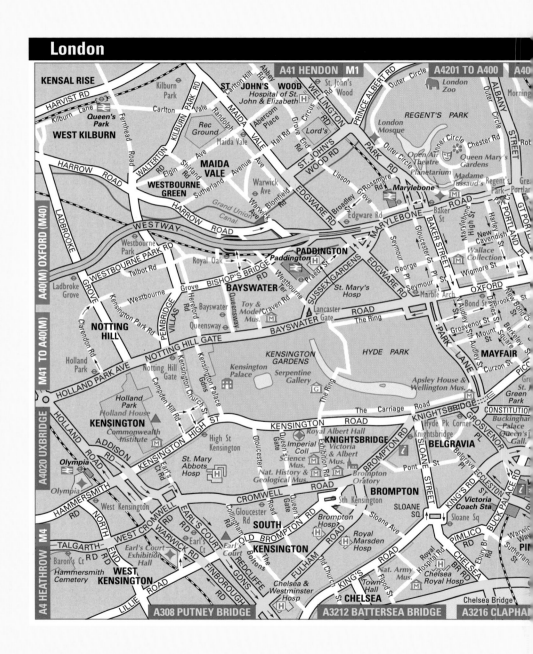

London

0   **Miles**   **1**

CMDEN TOWN **M1**   **A5203 TO A1**   **A1 HIGHGATE** **M1**   **A1200 TO A1**   **A10 TOTTENHAM, CAMBRIDGE**

HOXTON

King's Cross

PENTONVILLE RD

CITY ROAD

Grand Union Canal

Angel

SHOREDITCH

Shoreditch

St. Pancras

King's Cross Thameslink

Euston

CLERKENWELL

Old Street

Wesley's Chapel

Worship

Whitechapel Art Gall.

BLOOMSBURY

RUSSELL SQ

Farringdon

Barbican

Chiswell

Moorgate

Liverpool St

ZROVIA

British Museum

Barbican St. Barts

Mus. of London

CITY

Aldgate East

NEW OXFORD ST

HOLBORN

HOLBORN VIADUCT

NEWGATE

St. Paul's

Gresham

CHEAP

POULTRY

WALL

St. Helen's

Soane's Mus.

Chancery La

Bank

LEADENHALL ST

SOHO

City Thameslink

FLEET ST

LUDGATE HILL

SIDE

St. Paul's

Fenchurch St

Piccadilly Circus

Covent Gdn

Drury Lane

STRAND

Temple Ch.

Carter Lane

QN VICTORIA ST

CANNON ST

Cannon St

EAST

Tower Hill

Tower of London

Charing Cross

Transport Mus.

Leicester Sq

ALDWYCH

EMBANKMENT

UPR THAMES ST

LWR THAMES

Tower Gateway (DLR)

ST. JAMES'S

THE MALL

Charing Cross

Embankment

Waterloo Bridge

Blackfriars

SOUTHWARK

The Monument

HMS Belfast

Tower Br.

River Thames

Downing Street

Qn. Elizabeth & Royal Festival Halls

STAMFORD ST

SOUTHWARK ST

London Dungeon

London Bridge

St The Design Museum

WHITEHALL

Hayward Gall.

Waterloo East

Union St

Guy's Hosp

Jamaica Rd

Cabinet War Rooms

County Hall

YORK RD

THE CUT

SOUTHWARK BR RD

HIGH ST

LONG LANE

Abbey

St. James's Pk

Westminster

Waterloo

BOROUGH

Trinity

Spa Rd

PARLIAMENT

St. Thomas Hosp

St. George's Cath.(R.C.)

ST. GEORGE'S RD

Elephant & Castle

GREAT DOVER ST

Grange Rd

BERMONDSEY

Houses of Parliament

Westminster Abbey

Lambeth Pal.

NEWINGTON

Southwark Park Rd

VICTORIA

Westminster Cath.

Lambeth Bridge

LAMBETH RD

NEW KENT RD

Elephant & Castle

Rodney Rd

OLD KENT ROAD

A2 GREENWICH M2

Tate Gall.

LAMBETH

Imperial War Mus.

WALWORTH

Burgess Park

VAUXHALL BRIDGE RD

Vauxhall

Black Prince Rd

KENNINGTON LANE

NEWINGTON BUTTS

Cuming Mus.

Pimlico

ALBERT EMBANKMENT

A3

Kennington

WALWORTH ROAD

Vauxhall Bridge

KENNINGTON

The Oval

KENNINGTON PARK RD

Cook's Rd

Albany

Burgess Park

River Thames

A203 BRIXTON   The Oval   **A202 CAMBERWELL**

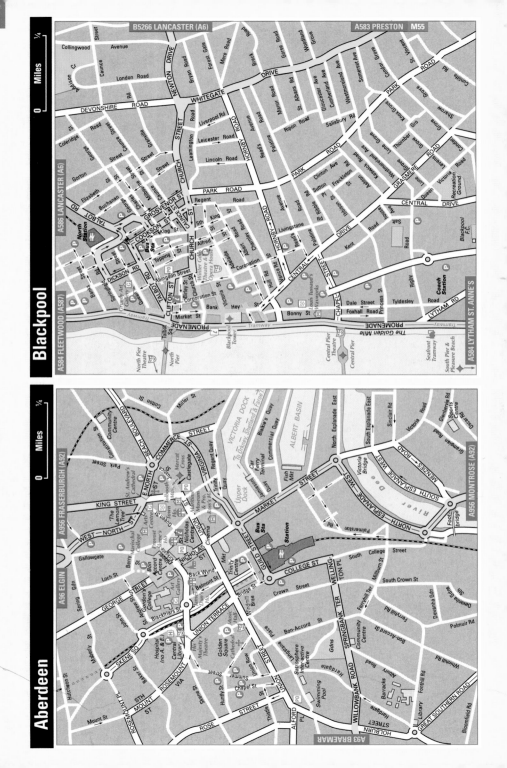

Blackpool

B5266 LANCASTER (A6)

A583 PRESTON M55

A584 PRESTON M55

A586 LANCASTER (A6)

A584 FLEETWOOD (A587)

A584 LYTHAM ST. ANNE'S

Aberdeen

A956 FRASERBURGH (A92)

A96 ELGIN

A956 MONTROSE (A92)

A93 BRAEMAR

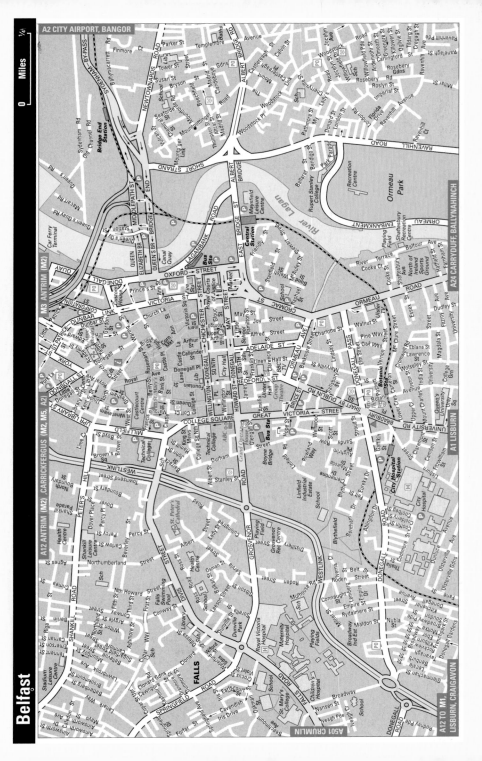

Belfast

47

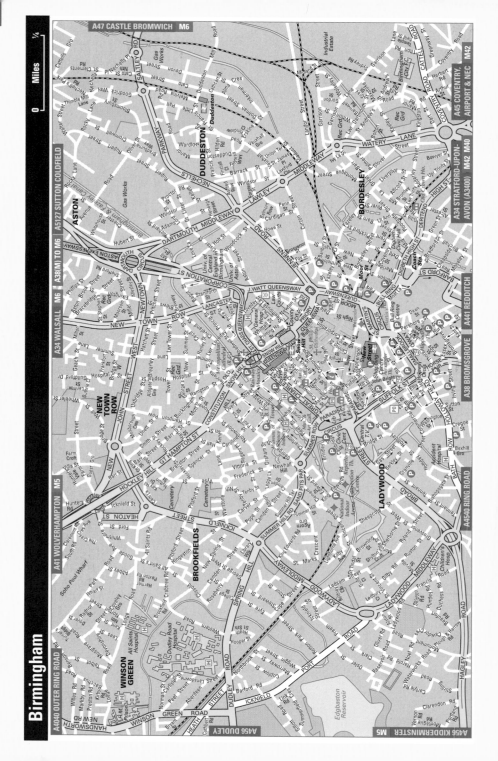

Birmingham

0 Miles ¼

A47 CASTLE BROMWICH M6

A45 COVENTRY, AIRPORT & NEC M42

A34 STRATFORD-UPON- M42 M40
AVON (A3400)

A441 REDDITCH

A38 BROMSGROVE

A456 KIDDERMINSTER M5

A456 DUDLEY

A4540 RING ROAD

HANDSWORTH NEW RD

A41 WOLVERHAMPTON M5

A4040 OUTER RING ROAD

A34 WALSALL M6 A38(M) TO M6

A5127 SUTTON COLDFIELD

ASTON
DUDDESTON
BORDESLEY
NEW TOWN ROW
LADYWOOD
BROOKFIELDS
WINSON GREEN

Edgbaston Reservoir

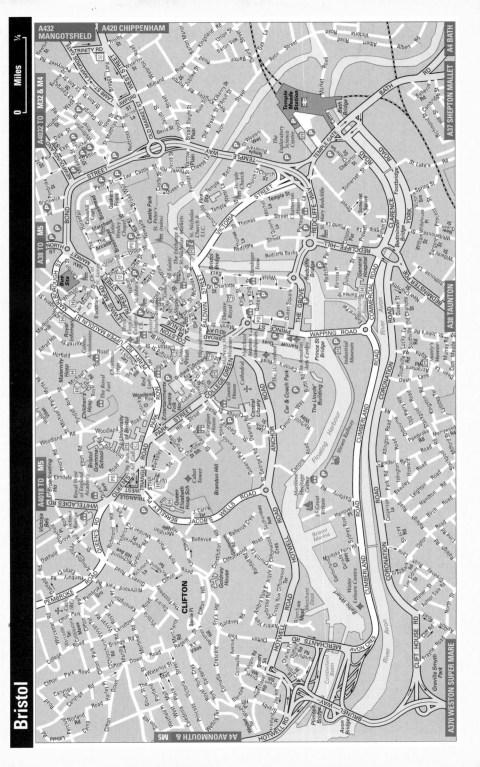

Bristol

A432 MANGOTSFIELD

A420 CHIPPENHAM

A4032 TO M32 & M4

A37 SHEPTON MALLET

A4 BATH

A38 TO M5

A38 TAUNTON

A4018 TO M5

A370 WESTON SUPER MARE

A4 AVONMOUTH & M5

¼

0

Miles

Temple Meads Station

The Exploratory Science Centre

CLIFTON

University of Bristol

Floating Harbour

River Avon

Bristol Marina

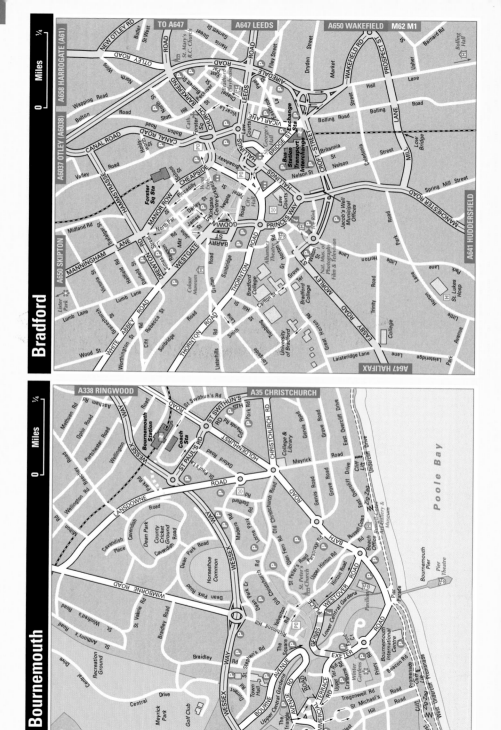

Bradford

Bournemouth

Cambridge

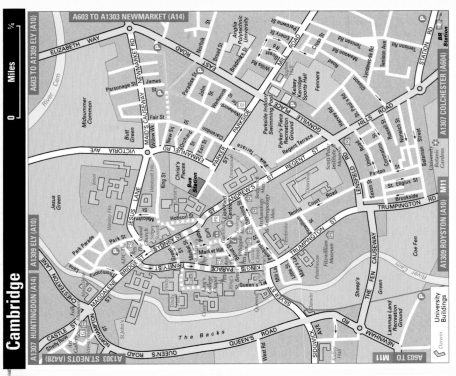

University Buildings

Brighton

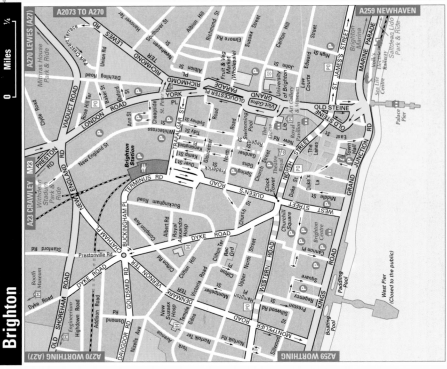

Cardiff

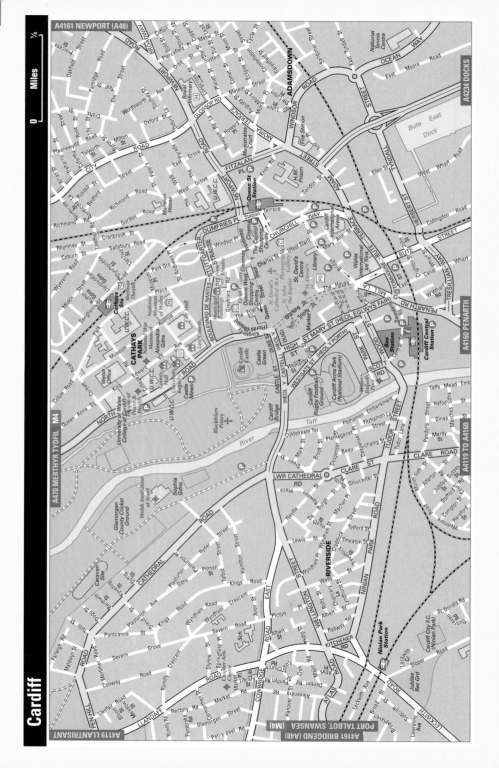

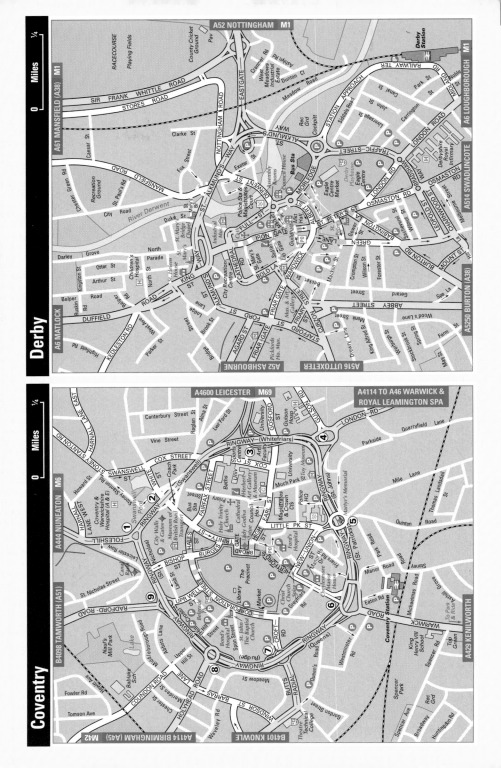

Derby

A52 NOTTINGHAM M1

A61 MANSFIELD (A38) M1

A6 MATLOCK

A6 LOUGHBOROUGH M1

A514 SWADLINCOTE

A5250 BURTON (A38)

A516 UTTOXETER

A52 ASHBOURNE

Derby Station

RACECOURSE
Playing Fields
Country Cricket Ground
Pav
County Cricket Ground

West Meadows Industrial Estate

SIR FRANK WHITTLE ROAD
STORES ROAD

MANSFIELD ROAD
NOTTINGHAM ROAD

RAILWAY TER

Clarke St
Fox Street

River Derwent

Recreation Ground
City Road

St Mary's Bridge Chapel

Police Sta & Magistrates Court

Assembly Rooms
Council House
Bus Sta

Derbyshire Royal Infirmary

OSMASTON RD

Eagle Centre
Eagle Centre Market

CATHEDRAL
IRON GATE
FRIAR GATE

ABBEY STREET

Miles 0 ¼

Coventry

A4600 LEICESTER M69

A4114 TO A46 WARWICK & ROYAL LEAMINGTON SPA

A444 NUNEATON M6

B4098 TAMWORTH (A51)

A4114 BIRMINGHAM (A45) M42

B4101 KNOWLE

A29 KENILWORTH

Canterbury Street
Vine Street
Raglan St
Alma St
Lwr Ford St

RINGWAY (Whitefriars)

COX STREET
SWANSWELL

University
GOSFORD ST
LONDON RD

Quarryfield Lane
Parkside
Mile Lane

Coventry & Warwickshire Hospital (A & E)

Coach Park

Holy Trinity Church
Lady Godiva
Cathedral

Coventry Station

King Henry VIII School

RINGWAY (St Johns)

RINGWAY (Queens)

WARWICK ROAD

Spencer Park

Miles 0 ¼

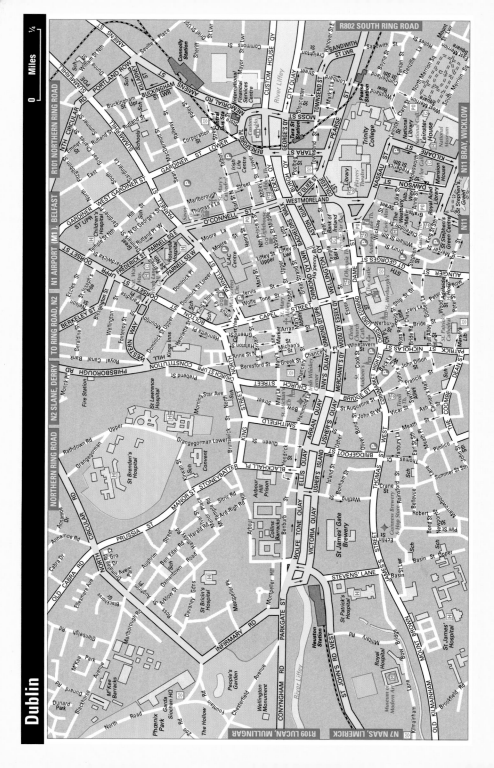

Exeter

Dundee

Edinburgh

A1 BERWICK UPON TWEED

¼ Miles 0

A90 LEITH

A7 GALASHIELS & JEDBURGH (A68)

TO A7

A702 CARLISLE & M74

HOLYROOD PARK

Salisbury Craigs

Radical Road

Queen's Drive

Queen's Drive

Deaconess Hospital

CALTON HILL

Nelson Monument

City Observatory

Calton Burial Ground

Palace of Holyrood House

Remains of Holyrood Abbey (A.D. 1128)

White Horse Close

Royal Terrace Gardens

Regent Gardens

National Monument

Old Royal High School

THE ROYAL MILE

CANONGATE

The People's Story

The Museum of Childhood

John Knox House

Holyrood

Museum of Scotland

Royal Infirmary

Simpson Memorial Maternity Hospital

Bus Sta

Edinburgh (Waverley) Station

Waverley Mkt

Tattoo Office

Festival Office

National Gallery of Scotland

St. Andrew's House

National Portrait Gallery & Museum of Antiquities

New Town Conservation Centre

B.B.C.

Scott Mon.

East Princes St Gdns

The Mound

Royal Scottish Academy

Assembly Rooms & Musical Hall

Floral Clock

Royal Lyceum Theatre

West Princes Street Gardens

Edinburgh Castle

National Library of Scotland

Greyfriars Kirk

George Heriot's Sch

College of Art

Usher Hall

St. Cuthbert's Church

Edinburgh International Conference Centre

Cameo Cinema

PRINCES STREET

GEORGE STREET

QUEEN STREET

CHARLOTTE SQUARE

SOUTH CHARLOTTE

HOPE STREET

Georgian House

Film House

Scottish National Gallery

St. John's Church

LOTHIAN ROAD

MORRISON STREET

QUEENSFERRY ROAD

Water of Leith

Dean Bridge

Dean Park

St. Mary's Scottish Episcopal Cathedral

Haymarket Station

HAY MARKET

A71 KILMARNOCK   A8 GLASGOW (M8)   & STIRLING (M9)   A90 FORTH ROAD BRIDGE & PERTH (M90)

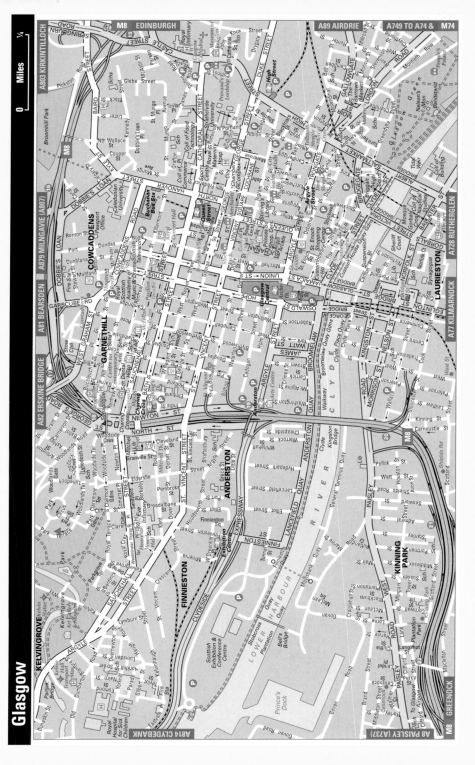

Glasgow

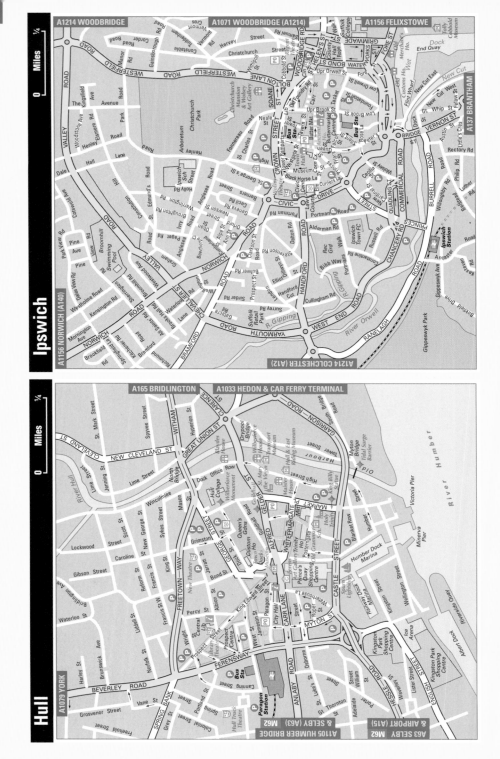

Ipswich

Hull

Leeds

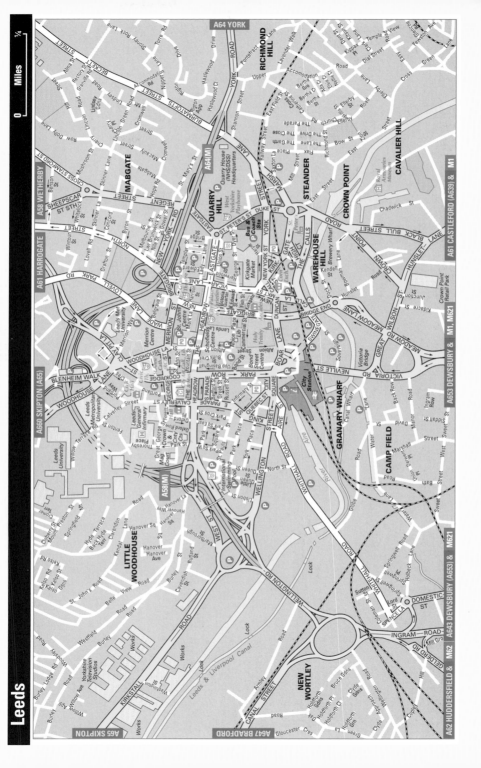

A64 YORK

A64(M)

A58 WETHERBY

A61 HARROGATE

A60 SKIPTON (A65)

A58(M)

A62 HUDDERSFIELD & M62

A63 DEWSBURY (A653) & M621

A653 DEWSBURY & M1, M621

A61 CASTLEFORD (A639) & M1

A647 BRADFORD

A65 SKIPTON

RICHMOND HILL

MABGATE

SHEEPSCAR

QUARRY HILL

STEANDER

WAREHOUSE HILL

CROWN POINT

CAVALIER HILL

GRANARY WHARF

CAMP FIELD

LITTLE WOODHOUSE

NEW WORTLEY

Leeds University

Leeds Metropolitan University

Leeds Met University

Merrion Centre

Kirkgate Market

Bus & Coach Sta

City Station

DOMESTIC ST

Leeds & Liverpool Canal

Yorkshire Television Studios

West Yorkshire Playhouse

Royal Armouries Museum

Crown Point Retail Park

Leeds General Infirmary

International Swimming Pool

River Aire

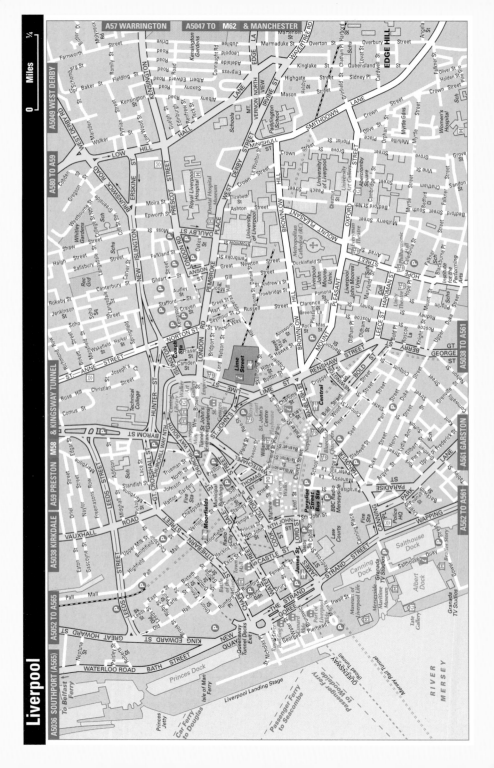

Liverpool

Leicester

A50 BURTON-UPON-TRENT M1
A6 LOUGHBOROUGH
A47 PETERBOROUGH
A6 MARKET HARBOROUGH
A607 NEWARK-ON-TRENT
A50 NORTHAMPTON
A426 RUGBY
A5460 COVENTRY M1 (M69)
A47 HINCKLEY

London Road Sta
De Montfort Hall
University of Leicester
St Matthew's Way
St Margaret's Way
Vaughan Way
Church Gate
Highcross St
Northgate St
Narborough Rd North
King Richards Rd
Duns La
River Soar
Belgrave Gate
Humberstone Gate
Charles St
St George's Way
Bus Sta
Shires Shopping Centre
Haymarket Shopping Centre
Town Hall
Cathedral
Guildhall
Civic Centre
Newarke St
Welford Rd
Oxford St
Waterloo Way
Lancaster Rd
University Rd
De Montfort University
Leicester Royal Infirmary
Leicester City Football Ground
Walnut Street
Western Boulevard

Middlesbrough

A66 REDCAR (A1085)
A1085 REDCAR
A178 HARTLEPOOL
A1046 STOCKTON ON TEES
A1046
A172 STOKESLEY & THIRSK (A19)
A1032 HEMLINGTON & A19
A19 THIRSK
A66 STOCKTON ON TEES
A1046 STOCKTON ON TEES
A1085 BILLINGHAM (A19)
A19 SUNDERLAND

River Tees
Transporter Bridge
Middlehaven
Middlesbrough FC
Clarence Road
Haverton Hill Rd
Newport Br Appr Rd
Newport Bridge
Tees Viaduct
I.C.I. Works
Riverside Park
Riverside Business Park
Middlesbrough By-Pass
North Rd
Bridge St West
Wilson Street
Middlesbrough Sta
Bus Sta
Hartington Rd
Newport Rd
Borough Rd
Marton Rd
Linthorpe Rd
Park Rd North
Ayresome Street
Acklam Rd
Northern Route
Albert Park
University of Teesside
Town Hall
Middlesbrough Gen Hosp
St Barnabas Rd
Marton Burn Rd
The Avenue

For LONDON see pages 42-45

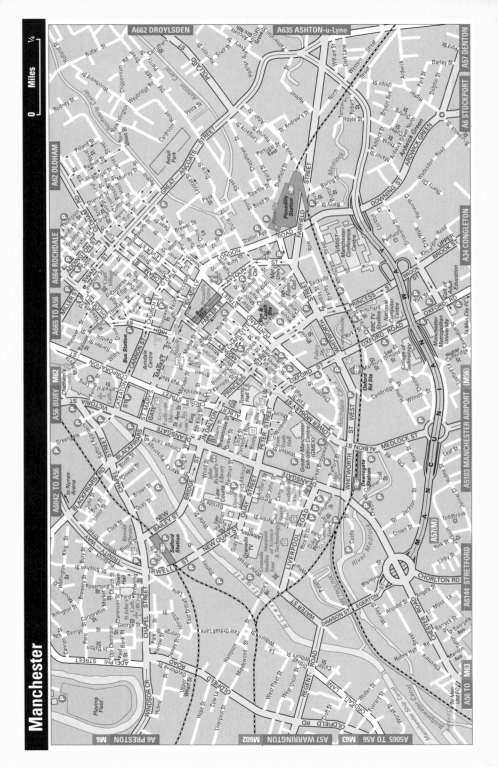

Manchester

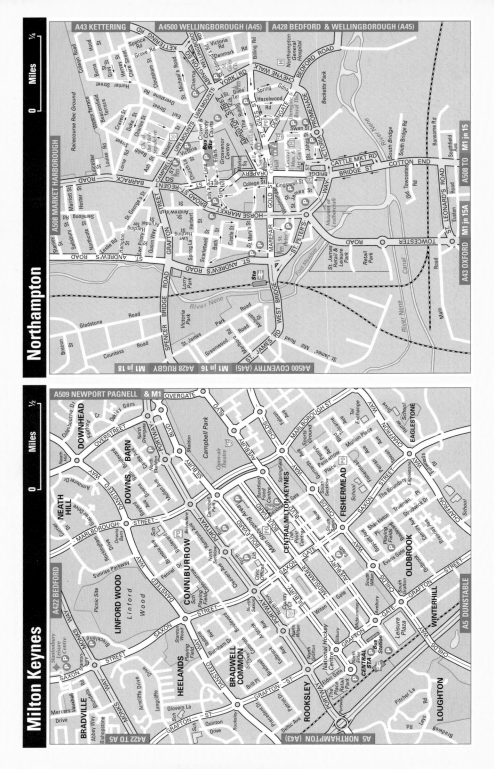

Northampton

A43 KETTERING   A4500 WELLINGBOROUGH (A45)   A428 BEDFORD & WELLINGBOROUGH (A45)

A508 MARKET HARBOROUGH

M1 jn 15   M1 jn 15A   A508 TO

A508 OXFORD   ST. LEONARD'S ROAD

A43 OXFORD

M1 jn 18   A428 RUGBY   M1 jn 16   A4500 COVENTRY (A45)

Milton Keynes

A509 NEWPORT PAGNELL & M1

A422 BEDFORD

A5 DUNSTABLE

A422 TO A5   A5 NORTHAMPTON (A43)

Newcastle

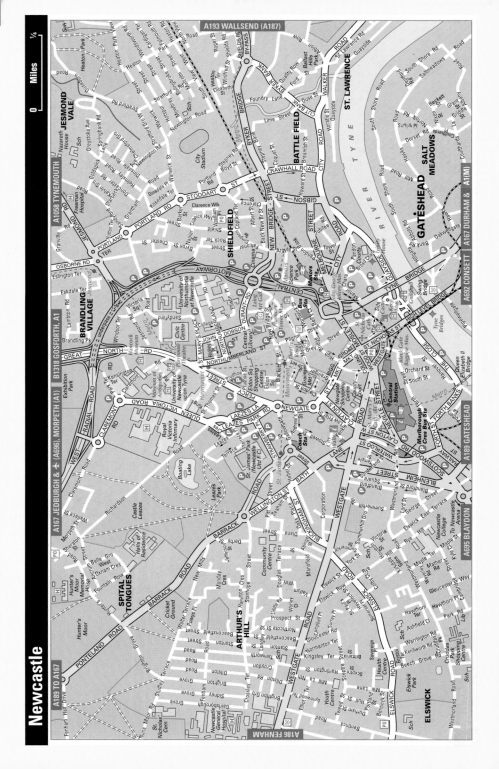

0   Miles   ¼

A189 TO A167 | A167 JEDBURGH & ✈ (A696), MORPETH (A1) | B1318 GOSFORTH, A1 | A1058 TYNEMOUTH

A193 WALLSEND (A187)

A692 CONSETT | A167 DURHAM & A1(M)

A189 GATESHEAD | A695 BLAYDON

A186 FENHAM

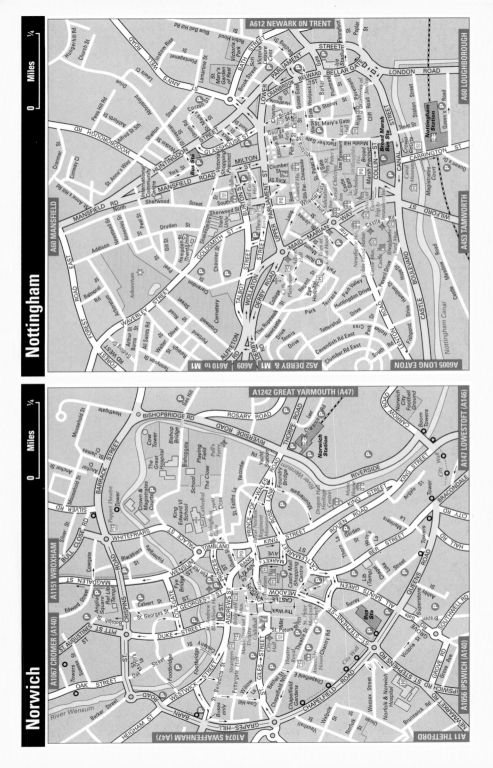

Nottingham

Norwich

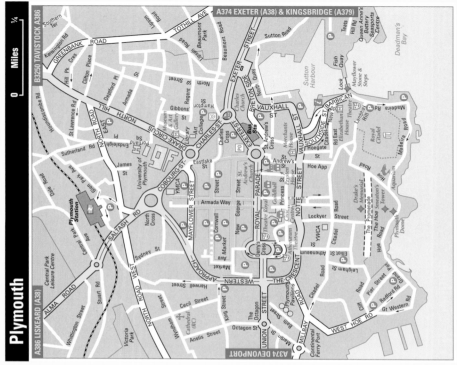

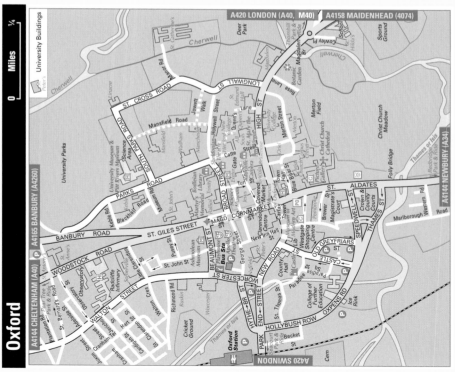

Portsmouth

Reading

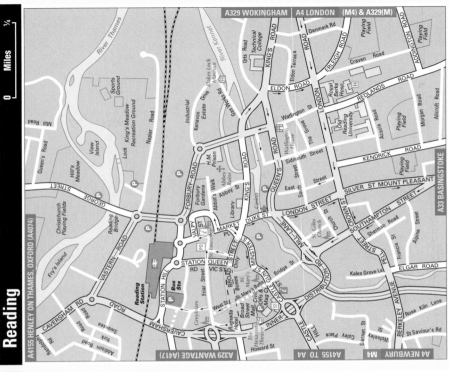

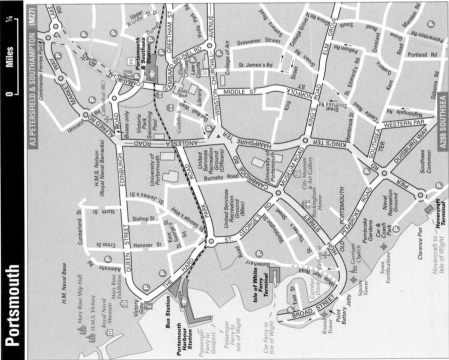

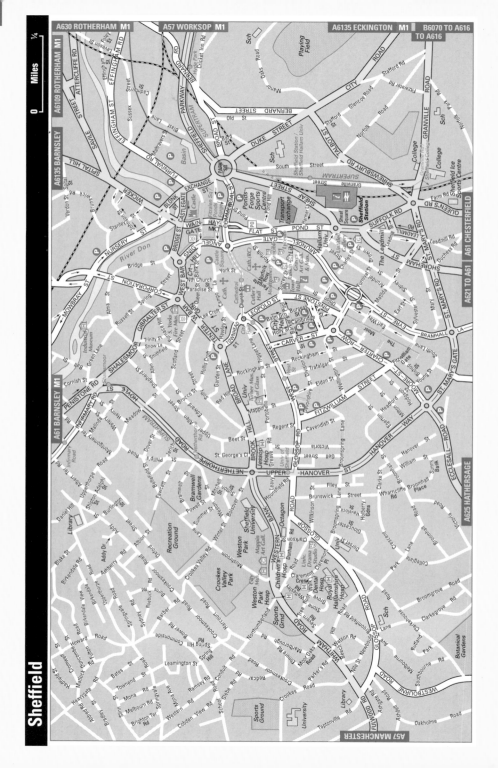

Sheffield

A630 ROTHERHAM M1
A57 WORKSOP M1
A6135 ECKINGTON M1
B6070 TO A616
TO A616

A6109 ROTHERHAM M1
A6135 BARNSLEY
A61 BARNSLEY M1

A61 CHESTERFIELD
A621 TO A61 | A61 CHESTERFIELD
A625 HATHERSAGE

A57 MANCHESTER

¼ Miles 0

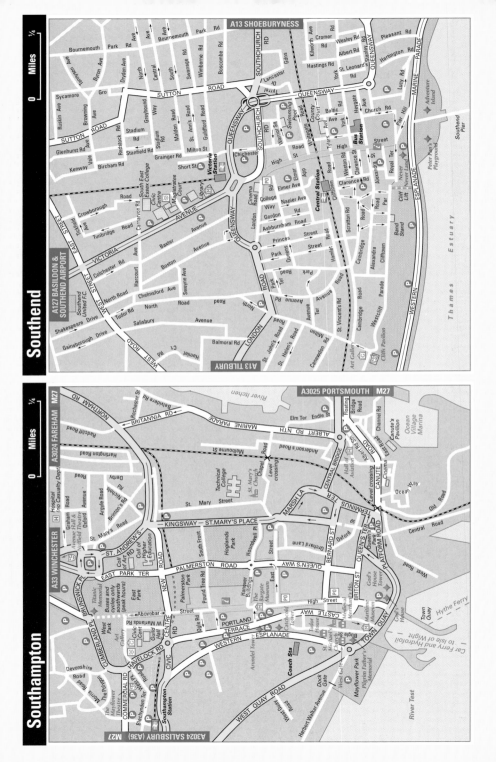

Southend

Southampton

Stratford-upon-Avon

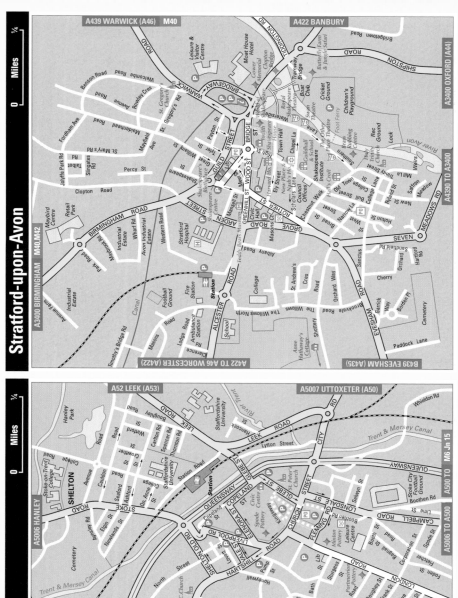

Stoke

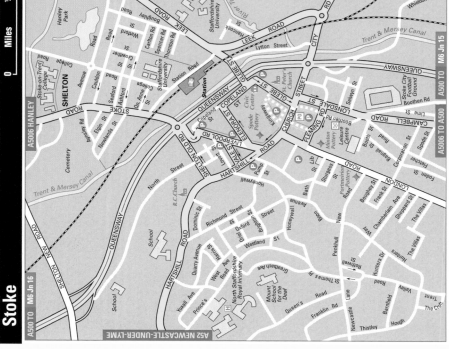

Swansea

Sunderland

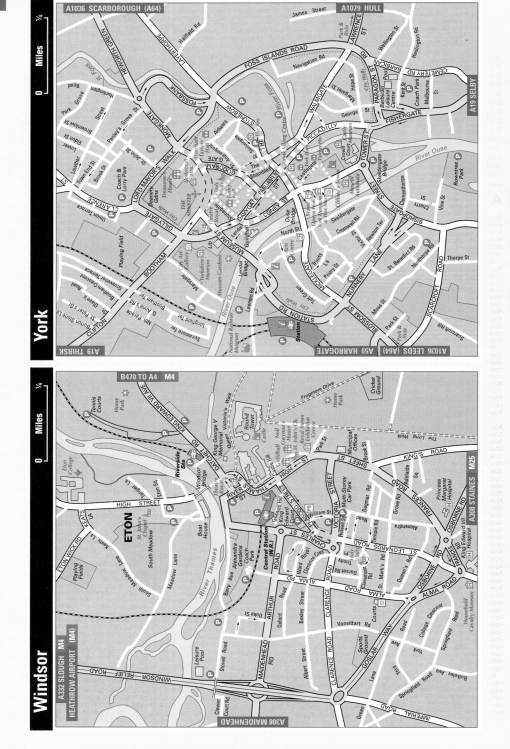

72

York

A1036 SCARBOROUGH (A64)

A1079 HULL

A19 SELBY

FISHERGATE

A19 THIRSK   A59 HARROGATE   A1036 LEEDS (A4)

Miles 0 ¼

Windsor

B470 TO A4 M4

A332 SLOUGH M4
HEATHROW AIRPORT (M4)

A308 MAIDENHEAD

A308 STAINES M25

Miles 0 ¼

ETON

Abbreviation	Full name		Abbreviation	Full name
Aberd C	Aberdeen City		Gtr Man	Greater Manchester
Aberds	Aberdeenshire		Gwyn	Gwynedd
Aber/Colw	Aberconwy & Colwyn		H'land	Highland
Angl	Anglesey		Hants	Hampshire
Arg/Bute	Argyll & Bute		Heref/Worcs	Hereford & Worcester
Beds	Bedfordshire		Herts	Hertfordshire
Berks	Berkshire		Humber	Humberside
Bl Gwent	Blaenau Gwent		I of Man	Isle of Man
Bridg	Bridgend		I of Scilly	Isles of Scilly
Bucks	Buckinghamshire		I of Wight	Isle of Wight
C of Edinb	City of Edinburgh		Invercl	Inverclyde
C of Glasg	City of Glasgow		Lancs	Lancashire
Caerph	Caerphilly		Leics	Leicestershire
Cambs	Cambridgeshire		Lincs	Lincolnshire
Card	Cardiff		Mersey	Merseyside
Cards	Cardiganshire		Merth Tyd	Merthyr Tydfil
Carms	Carmarthenshire		Midloth	Midlothian
Chan Is	Channel Is		Monmouths	Monmouthshire
Ches	Cheshire		N Ayrs	North Ayrshire
Clack	Clackmannanshire		N Lanarks	North Lanarkshire
Clevl'd	Cleveland		N Yorks	North Yorkshire
Cornw'l	Cornwall		Neath P Talb	Neath Port Talbot
Cumb	Cumbria		Newp	Newport
Denbs	Denbighshire		Notts	Nottinghamshire
Dumf/Gal	Dumfries & Galloway		Northants	Northamptonshire
Dundee C	Dundee City		Northum	Northumberland
E Ayrs	East Ayrshire		Oxon	Oxfordshire
E Dunb	East Dunbartonshire		Pembs	Pembrokeshire
E Loth	East Lothian		Perth/Kinr	Perth & Kinross
E Renf	East Renfrewshire *		Renf	Renfrewshire
E Sussex	East Sussex		Rh Cyn Taff	Rhondda Cynon Taff
Falk	Falkirk		S Ayrs	South Ayrshire
Flints	Flintshire		S Lanarks	South Lanarkshire
Glos	Gloucestershire		S Yorks	South Yorkshire
			Shetl'd	Shetland

Abbreviation	Full name
Shrops	Shropshire
Som'set	Somerset
Staffs	Staffordshire
Stirl	Stirling
Swan	Swansea
Torf	Torfaen
Tyne/Wear	Tyne & Wear
V of Glam	Vale of Glamorgan
W Dunb	West Dunbartonshire
W Isles	Western Isles
W Loth	West Lothian
W Midlands	West Midlands
W Sussex	West Sussex
W Yorks	West Yorkshire
Warwick	Warwickshire
Wilts	Wiltshire
Wrex	Wrexham

A

Abbey Galway 35 R7
Abbey Town Cumb 20 N17
Abbeydorney Kerry 38 T4
Abbeyfeale Limerick 38 T5
Abbeyleix Laois 40 S9
Abbots Bromley Staffs 11 S20
Abbotsbury Dorset 4 W18
Aberaeron Card 9 ST1
Aberarth Card 9 ST1
Abercarn Caerph 4 U17
Aberchirder Aberds 29 G18
Abercrave Powys 9 U16
Aberdare Rh Cyn Taff 9 U16
Aberdaron Gwyn 8 S14
Aberdeen Aberd C 25 H19
Aberdour Fife 24 K17
Aberdulais Neath P Talb 9 U16
Aberdyfi Gwyn 8 S15
Aberfeldy Perth/Kinr 24 J16
Aberffraw Angl 8 R15
Aberfoyle Stirl 24 K15
Abergavenny Monmouths 4 U17
Abergele Aber/Colw 8 R16
Abergwili Carms 9 U15
Abergwyngregyn Gwyn 8 R15
Aberlady E Loth 25 K18
Abernethy Perth/Kinr 24 K17
Aberporth Card 9 ST1
Abersoch Gwyn 8 S14
Abersychan Torf 4 U17
Abertillery Bl Gwent 4 U17
Aberystwyth Card 9 ST1
Abingdon Oxon 5 U21
Abington Limerick 39 S7
Abington S Lanarks 20 L16
Aboyne Aberds 25 H18
Accrington Lancs 15 Q19
Acha Arg/Bute 22 J10
Achanalt H'land 27 G14
Achaphubuil H'land 23 J13
Acharacle H'land 23 J12
Achavanich H'land 28 F17
Achavraie H'land 27 E14
Achill Mayo 34 Q4
Achiltibuie H'land 27 E14
Achnacroish Arg/Bute 23 J12
Achnasheen H'land 27 G13
Achnashellach H'land 27 H13
Achosnich H'land 22 J11
Achriabhach H'land 23 J13
Acklam N Yorks 17 P22
Aclare Sligo 35 P6
Acle Norfolk 13 S27
Acomb N Yorks 16 Q21
Acton Burnell Shrops 10 S18
Acton Armagh 33 P11
Adamstown Waterford 40 T9
Adare Limerick 39 S6
Adcarn Roscommon 35 Q7
Addingham W Yorks 15 P20
Adlington Lancs 15 Q18
Adrigole Cork 38 U4
Adwick le Street S Yorks 16 Q21

Affric Lodge H'land 27 H13
Aghagower Mayo 34 Q5
Aghalee Antrim 33 N11
Aghavannagh Wicklow 40 S11
Aghaville Cork 38 U5
Aghern Cork 39 T7
Aghnacliff Longford 36 Q8
Aglish Waterford 39 T8
Ahascragh Galway 35 R7
Ahoghill Antrim 33 N11
Ainsdale Mersey 15 Q17
Aird a Mhulaidh W Isles 26 G10
Aird Asaig Tairbeart W Isles 26 G10
Aird Arg/Bute 23 K12
Aird Uig W Isles 26 F9
Airdrie N Lanarks 19 L16
Airor H'land 23 H12
Airth Falk 24 K16
Aisgill Cumb 15 P19
Aith Orkney 30 D18
Aith Shetl'd 31 B21
Akeley Bucks 11 T22
Albrighton Shrops 10 S19
Alcester Warwick 11 T20
Aldborough N Yorks 16 P21
Aldbourne Wilts 5 V20
Aldbrough Humber 17 Q23
Aldeburgh Suffolk 13 T27
Alderbury Wilts 5 V20
Alderley Edge Ches 15 R19
Aldermaston Berks 5 V21
Aldershot Hants 6 V22
Aldridge W Midlands 11 S20
Aldsworth Glos 5 U20
Aldwick W Sussex 6 W22
Alexandria W Dunb 24 L14
Alford Aberds 25 H18
Alford Lincs 17 R24
Alfreton Derby 11 R21
Alfriston E Sussex 6 W24
Alkham Kent 7 V26
Allen Kildare 37 R10
Allendale Town Northum 21 N19
Allenheads Northum 21 N19
Allenwood Kildare 37 R10
Allihies Cork 38 U3
Alloa Clack 24 K16
Allonby Cumb 20 N17
Almondsbury Avon 4 U18
Alness H'land 28 G15
Alnmouth Northum 21 M20
Alnwick Northum 21 M20
Alphington Devon 4 W16
Alrewas Staffs 11 S20
Alsager Ches 10 R19
Alston Cumb 21 N19
Alt na h'Airbhe H'land 27 G13
Altanduino H'land 28 F15
Altarnun Cornw'l 2 W14
Altass H'land 28 G14
Althorne Essex 7 U25
Althorpe Humber 17 Q22
Altnaharra H'land 28 F15
Alton Hants 6 V22
Alton Staffs 11 S20
Altrincham Gtr Man 15 R19
Alva Clack 24 K16
Alvechurch Heref/Worcs 11 T20
Alveley Shrops 10 T19
Alveston Avon 4 U18

Alvie H'land 24 H16
Alwinton Northum 21 M19
Alyth Perth/Kinr 25 J17
Amble Northum 21 M20
Ambleside Cumb 15 P18
Ambrosden Oxon 11 U21
Amersham Bucks 6 U22
Amesbury Wilts 5 V20
Amlwch Angl 8 R15
Ammanford Carms 9 U16
Ampleforth N Yorks 16 P21
Ampthill Beds 12 T23
Amulree Perth/Kinr 24 J16
An Geata Mór Mayo 34 P3
An t-Ob N Isles 26 G9
Anacotty Limerick 39 S6
Anascaul Kerry 38 T3
Ancaster Lincs 12 S22
Ancroft Northum 21 L19
Ancrum Borders 21 L18
Andover Hants 5 V21
Andoversford Glos 11 U20
Andreas I of Man 14 P15
Angle Pembs 9 U13
Angmering W Sussex 6 W23
Annacarty Tipperary 39 S7
Annacloy Down 33 P12
Annagassan Louth 37 Q11
Annahilt Down 33 P12
Annalong Down 37 P12
Annan Dumf/Gal 20 N17
Annbank S Ayrs 19 M14
Annestown Waterford 40 T9
Annfield Plain Durham 21 N20
Anstey Leics 11 S21
Anstruther Fife 25 K18
Antrim Antrim 33 N11
Appleby-in-Westmorland Cumb 21 N19
Applecross H'land 27 H12
Appledore Devon 3 V15
Appledore Kent 7 V25
Araglin Tipperary 39 T7
Arboe Tyrone 33 N10
Arbroath Angus 25 J18
Archiestown Moray 28 H17
Ardagh Limerick 38 T5
Ardagh Longford 36 Q8
Ardahy Monaghan 33 P10
Ardara Donegal 32 N7
Ardarroch H'land 27 H12
Ardbeg Arg/Bute 18 L11
Ardcath Meath 37 Q11
Ardcharnich H'land 27 G13
Ardchyle Stirl 24 K15
Ardcrony Tipperary 36 S7
Ardee Louth 37 Q10
Ardentinny Arg/Bute 23 K14
Ardersier H'land 28 G15
Ardessie H'land 27 G13
Ardfert Kerry 38 T4
Ardfinnane Tipperary 39 T8
Ardgay H'land 28 G15
Ardglass Down 33 P12
Ardgroom Cork 38 U4
Ardhasig W Isles 26 G10
Ardingly W Sussex 6 V23
Ardkearagh Kerry 38 U3
Ardkeen Down 33 P12
Ardleigh Essex 13 U26
Ardley Oxon 11 U21
Ardlui Arg/Bute 24 K14
Ardlussa Arg/Bute 23 K12
Ardmore Galway 34 R4
Ardmore Waterford 39 U8

Ardnacrusha Clare 39 S6
Ardnamona Donegal 32 N7
Ardnaree Mayo 35 P5
Ardnasodan Galway 35 R6
Ardnave Arg/Bute 18 L11
Ardpatrick Limerick 39 T6
Ardrahan Galway 35 R6
Ardreagh Londonderry 33 M10
Ardrishaig Arg/Bute 23 K13
Ardrossan N Ayrs 18 L14
Ardscull Kildare 40 R10
Ardstraw Tyrone 32 N9
Ardtalnaig Perth/Kinr 24 J15
Ardvasar H'land 23 H12
Ardwell Dumf/Gal 18 N14
Ardwell Moray 29 H17
Arinagour Arg/Bute 22 J10
Arisaig H'land 23 J12
Arklow Wicklow 40 S11
Arless Laois 40 S9
Armadale H'land 23 H12
Armadale W Loth 24 L16
Armagh Armagh 33 P10
Armathwaite Cumb 20 N18
Armitage Staffs 11 S20
Armoy Antrim 33 M11
Armthorpe S Yorks 16 Q21
Arncliffe N Yorks 15 P19
Arncott Oxon 6 U21
Arney Fermanagh 32 P8
Arnisdale H'land 23 H12
Arnold Notts 11 R21
Arnside Cumb 15 P18
Arreton I of Wight 5 W21
Arrochar Arg/Bute 24 K14
Arthurstown Wexford 40 T10
Articlave Londonderry 33 M10
Artigarvan Tyrone 32 N9
Arundel W Sussex 6 W22
Ascot Berks 6 V22
Asfordby Leics 11 S22
Ash Kent 7 V26
Ash Surrey 6 V22
Ashbourne Meath 37 Q11
Ashbourne Derby 11 R20
Ashburton Devon 3 W16
Ashbury Oxon 5 U20
Ashby de-la-Zouch Leics 11 S21
Ashchurch Glos 10 U19
Ashford Wicklow 40 R11
Ashford Derby 16 R20
Ashford Kent 7 V25
Ashingdon Essex 7 U25
Ashington Northum 21 M20
Ashley Staffs 10 S19
Ashton Keynes Wilts 5 U20
Ashton Ches 15 R18
Ashton under Hill Heref/Worcs 11 T20
Ashton under Lyne Gtr Man 15 R19
Ashton-in-Makerfield Gtr Man 15 R18
Ashurst Hants 5 W20
Ashville Louth 37 Q10
Ashwater Devon 3 W15
Ashwell Herts 12 T23
Ashwell Som'set 4 V18
Askam-in-Furness Cumb 14 P17
Askeaton Limerick 39 S6
Askern S Yorks 16 Q21

Askrigg N Yorks 15 P19
Aslackby Lincs 12 S23
Aspatria Cumb 20 N17
Astee Kerry 38 S4
Astwood Bank Heref/Worcs 11 T20
Athboy Meath 37 Q10
Athea Limerick 38 T5
Athenry Galway 35 R6
Atherstone Warwick 11 S20
Atherton Gtr Man 15 Q19
Athlacca Limerick 39 T6
Athleague Roscommon 35 Q7
Athlone Westmeath 36 R8
Athy Kildare 40 S10
Attical Down 37 P11
Attleborough Norfolk 13 S26
Attymon Galway 35 R6
Atworth Wilts 5 V19
Auchenblae Aberds 25 J19
Auchencairn Dumf/Gal 19 N16
Auchengray S Lanarks 20 L16
Auchertool Fife 25 K17
Auchinleck E Ayrs 19 M15
Auchronie Angus 25 J18
Auchterarder Perth/Kinr 24 K16
Auchterderran Fife 24 K17
Auchtermuchty Fife 25 K17
Auchtertyre H'land 27 H12
Aucloggeen Galway 35 R6
Audlem Ches 10 S18
Audley Staffs 10 R19
Augher Tyrone 32 P9
Aughnacloy Tyrone 33 P10
Aughrim Clare 35 R6
Aughrim Galway 35 R7
Aughrim Wicklow 40 S11
Auldearn H'land 28 G16
Aultbea H'land 27 G12
Austwick N Yorks 15 P19
Avebury Wilts 5 V20
Avening Glos 5 U19
Aveton Gifford Devon 3 X16
Aviemore H'land 24 H16
Avoca Wicklow 40 S11
Avoch H'land 28 G15
Avonmouth Avon 4 U18
Axbridge Som'set 4 V18
Axminster Devon 4 W17
Axmouth Devon 4 W17
Aylesbury Bucks 6 U22
Aylesford Kent 7 V24
Aylesham Kent 7 V26
Aylsham Norfolk 13 S26
Aynho Northants 11 U21
Ayr S Ayrs 19 M14
Aysgarth N Yorks 15 P19
Ayton Borders 21 L19
Ayton N Yorks 17 P23

B

Bac W Isles 26 F11
Backwell Avon 4 V18
Bacton Norfolk 13 S26
Bacup Lancs 15 Q19
Badenscoth Aberds 29 H19
Badenyon Aberds 25 H17

Place	County	No.	Grid
Badrallach	*H'land*	27	G13
Bagh a Chaisteil *W Isles*		22	J8
Bagillt	*Flints*	15	R17
Bagshot	*Surrey*	6	V22
Baildon	*W Yorks*	15	Q20
Baile Ailein	*W Isles*	26	F10
Bailieborough	*Cavan*	37	Q10
Bainbridge	*N Yorks*	15	P19
Bainton	*Humber*	17	Q22
Bakewell	*Derby*	11	R20
Bala	*Gwyn*	8	S16
Balbeggie	*Perth/Kinr*	24	K17
Balblair	*H'land*	28	G15
Balbriggan	*Dublin*	37	Q11
Balcombe	*W Sussex*	6	V23
Balderton	*Notts*	11	R22
Baldock	*Herts*	12	U23
Baldoyle	*Dublin*	37	R11
Balfour	*Orkney*	30	D18
Balfron	*Stirl*	24	K15
Balintore	*H'land*	28	G16
Balla	*Mayo*	35	Q5
Ballachulish	*H'land*	23	J13
Ballagh	*Galway*	35	R5
Ballagh	*Limerick*	38	T5
Ballagh	*Tipperary*	39	S8
Ballaghaderreen *Roscommon*		35	Q6
Ballantrae	*S Ayrs*	18	M14
Ballasalla	*I of Man*	14	P14
Ballater	*Aberds*	25	H17
Ballaugh	*I of Man*	14	P14
Ballickmoyler	*Laois*	40	S9
Ballin Cloher	*Kerry*	38	T4
Ballina	*Mayo*	35	P5
Ballina	*Tipperary*	39	S7
Ballinadee	*Cork*	39	U6
Ballinafad	*Sligo*	35	P7
Ballinagar	*Offaly*	36	R9
Ballinakill	*Laois*	40	S9
Ballinalack *Westmeath*		36	Q9
Ballinalea	*Wicklow*	40	R11
Ballinalee	*Longford*	36	Q8
Ballinamallard *Fermanagh*		32	P8
Ballinameen *Roscommon*		35	Q7
Ballinamore Bridge *Galway*		35	R7
Ballinamore	*Leitrim*	36	P8
Ballinascarty	*Cork*	39	U6
Ballinasloe	*Galway*	35	R7
Ballincollig	*Cork*	39	U6
Ballincurrig	*Cork*	39	U7
Ballindaggan	*Wexford*	40	S10
Ballinderreen	*Galway*	35	R6
Ballinderry	*Tipperary*	35	R7
Ballinderry Upr. *Antrim*		33	N11
Ballindine	*Mayo*	35	Q6
Ballindooly	*Galway*	35	R5
Ballineen	*Cork*	39	U6
Ballingarry	*Limerick*	39	T6
Ballingarry	*Tipperary*	39	T6
Ballingarry	*Tipperary*	39	S8
Ballingeary	*Cork*	38	U5
Ballinhassig	*Cork*	39	U6
Ballinlea	*Antrim*	33	M11
Ballinlough *Roscommon*		35	Q6
Ballinluig	*Perth/Kinr*	24	J16
Ballinrobe	*Mayo*	35	Q5
Ballinskelligs	*Kerry*	38	U3
Ballinspittle	*Cork*	39	U6
Ballintober	*Mayo*	34	Q5
Ballintober *Roscommon*		35	Q7
Ballintoy	*Antrim*	33	M11
Ballintra	*Donegal*	32	N7
Ballintroohan	*Donegal*	33	M9
Ballinunty	*Tipperary*	39	S8
Ballinure	*Tipperary*	39	S8
Ballitore	*Kildare*	40	R10
Ballivor	*Meath*	37	Q10
Balloch	*H'land*	28	H15
Balloch	*W Dunb*	24	K14
Ballochan	*Aberds*	25	H18
Ballon	*Carlow*	40	S10
Ballure	*Donegal*	32	N7
Ballyagran	*Limerick*	39	T6
Ballybay	*Monaghan*	37	P10
Ballybofey	*Donegal*	32	N8
Ballybohil	*Dublin*	37	Q11
Ballybogy	*Antrim*	33	M10
Ballybritt	*Offaly*	36	R8
Ballybrittas	*Laois*	36	R9
Ballybrophy	*Laois*	39	S8
Ballybunion	*Kerry*	38	S4
Ballycahill	*Tipperary*	39	S8
Ballycanew	*Wexford*	40	S11
Ballycarney	*Wexford*	40	S10
Ballycarry	*Antrim*	33	N12
Ballycastle	*Antrim*	33	M11
Ballycastle	*Mayo*	34	P5
Ballyclare	*Antrim*	33	N12
Ballyclerahan *Tipperary*		39	T8
Ballyclogh	*Cork*	39	T6
Ballycolla	*Laois*	40	S9
Ballyconneely	*Galway*	34	R3
Ballyconnell	*Cavan*	36	P8
Ballyconnell	*Sligo*	32	P6
Ballycotton	*Cork*	39	U7
Ballycrossaun	*Galway*	36	R7
Ballycroy	*Mayo*	34	P4
Ballycumber	*Offaly*	36	R8
Ballydangan *Roscommon*		36	R7
Ballydavid	*Galway*	35	R7
Ballydavid	*Kerry*	38	T3
Ballydavis	*Laois*	40	R9
Ballydehob	*Cork*	38	U5
Ballydonegan	*Cork*	38	U3
Ballyduff	*Kerry*	38	T4
Ballyduff	*Waterford*	39	T7
Ballydugan	*Down*	33	P12
Ballyfarnan *Roscommon*		35	P7
Ballyferriter	*Kerry*	38	T3
Ballyfin	*Laois*	40	R9
Ballyforan *Roscommon*		35	R7
Ballygar	*Galway*	35	Q7
Ballygarrett	*Wexford*	40	S11
Ballygawley	*Sligo*	32	P7
Ballygawley	*Tyrone*	33	P9
Ballyglass	*Mayo*	35	Q5
Ballygorman	*Donegal*	32	M9
Ballygowan	*Down*	33	N12
Ballygrant	*Arg/Bute*	18	L11
Ballyhaght	*Limerick*	39	T6
Ballyhahill	*Limerick*	38	S5
Ballyhaise	*Cavan*	36	P9
Ballyhalbert	*Down*	33	P13
Ballyhale	*Galway*	35	R5
Ballyhaunis	*Mayo*	35	Q6
Ballyhean	*Mayo*	34	Q5
Ballyheige	*Kerry*	38	T4
Ballyhooly	*Cork*	39	T7
Ballyhornan	*Down*	33	P12
Ballyjamesduff	*Cavan*	36	Q9
Ballykelly *Londonderry*		33	M9
Ballykillin	*Donegal*	32	M9
Ballylanders	*Limerick*	39	T7
Ballylaneen	*Waterford*	39	T9
Ballyliffin	*Donegal*	32	M9
Ballylongford	*Kerry*	38	S5
Ballylooby	*Tipperary*	39	T8
Ballylynan	*Laois*	40	S9
Ballymacarbry *Waterford*		39	T8
Ballymacoda	*Cork*	39	U8
Ballymagorry	*Tyrone*	32	N9
Ballymahon	*Longford*	36	Q8
Ballymakenny	*Louth*	37	Q11
Ballymartin	*Down*	37	P12
Ballymena	*Antrim*	33	N11
Ballymoe	*Galway*	35	Q7
Ballymoney	*Antrim*	33	M10
Ballymore Eustace *Kildare*		37	R10
Ballymore	*Westmeath*	36	Q8
Ballymote	*Sligo*	35	P6
Ballymullakill *Roscommon*		36	R7
Ballymurphy	*Carlow*	40	S10
Ballymurray *Roscommon*		36	Q7
Ballynabola	*Wexford*	40	T10
Ballynacally	*Clare*	38	S5
Ballynacarrigy *Westmeath*		36	Q8
Ballynacorra	*Cork*	39	U7
Ballynagore	*Westmeath*	36	R9
Ballynahinch	*Down*	33	P12
Ballynahown *Westmeath*		36	R8
Ballynamona	*Cork*	39	T6
Ballynamult	*Waterford*	39	T8
Ballyneety	*Limerick*	39	S6
Ballynure	*Antrim*	33	N12
Ballyporeen	*Tipperary*	39	T7
Ballyragget	*Kilkenny*	40	S9
Ballyroan	*Laois*	40	S9
Ballyroe	*Cork*	39	T7
Ballyronan *Londonderry*		33	N10
Ballyroney	*Down*	33	P11
Ballysadare	*Sligo*	32	P6
Ballyshannon	*Donegal*	32	P7
Ballyshannon	*Kildare*	37	R10
Ballyshrule	*Galway*	35	R7
Ballysloe	*Tipperary*	39	S8
Ballysteen	*Limerick*	39	S6
Ballyvaghan	*Clare*	35	R5
Ballyvourney	*Cork*	38	U5
Ballyvoy	*Antrim*	33	M11
Ballywalter	*Down*	33	N13
Ballyward	*Down*	33	P11
Ballywilliam	*Wexford*	40	T10
Balmaclellan *Dumf/Gal*		19	M15
Balmedie	*Aberds*	25	H19
Balnapaling	*H'land*	28	G15
Balquhidder	*Stirl*	24	K15
Balrath	*Meath*	37	Q11
Balrothery	*Dublin*	37	Q11
Balsall	*W Midlands*	11	T20
Balsham	*Cambs*	12	T24
Baltasound	*Shetl'd*	31	A22
Baltimore	*Cork*	39	V5
Baltinglass	*Wicklow*	40	S10
Baltracey	*Kildare*	37	R10
Baltray	*Louth*	37	Q11
Balvicar	*Arg/Bute*	23	K12
Bamber Bridge	*Lancs*	15	Q18
Bamburgh	*Northum*	21	L20
Bamford	*Derby*	16	R20
Bampton	*Devon*	4	W17
Bampton	*Oxon*	5	U20
Banagher	*Offaly*	36	R8
Banbridge	*Down*	33	P11
Banbury	*Oxon*	11	T21
Banchory	*Aberds*	25	H18
Bandon	*Cork*	39	U6
Banff	*Aberds*	29	G18
Bangor	*Down*	33	N12
Bangor	*Mayo*	34	P4
Bangor	*Gwyn*	8	R15
Bangor-is-y-coed *Wrex*		10	S18
Banham	*Norfolk*	13	T26
Bankend	*Dumf/Gal*	20	M16
Bankfoot	*Perth/Kinr*	24	J16
Bankhead	*Aberd C*	25	H19
Banks	*Lancs*	15	Q18
Bannockburn	*Stirl*	24	K16
Bannow	*Wexford*	40	T10
Banstead	*Surrey*	6	V23
Banteer	*Cork*	39	T6
Bantry	*Cork*	38	U5
Banwell	*Avon*	4	V18
Bar Hill	*Cambs*	12	T24
Barabhas	*W Isles*	26	F10
Baranailt	*Londonderry*	33	N9
Barassie	*S Ayrs*	19	L14
Barbon	*Cumb*	15	P18
Bardney	*Lincs*	17	R23
Barefield	*Clare*	39	S6
Barford	*Warwick*	11	T20
Bargoed	*Caerph*	4	U17
Bargrennan	*Dumf/Gal*	19	M14
Barham	*Kent*	7	V26
Barkway	*Herts*	12	U24
Barlborough	*Derby*	16	R21
Barlby	*N Yorks*	16	Q21
Barley	*Herts*	12	T24
Barmby Moor *Humber*		17	Q22
Barmoor Castle *Northum*		21	L19
Barmouth	*Gwyn*	8	S15
Barna	*Galway*	35	R5
Barnadeg	*Galway*	35	R6
Barnard Castle *Durham*		21	N20
Barnesmore	*Donegal*	32	N7
Barnet	*London*	6	U23
Barnetby le Wold *Humber*		17	Q23
Barnham	*Suffolk*	13	T25
Barnhill	*Moray*	28	G17
Barnoldswick	*Lancs*	15	Q19
Barnsley	*S Yorks*	16	Q21
Barnstaple	*Devon*	3	V15
Barnt Green *Heref/Worcs*		11	T20
Barr	*S Ayrs*	19	M14
Barraduff	*Kerry*	38	T5
Barran	*Cavan*	32	P8
Barrhead	*E Renf*	19	L15
Barrhill	*S Ayrs*	18	M14
Barrow upon Humber *Humber*		17	Q23
Barrowford	*Lancs*	15	Q19
Barrow-in-Furness *Cumb*		15	P17
Barry	*Angus*	25	K18
Barry	*V of Glam*	4	V17
Barton	*N Yorks*	16	P20
Barton upon Humber *Humber*		17	Q23
Barton-le-Clay	*Beds*	12	U23
Barwell	*Leics*	11	S21
Baschurch	*Shrops*	10	S18
Basildon	*Essex*	7	U25
Basingstoke	*Hants*	5	V21
Baslow	*Derby*	16	R20
Baston	*Lincs*	12	S23
Bath	*Avon*	5	V19
Bathford	*Avon*	5	V19
Bathgate	*W Loth*	24	L16
Batley	*W Yorks*	16	Q20
Batterstown	*Meath*	37	R10
Battle	*E Sussex*	7	W24
Bawdeswell	*Norfolk*	13	S26
Bawdsey	*Suffolk*	13	T26
Bawnboy	*Cavan*	36	P8
Bawtry	*S Yorks*	16	R21
Bayston Hill	*Shrops*	10	S18
Beachley	*Glos*	4	U18
Beaconsfield	*Bucks*	6	U22
Beadnell	*Northum*	21	L20
Bealin	*Westmeath*	36	R8
Bealnablath	*Cork*	39	U6
Beaminster	*Dorset*	4	W18
Bearsden	*E Dunb*	19	L15
Bearsted	*Kent*	7	V25
Beattock	*Dumf/Gal*	20	M17
Beaufort	*Kerry*	38	T4
Beaufort	*Bl Gwent*	4	U17
Beaulieu	*Hants*	5	W21
Beauly	*H'land*	28	H15
Beaumaris	*Angl*	8	R15
Bebington	*Mersey*	15	R17
Beccles	*Suffolk*	13	T27
Beck Row	*Suffolk*	12	T24
Beckermet	*Cumb*	14	P16
Beckfoot	*Cumb*	20	N17
Beckhampton	*Wilts*	5	V20
Beckingham	*Notts*	17	R22
Beckington	*Som'set*	5	V19
Bedale	*N Yorks*	16	P20
Beddgelert	*Gwyn*	8	R15
Bedford	*Beds*	12	T23
Bedlington	*Northum*	21	M20
Bedwas	*Caerph*	4	U17
Bedworth	*Warwick*	11	T21
Beech Hill	*Down*	33	P11
Beeford	*Humber*	17	Q23
Beelaha	*Clare*	38	S4
Beer	*Devon*	4	W17
Beeston	*Notts*	11	S21
Beeswing	*Dumf/Gal*	19	M16
Begelly	*Pembs*	9	U14
Beguildy	*Powys*	10	T17
Beighton	*S Yorks*	16	R21
Beith	*N Ayrs*	19	L14
Belbroughton *Heref/Worcs*		10	T19
Belchford	*Lincs*	17	R23
Belclare	*Galway*	35	R6
Belcoo	*Fermanagh*	32	P8
Beldeg	*Mayo*	34	P4
Belfast	*Antrim*	33	N12
Belford	*Northum*	21	L20
Belgooly	*Cork*	39	U7
Bellacorick	*Mayo*	34	P4
Bellaghy	*Londonderry*	33	N10
Bellahy	*Sligo*	35	Q6
Bellanagare *Roscommon*		35	Q7
Bellanaleck *Fermanagh*		32	P8
Bellanamore	*Donegal*	32	N7
Bellananagh	*Cavan*	36	Q9
Bellavary	*Mayo*	35	Q6
Belleek	*Armagh*	33	P11
Belleek	*Donegal*	32	P7
Belleville	*Galway*	35	R6
Bellinamuck	*Longford*	36	Q8
Bellingham	*Northum*	21	M19
Bellsbank	*E Ayrs*	19	M15
Bellshill	*N Lanarks*	19	L15
Belmont	*Lancs*	15	Q19
Belmont	*Shetl'd*	31	A22
Belmullet	*Mayo*	34	P4
Belper	*Derby*	11	R21
Belsay	*Northum*	21	M20
Beltinge	*Kent*	7	V26
Belton	*Humber*	17	Q22
Belton	*Norfolk*	13	S27
Beltra	*Mayo*	34	Q5
Beltra	*Sligo*	32	P6
Belturbet	*Cavan*	36	P9
Bembridge	*I of Wight*	5	W21
Benburb	*Tyrone*	33	P10
Benington	*Lincs*	12	R24
Benllech	*Angl*	8	R15
Bennettsbridge *Kilkenny*		40	S9
Benson	*Oxon*	5	U21
Bentley	*Hants*	6	V22
Bentley	*S Yorks*	16	Q21
Benwick	*Cambs*	12	T23
Beragh	*Tyrone*	32	N9
Bere Alston	*Devon*	3	X15
Bere Regis	*Dorset*	5	W19
Berkeley	*Glos*	5	U19
Berkhamsted	*Herts*	6	U22
Berriedale	*H'land*	28	F17
Berriew	*Powys*	10	S17
Berrow	*Som'set*	4	V17
Berwick	*E Sussex*	6	W24
Berwick-upon-Tweed *Northum*		21	L19
Bessbrook	*Armagh*	33	P11
Bethersden	*Kent*	7	V25
Bethesda	*Gwyn*	8	R15
Bettws Bledrws *Card*		9	ST1
Bettyhill	*H'land*	28	E15
Bettystown	*Meath*	37	Q11
Betws	*Bridg*	9	U16
Betws-y-Coed *Aber/Colw*		8	R16
Beulah	*Powys*	9	T16
Beverley	*Humber*	17	Q23
Beville	*Mayo*	34	P5
Bewcastle	*Cumb*	21	M18
Bewdley	*Heref/Worcs*	10	T19
Bexhill	*E Sussex*	7	W24
Bexley	*London*	6	V24
Bibury	*Glos*	5	U20
Bicester	*Oxon*	11	U21
Bickington	*Devon*	4	W16
Bicton	*Shrops*	10	S18
Biddenden	*Kent*	7	V25
Biddulph	*Staffs*	10	R19
Bideford	*Devon*	3	V15
Bidford-on-Avon *Warwick*		11	T20
Bigbury	*Devon*	3	X16
Biggar	*S Lanarks*	20	L16
Biggin Hill	*London*	6	V24
Biggleswade	*Beds*	12	T23
Bildeston	*Suffolk*	13	T25
Billericay	*Essex*	7	U24
Billesdon	*Leics*	11	S22
Billingborough	*Lincs*	12	S23
Billingham	*Clevl'd*	21	N21
Billinghay	*Lincs*	12	R23
Billingshurst *W Sussex*		6	V23
Bilston	*W Midlands*	10	S19
Binbrook	*Lincs*	17	R23
Bingham	*Notts*	11	S22
Bingley	*W Yorks*	15	Q20
Birchgrove	*Swan*	9	U16
Birchington	*Kent*	7	V26
Birdhill	*Tipperary*	39	S7
Birdlip	*Glos*	5	U19
Birkdale	*Mersey*	15	Q17
Birkenhead	*Mersey*	15	R17
Birmingham	*W Midlands*	11	T20
Birr	*Offaly*	36	R8
Birtley	*Northum*	21	M19
Birtley	*Tyne/Wear*	21	N20
Bishop Auckland *Durham*		21	N20
Bishop Monkton *N Yorks*		16	P21
Bishopbriggs	*E Dunb*	19	L15
Bishop's Castle *Shrops*		10	S18
Bishop's Cleeve *Glos*		10	U19
Bishop's Frome *Heref/Worcs*		10	T19
Bishops Lydeard *Som'set*		4	V17

Bishop's Nympton *Devon* 3 W16
Bishop's Stortford *Herts* 6 U24
Bishop's Tawton *Devon* 3 V15
Bishop's Waltham *Hants* 5 W21
Bishopsteignton *Devon* 4 W16
Bishopstoke *Hants* 5 W21
Bishopston *Swan* 9 U15
Bitton *Avon* 5 V19
Blaby *Leics* 11 S21
Black Rock *Louth* 37 Q11
Blackburn *Lancs* 15 Q19
Blackford *Cumb* 20 N18
Blackford *Perth/Kinr* 24 K16
Blackpool *Lancs* 15 Q17
Blackridge *W Loth* 19 L16
Blackrock *Dublin* 37 R11
Blackwater *Wexford* 40 T11
Blackwaterfoot *N Ayrs* 18 L13
Blackwood *Caerph* 4 U17
Blackwood *S Lanarks* 19 L16
Blaenau Ffestiniog *Gwyn* 8 S16
Blaenavon *Torf* 4 U17
Blagdon *Avon* 4 V18
Blaina *Bl Gwent* 4 U17
Blair Atholl *Perth/Kinr* 24 J16
Blairgowrie *Perth/Kinr* 24 J17
Blakeney *Glos* 5 U19
Blakeney *Norfolk* 13 S26
Blanchland *Northum* 21 N19
Blanchardstown *Dublin* 37 R11
Blandford Forum *Dorset* 5 W19
Blaney *Fermanagh* 32 P8
Blarney *Cork* 39 U6
Blaydon *Tyne/Wear* 21 N20
Bleadon *Avon* 4 V18
Blean *Kent* 7 V26
Blessington *Wicklow* 37 R10
Bletchingdon *Oxon* 5 U21
Bletchley *Bucks* 12 U22
Blewbury *Oxon* 5 U21
Blidworth *Notts* 11 R21
Blisworth *Northants* 11 T22
Blockley *Glos* 11 T20
Blofield *Norfolk* 13 S26
Bloxham *Oxon* 11 T21
Blubberhouses *N Yorks* 16 Q20
Blundeston *Norfolk* 13 S27
Blyth Bridge *Borders* 20 L17
Blyth *Northum* 21 M20
Blyth *Notts* 16 R21
Blythburgh *Suffolk* 13 T27
Blythe Bridge *Staffs* 10 S19
Blyton *Lincs* 17 R22
Boat of Garten *H'land* 24 H16
Boddam *Aberds* 29 H20
Boddam *Shetl'd* 31 C21
Bodedern *Angl* 8 R14
Bodenham *Heref/Worcs* 10 T18
Bodiam *E Sussex* 7 V25
Bodinnick *Cornw'l* 2 X14
Bodmin *Cornw'l* 2 X14
Bodyke *Clare* 39 S6
Boggaun *Leitrim* 32 P7
Bognor Regis *W Sussex* 6 W22
Boheraphuca *Offaly* 36 R8
Boherboy *Cork* 38 T5
Boherlahan *Tipperary* 39 S8
Boho *Fermanagh* 32 P8
Bohola *Mayo* 35 Q5
Boldon *Tyne/Wear* 21 N21
Bolea *Londonderry* 33 M10
Boley *Kildare* 40 R10
Bollington *Ches* 15 R19
Bolney *W Sussex* 6 W23
Bolsover *Derby* 16 R21
Bolton Abbey *N Yorks* 15 Q20
Bolton Bridge *N Yorks* 15 Q20
Bolton by Bowland *Lancs* 15 Q19
Bolton le Sands *Lancs* 15 P18
Bolton *Gtr Man* 15 Q19
Bonarbridge *H'land* 28 G15

Bonby *Humber* 17 Q23
Bonchester Bridge *Borders* 21 M18
Bonchurch *I of Wight* 5 W21
Bo'ness *Falk* 24 K16
Bonhill *W Dunb* 24 L14
Bonnybridge *Falk* 24 K16
Bonnyrigg *Midloth* 20 L17
Bonvilston *V of Glam* 4 U16
Boot *Cumb* 15 P17
Bootle *Cumb* 14 P17
Bootle *Mersey* 15 R17
Bordon *Hants* 6 V22
Borehamwood *Herts* 6 U23
Boreland *Dumf/Gal* 20 M17
Borgh *W Isles* 26 F11
Borgue *Dumf/Gal* 19 N15
Borough Green *Kent* 7 V24
Boroughbridge *N Yorks* 16 P21
Borris *Carlow* 40 S10
Borris-in-Ossory *Laois* 36 S8
Borrisokane *Tipperary* 36 S7
Borrisoleigh *Tipperary* 39 S8
Borrowdale *Cumb* 15 N17
Borth *Card* 8 ST1
Bosbury *Heref/Worcs* 10 T19
Boscastle *Cornw'l* 2 W14
Bosham *W Sussex* 6 W22
Boston Spa *W Yorks* 16 Q21
Boston *Lincs* 12 S23
Botesdale *Suffolk* 13 T25
Bothel *Cumb* 20 N17
Bothenhampton *Dorset* 4 W18
Botley *Oxon* 5 U21
Bottesford *Leics* 11 S22
Bottisham *Cambs* 12 T24
Botwnnog *Gwyn* 8 S14
Bouladuff *Tipperary* 39 S8
Bourne End *Bucks* 6 U22
Bourne *Lincs* 12 S23
Bournemouth *Dorset* 5 W20
Bourton-on-the-Water *Glos* 11 U20
Bovey Tracey *Devon* 4 W16
Bow *Devon* 3 W16
Bowes *Durham* 15 P20
Bowmore *Arg/Bute* 18 L11
Bowness-on-Solway *Cumb* 20 N17
Bowness-on-Windermere *Cumb* 15 P18
Box *Wilts* 5 V19
Boyle *Roscommon* 35 Q7
Bozeat *Northants* 12 T22
Brabourne Lees *Kent* 7 V25
Brabourne *Kent* 7 V25
Bracadale *H'land* 26 H11
Bracebridge Heath *Lincs* 12 R22
Brackelsham *W Sussex* 6 W22
Brackley *Northants* 11 T21
Bracklin *Cavan* 37 Q10
Bracknagh *Offaly* 36 R9
Bracknell *Berks* 6 V22
Braco *Perth/Kinr* 24 K16
Bradford on Avon *Wilts* 5 V19
Bradford *W Yorks* 15 Q20
Brading *I of Wight* 5 W21
Bradpole *Dorset* 4 W18
Bradwell-on-Sea *Essex* 7 U25
Bradworthy *Devon* 3 W15
Brae Roy Lodge *H'land* 24 J14
Brae *Shetl'd* 31 B21
Braemar *Aberds* 24 H17
Braemore *H'land* 27 G13
Braemore *H'land* 28 F16
Brailsford *Derby* 11 S20
Braintree *Essex* 7 U25
Bramford *Suffolk* 13 T26
Bramhall *Gtr Man* 15 R19
Bramhope *W Yorks* 16 Q20
Brampton *Cambs* 12 T23
Brampton *Cumb* 21 N18
Brampton *Suffolk* 13 T25
Brancaster *Norfolk* 13 S25
Branden *Kerry* 38 T3
Branderburgh *Moray* 29 G17
Brandon *Durham* 21 N20
Brandon *Suffolk* 13 T25
Branston *Lincs* 17 R23
Brantham *Suffolk* 13 U26

Bratton Fleming *Devon* 3 V16
Braunston *Northants* 11 T21
Braunton *Devon* 3 V15
Bray *Wicklow* 37 R11
Bray *Berks* 6 U22
Breage *Cornw'l* 2 X13
Breaghva *Clare* 38 S4
Breakish *H'land* 23 H12
Bream *Glos* 4 U18
Breanais *W Isles* 26 F9
Brechfa *Carms* 9 U15
Brechin *Angus* 25 J18
Brecon *Powys* 9 U17
Brede *E Sussex* 7 W25
Bredenbury *Heref/Worcs* 10 T18
Breedoge *Roscommon* 35 Q7
Breenagh *Donegal* 32 N8
Brent *London* 6 U23
Brentwood *Essex* 7 U24
Bretforton *Heref/Worcs* 11 T20
Brewood *Staffs* 10 S19
Bride *I of Man* 14 P15
Bridestowe *Devon* 3 W15
Brideswell *Roscommon* 36 R7
Bridge End *Donegal* 32 M9
Bridge of Allan *Stirl* 24 K16
Bridge of Balgie *Perth/Kinr* 24 J15
Bridge of Cally *Perth/Kinr* 24 J17
Bridge of Don *Aberd C* 25 H19
Bridge of Earn *Perth/Kinr* 24 K17
Bridge of Orchy *Arg/Bute* 24 J14
Bridge of Weir *Renf* 19 L14
Bridge *Kent* 7 V26
Bridgend *Arg/Bute* 18 L11
Bridgend *Bridg* 4 U16
Bridgetown *Wexford* 40 T10
Bridgnorth *Shrops* 10 S19
Bridgwater *Som'set* 4 V18
Bridlington *Humber* 17 P23
Bridport *Dorset* 4 W18
Brierfield *Lancs* 15 Q19
Brierley Hill *W Midlands* 10 T19
Brigg *Humber* 17 Q23
Brighouse *W Yorks* 15 Q20
Brighstone *I of Wight* 5 W21
Brightlingsea *Essex* 7 U26
Brighton *E Sussex* 6 W23
Brigstock *Northants* 12 T22
Brill *Bucks* 6 U21
Brimfield *Heref/Worcs* 10 T18
Brinklow *Warwick* 11 T21
Brinkworth *Wilts* 5 U20
Brinyan *Orkney* 30 D17
Bristol *Avon* 4 V18
Briston *Norfolk* 13 S26
Briton Ferry *Neath P Talb* 9 U16
Brittas *Dublin* 37 R11
Brixham *Devon* 3 X16
Brixton *Devon* 3 X15
Brixworth *Northants* 11 T22
Brize Norton *Oxon* 5 U20
Broad Chalke *Wilts* 5 V20
Broad Haven *Pembs* 9 U13
Broad Hinton *Wilts* 5 V20
Broadclyst *Devon* 4 W17
Broadford *Clare* 39 S6
Broadford *Limerick* 39 T6
Broadford *H'land* 23 H12
Broadhembury *Devon* 4 W17
Broadmayne *Dorset* 5 W19
Broadstairs *Kent* 7 V26
Broadstone *Dorset* 5 W19
Broadwas *Heref/Worcs* 10 T19
Broadway *Wexford* 40 T11
Broadway *Heref/Worcs* 11 T20
Broadwey *Dorset* 5 W19
Broadwindsor *Dorset* 4 W18
Brochel *H'land* 27 H11
Brockenhurst *Hants* 5 W20
Brockworth *Glos* 5 U19
Brocton *Staffs* 10 S19
Brodick *N Ayrs* 18 L13
Bromfield *Shrops* 10 T18

Bromham *Beds* 12 T22
Bromham *Wilts* 5 V19
Bromley Green *Kent* 7 V25
Bromley *London* 6 V24
Brompton Regis *Som'set* 4 V16
Brompton *N Yorks* 16 P21
Bromsgrove *Heref/Worcs* 10 T19
Bromyard *Heref/Worcs* 10 T19
Brooke *Norfolk* 13 S26
Brookeborough *Fermanagh* 32 P9
Broomfield *Monaghan* 37 P10
Broomfield *Essex* 7 U24
Broomhaugh *Northum* 21 N20
Broomhill *Northum* 21 M20
Brora *H'land* 28 F16
Broseley *Shrops* 10 S19
Brothertoft *Lincs* 12 R23
Brotton *Clevl'd* 17 N22
Brough *Cumb* 15 N19
Brough *H'land* 28 E17
Brough *Humber* 17 Q22
Broughderg *Tyrone* 33 N10
Broughshane *Antrim* 33 N11
Broughton Astley *Leics* 11 S21
Broughton *Borders* 20 L17
Broughton *Cumb* 20 N17
Broughton *Hants* 5 V20
Broughton *Humber* 17 Q22
Broughton *Lancs* 15 Q18
Broughton *Northants* 11 T22
Broughton-in-Furness *Cumb* 15 P17
Broughty Ferry *Dundee C* 25 K18
Brownhills *W Midlands* 11 S20
Broxburn *W Loth* 24 L17
Broxton *Ches* 10 R18
Bruff *Limerick* 39 T6
Bruichladdich *Arg/Bute* 18 L11
Brundall *Norfolk* 13 S26
Brunton *Northum* 21 L20
Brunton *Northum* 21 M19
Bruree *Limerick* 39 T6
Bruton *Som'set* 5 V19
Brymbo *Wrex* 10 R17
Brynamman *Carms* 9 U16
Bryncrug *Gwyn* 8 S15
Brynmawr *Bl Gwent* 4 U17
Brynsiencyn *Angl* 8 R15
Bubwith *Humber* 17 Q22
Buchlyvie *Stirl* 24 K15
Buckden *Cambs* 12 T23
Buckden *N Yorks* 15 P19
Buckfast *Devon* 3 X16
Buckfastleigh *Devon* 3 X16
Buckhaven *Fife* 25 K17
Buckie *Moray* 29 G18
Buckingham *Bucks* 11 T22
Buckland Brewer *Devon* 3 W15
Buckland Newton *Dorset* 5 W19
Buckland *Oxon* 5 U21
Buckley *Flints* 10 R17
Buck's Cross *Devon* 3 W15
Bucksburn *Aberd C* 25 H19
Bude *Cornw'l* 2 W14
Budleigh Salterton *Devon* 4 W17
Bugbrooke *Northants* 11 T22
Buggan *Fermanagh* 32 P8
Bugle *Cornw'l* 2 X14
Builth Wells *Powys* 9 T17
Bulford *Wilts* 5 V20
Bulkington *Warwick* 11 T21
Bullaun *Galway* 35 R6
Bulwell *Notts* 11 R21
Bunahowen *Mayo* 34 P4
Bunalunn *Cork* 38 U5
Bunaw *Kerry* 38 U4
Bunbeg *Donegal* 32 M7
Bunbrosna *Westmeath* 36 Q9
Bunbury *Ches* 10 R18
Bunclody *Wexford* 40 S10
Buncrana *Donegal* 32 M9
Bundoran *Donegal* 32 P7
Bunessan *Arg/Bute* 22 K11
Bungay *Suffolk* 13 T26
Bunmahon *Waterford* 40 T9

Bunnaglass *Galway* 35 R6
Bunnahabhain *Arg/Bute* 18 L11
Bunnanaddan *Sligo* 35 P6
Bunnyconnellan *Mayo* 35 P5
Bunratty *Clare* 39 S6
Buntingford *Herts* 12 U23
Bunwell *Norfolk* 13 S26
Burbage *Derby* 15 R20
Burbage *Leics* 11 S21
Burbage *Wilts* 5 V20
Bures *Suffolk* 13 U25
Burford *Oxon* 5 U20
Burgess Hill *W Sussex* 6 W23
Burgh le Marsh *Lincs* 12 R24
Burgh-by-Sands *Cumb* 20 N17
Burghclere *Hants* 5 V21
Burghead *Moray* 28 G17
Burghfield Common *Berks* 6 V21
Burley *Hants* 5 W20
Burley *W Yorks* 15 Q20
Burlton *Shrops* 10 S18
Burneside *Cumb* 15 P18
Burness *Orkney* 30 D18
Burnfoot *Cork* 39 T6
Burnfoot *Donegal* 32 M9
Burnham Market *Norfolk* 13 S25
Burnham *Bucks* 6 U22
Burnham-on-Crouch *Essex* 7 U25
Burnham-on-Sea *Som'set* 4 V18
Burniston *N Yorks* 17 P23
Burnley *Lancs* 15 Q19
Burnmouth *Borders* 21 L19
Burntisland *Fife* 25 K17
Burntwood *Staffs* 11 S20
Burravoe *Shetl'd* 31 A21
Burrelton *Perth/Kinr* 24 J17
Burren *Clare* 35 R5
Burren *Down* 37 P11
Burry Port *Carms* 9 U15
Burscough Bridge *Lancs* 15 Q18
Burstwick *Humber* 17 Q23
Burton Agnes *Humber* 17 P23
Burton Bradstock *Dorset* 4 W18
Burton Fleming *Humber* 17 P23
Burton in Lonsdale *N Yorks* 15 P18
Burton Latimer *Northants* 12 T22
Burton *Cumb* 15 P18
Burton upon Stather *Humber* 17 Q22
Burton upon Trent *Staffs* 11 S20
Burtonport *Donegal* 32 N7
Burwash *E Sussex* 7 W24
Burwell *Cambs* 12 T24
Burwick *Orkney* 30 E18
Bury St. Edmunds *Suffolk* 13 T25
Bury *Gtr Man* 15 Q19
Bushey *Herts* 6 U23
Bushmills *Antrim* 33 M10
Butler's Bridge *Cavan* 36 P9
Butlerstown *Cork* 39 U6
Buttermere *Cumb* 20 N17
Buttevant *Cork* 39 T6
Buxted *E Sussex* 6 W24
Buxton *Derby* 15 R20
Bweeng *Cork* 39 T6
Byfield *Northants* 11 T21
Byfleet *Surrey* 6 V23
Bylchau *Aber/Colw* 8 R16

C

Cabinteely *Dublin* 37 R11
Cabrach *Moray* 29 H17
Cabragh *Tyrone* 33 P10
Cadamstown *Offaly* 36 R8
Caenby Corner *Lincs* 17 R22
Caergwrle *Flints* 10 R17
Caerleon *Newp* 4 U18
Caernarfon *Gwyn* 8 R15

Caerphilly *Caerph*	4	U17
Caersws *Powys*	8	S17
Caerwent *Monmouths*	4	U18
Caher *Clare*	35	S6
Caher *Galway*	34	R5
Caher *Tipperary*	39	T8
Caherciveen *Kerry*	38	U3
Caherconlish *Limerick*	39	S7
Caherdaniel *Kerry*	38	U3
Cahermore *Cork*	38	U3
Cahermurphy *Clare*	38	S5
Cairinis *W Isles*	26	G9
Cairndow *Arg/Bute*	23	K14
Cairnryan *Dumf/Gal*	18	N13
Caister-on-Sea		
Norfolk	13	S27
Caistor *Lincs*	17	R23
Calanais *W Isles*	26	F10
Caldbeck *Cumb*	20	N17
Calder Bridge *Cumb*	14	P17
Caldicot *Monmouths*	4	U18
Caledon *Tyrone*	33	P10
Calfsound *Orkney*	30	D18
Calgary *Arg/Bute*	22	J11
Callan *Kilkenny*	40	S9
Callander *Stirl*	24	K15
Callington *Cornw'l*	3	X15
Callow *Galway*	34	R3
Callow *Mayo*	35	Q5
Calne *Wilts*	5	V20
Calshot *Hants*	5	W21
Calstock *Cornw'l*	3	X15
Calta *Galway*	35	R7
Calverton *Notts*	11	R21
Cam *Glos*	5	U19
Camber *E Sussex*	7	W25
Camberley *Surrey*	6	V22
Cambo *Northum*	21	M20
Camborne *Cornw'l*	2	X13
Cambridge *Cambs*	12	T24
Camden *London*	6	U23
Camelford *Cornw'l*	2	W14
Camlough *Armagh*	33	P11
Cammachmore		
Aberds	25	H19
Camolin *Wexford*	40	S11
Camp *Kerry*	38	T4
Campbeltown		
Arg/Bute	18	M12
Campile *Wexford*	40	T10
Camrose *Pembs*	9	U13
Camross *Wexford*	40	T10
Canisbay *H'land*	29	E17
Cannich *H'land*	27	H14
Canningstown *Cavan*	36	Q9
Cannington *Som'set*	4	V17
Cannock *Staffs*	10	S19
Canonbie *Dumf/Gal*	20	M18
Canterbury *Kent*	7	V26
Canvey *Essex*	7	U25
Caol *H'land*	23	J13
Caolas Stocinis		
W Isles	26	G10
Caoles *Arg/Bute*	22	J10
Capel Curig		
Aber/Colw	8	R16
Capel St. Mary		
Suffolk	13	T26
Capel *Surrey*	6	V23
Cappagh *Cork*	39	T7
Cappagh *Galway*	35	R7
Cappagh White		
Tipperary	39	S7
Cappamore *Limerick*	39	S7
Cappeen *Cork*	39	U6
Cappoquin *Waterford*	39	T8
Carbis Bay *Cornw'l*	2	X13
Carbost *H'land*	26	H11
Carbost *H'land*	26	H11
Carbury *Kildare*	37	R10
Cardiff *Card*	4	V17
Cardigan *Card*	9	ST1
Cardington *Beds*	12	T22
Cardross *Arg/Bute*	19	L14
Cargill *Perth/Kinr*	24	J17
Carhampton *Som'set*	4	V17
Carisbrooke		
I of Wight	5	W21
Cark *Cumb*	15	P18
Carlabhagh *W Isles*	26	F10
Carlanstown *Meath*	37	Q10
Carleton Rode		
Norfolk	13	S26
Carlingford *Louth*	37	P11
Carlisle *Cumb*	20	N18
Carlops *Borders*	20	L17
Carlow *Carlow*	40	S10
Carlton Colville		
Suffolk	13	T27
Carlton Miniott		
N Yorks	16	P21
Carlton *N Yorks*	16	Q21
Carlton *Notts*	11	S21
Carlton-in-Lindrick		
Notts	16	R21
Carluke *S Lanarks*	19	L16
Carmarthen *Carms*	9	U15
Carmyllie *Angus*	25	J18
Carna *Galway*	34	R4
Carnachuin *H'land*	24	H16
Carnaross *Meath*	37	Q10
Carncastle *Antrim*	33	N12
Carndonagh *Donegal*	32	M9
Carnew *Wicklow*	40	S11
Carney *Sligo*	32	P6
Carnforth *Lancs*	15	P18
Carnlough *Antrim*	33	N12
Carno *Powys*	8	S16
Carnoustie *Angus*	25	J18
Carnwath *S Lanarks*	20	L16
Carracastle *Mayo*	35	Q6
Carradale *Arg/Bute*	18	L13
Carragh *Kildare*	37	R10
Carran *Clare*	35	R5
Carraroe *Galway*	34	R4
Carrbridge *H'land*	28	H16
Carrick *Donegal*	32	N6
Carrick *Arg/Bute*	23	K14
Carrickart *Donegal*	32	M8
Carrickbeg *Waterford*	40	T9
Carrickboy *Longford*	36	Q8
Carrickfergus *Antrim*	33	N12
Carrickmacross		
Monaghan	37	Q10
Carrickmore *Tyrone*	33	N9
Carrick-on-Shannon		
Roscommon	36	Q7
Carrick-on-Suir		
Tipperary	40	T9
Carrigaholt *Clare*	38	S4
Carrigahorig		
Tipperary	36	R7
Carrigaline *Cork*	39	U7
Carrigallen *Leitrim*	36	Q8
Carriganimmy *Cork*	38	U5
Carrigfadda *Cork*	38	U5
Carrigkerry *Limerick*	38	T5
Carrignavar *Cork*	39	U7
Carrigtohill *Cork*	39	U7
Carronbridge		
Dumf/Gal	19	M16
Carrowbehy		
Roscommon	35	Q6
Carrowkeel *Donegal*	32	M8
Carrowkeel *Donegal*	32	M9
Carrowkeel *Galway*	35	R7
Carrowkennedy *Mayo*	34	Q4
Carrowreilly *Sligo*	35	P6
Carrowroe *Longford*	36	Q8
Carryduff *Down*	33	N12
Carsaig *Arg/Bute*	23	K12
Carsphairn *Dumf/Gal*	19	M15
Carstairs *S Lanarks*	20	L16
Carterton *Oxon*	5	U20
Cartmel *Cumb*	15	P18
Cashel *Galway*	35	Q6
Cashel *Tipperary*	39	S8
Castle Acre *Norfolk*	13	S25
Castle Cary *Som'set*	4	V18
Castle Donington		
Leics	11	S21
Castle Douglas		
Dumf/Gal	19	N16
Castlebar *Mayo*	34	Q5
Castlebay = Bagh a		
Chaisteil *W Isles*	22	J8
Castlebellingham		
Louth	37	Q11
Castleblakeney		
Galway	35	R7
Castleblaney		
Monaghan	37	P10
Castlebridge *Wexford*	40	T11
Castlecomer *Kilkenny*	40	S9
Castleconnell		
Limerick	39	S7
Castlecor *Cork*	39	T6
Castledawson		
Londonderry	33	N10
Castlederg *Tyrone*	32	N8
Castledermot *Kildare*	40	S10
Castlefinn *Donegal*	32	N8
Castleford *W Yorks*	16	Q21
Castlegregory *Kerry*	38	T3
Castlehill *Mayo*	34	P4
Castleisland *Kerry*	38	T5
Castlelyons *Cork*	39	T7
Castlemaine *Kerry*	38	T4
Castlemartin *Pembs*	9	U13
Castlemartyr *Cork*	39	U7
Castleplunket		
Roscommon	35	Q7
Castlepollard		
Westmeath	36	Q9
Castlerea		
Roscommon	35	Q7
Castlerock		
Londonderry	33	M10
Castleside *Durham*	21	N20
Castleton *Derby*	15	R20
Castleton *N Yorks*	17	P22
Castletown		
Bearhaven *Cork*	38	U4
Castletown		
Geoghegan		
Westmeath	36	R9
Castletown *Laois*	36	S9
Castletown *Meath*	37	Q10
Castletown *H'land*	28	E17
Castletown *I of Man*	14	P14
Castletownroche *Cork*	39	T7
Castletownshend		
Cork	38	U5
Castlewellan *Down*	33	P12
Caston *Norfolk*	13	S25
Castor *Cambs*	12	S23
Catcleugh *Northum*	21	M19
Caterham *Surrey*	6	V23
Caton *Lancs*	15	P18
Catrine *E Ayrs*	19	L15
Catsfield *E Sussex*	7	W24
Catterall *Lancs*	15	Q18
Catterick Camp		
N Yorks	16	P20
Catterick *N Yorks*	16	P20
Catton *Northum*	21	N19
Caulkerbush		
Dumf/Gal	20	N16
Causeway *Kerry*	38	T4
Cavan *Cavan*	36	Q9
Cavangarden *Donegal*	32	N7
Cawdor *H'land*	28	G16
Cawood *N Yorks*	16	Q21
Cawston *Norfolk*	13	S26
Caythorpe *Lincs*	12	R22
Cefn-mawr *Wrex*	10	S17
Celbridge *Kildare*	37	R10
Cemaes *Angl*	8	R15
Cemmaes Road		
Powys	8	S16
Cenarth *Carms*	9	T14
Ceres *Fife*	25	K18
Cerne Abbas *Dorset*	5	W19
Cerrigydrudion		
Aber/Colw	8	R16
Chacewater *Cornw'l*	2	X13
Chaddesley Corbet		
Heref/Worcs	10	T19
Chadwell St. Mary		
Essex	7	V24
Chagford *Devon*	3	W16
Chalfont St. Giles		
Bucks	6	U22
Chalford *Glos*	5	U19
Chalgrove *Oxon*	6	U21
Challacombe *Devon*	3	V16
Challock *Kent*	7	V25
Chandler's Ford		
Hants	5	W21
Chanonrock *Louth*	37	Q10
Chapel en le Frith		
Derby	15	R20
Chapel St. Leonards		
Lincs	17	R24
Chapeltown		
S Lanarks	19	L15
Chapeltown *S Yorks*	16	R21
Chard *Som'set*	4	W18
Charing *Kent*	7	V25
Charlbury *Oxon*	11	U21
Charlemont *Armagh*	33	P10
Charlestown *Mayo*	35	Q6
Charlestown of		
Aberlour *Moray*	29	H17
Charleville *Cork*	39	T6
Charlton Horethorne		
Som'set	5	W19
Charlton Kings *Glos*	10	U19
Charlton *Wilts*	5	U19
Charlwood *Surrey*	6	V23
Charminster *Dorset*	5	W19
Charmouth *Dorset*	4	W18
Chartham *Kent*	7	V26
Chasel *Mayo*	34	Q4
Chatham *Kent*	7	V25
Chathill *Northum*	21	L20
Chatteris *Cambs*	12	T24
Chatton *Northum*	21	L20
Chawleigh *Devon*	3	W16
Cheadle *Gtr Man*	15	R19
Cheadle *Staffs*	11	S20
Chedburgh *Suffolk*	13	T25
Cheddar *Som'set*	4	V18
Cheddleton *Staffs*	10	R19
Chellaston *Derby*	11	S21
Chelmarsh *Shrops*	10	T19
Chelmsford *Essex*	7	U24
Cheltenham *Glos*	10	U19
Chepstow		
Monmouths	4	U18
Cherhill *Wilts*	5	V20
Cheriton Fitzpaine		
Devon	4	W16
Cheriton *Hants*	5	V21
Chertsey *Surrey*	6	V23
Chesham *Bucks*	6	U22
Cheshunt *Herts*	6	U23
Chester *Ches*	10	R18
Chesterfield *Derby*	16	R21
Chester-le-Street		
Durham	21	N20
Chew Magna *Avon*	4	V18
Chewton Mendip		
Som'set	4	V18
Chichester *W Sussex*	6	W22
Chiddingfold *Surrey*	6	V22
Chideock *Dorset*	4	W18
Chigwell *Essex*	6	U24
Chilcompton *Som'set*	4	V18
Chilham *Kent*	7	V25
Chillington *Devon*	3	X16
Chilton *Durham*	21	N20
Chingford *London*	6	U24
Chinnor *Oxon*	6	U22
Chippenham *Wilts*	5	V19
Chipping Campden		
Glos	11	T20
Chipping Norton		
Oxon	11	U20
Chipping Ongar		
Essex	7	U24
Chipping Sodbury		
Avon	5	U19
Chirbury *Shrops*	10	S17
Chirk *Wrex*	10	S17
Chirnside *Borders*	21	L19
Chiseldon *Wilts*	5	U20
Chitterne *Wilts*	5	V19
Chobham *Surrey*	6	V22
Chollerton *Northum*	21	M19
Cholsey *Oxon*	5	U21
Chorley *Lancs*	15	Q18
Chorleywood *Herts*	6	U22
Christchurch *Cambs*	12	S24
Christchurch *Dorset*	5	W20
Christow *Devon*	4	W16
Chudleigh *Devon*	4	W16
Chulmleigh *Devon*	3	W16
Church Hill *Donegal*	32	N8
Church Hill		
Fermanagh	32	P8
Church Stretton		
Shrops	10	S18
Church Village		
Rh Cyn Taff	9	U17
Churchdown *Glos*	10	U19
Churchill *Oxon*	11	U20
Churchstow *Devon*	3	X16
Churchtown *Cork*	39	U7
Churchtown *Wexford*	40	T11
Chwilog *Gwyn*	8	S15
Cilgerran *Pembs*	9	T14
Cille Bhrighde *W Isles*	22	H9
Cilycwm *Carms*	9	T16
Cinderford *Glos*	5	U19
Clabby *Fermanagh*	32	P8
Clabhach *Arg/Bute*	22	J10
Clachan na Luib		
W Isles	26	G9
Clachan *Arg/Bute*	18	L12
Clachan *H'land*	27	H11
Clackmannan *Clack*	24	K16
Clacton-on-Sea		
Essex	7	U26
Cladich *Arg/Bute*	23	K13
Clady *Tyrone*	32	N8
Clady Milltown		
Armagh	33	P10
Claggan *H'land*	23	J12
Claigan *H'land*	26	H10
Clanabogan *Tyrone*	32	N9
Clane *Kildare*	37	R10
Clanfield *Hants*	6	W22
Claonaig *Arg/Bute*	18	L13
Clapham *Beds*	12	T23
Clapham *N Yorks*	15	P19
Clara *Offaly*	36	R8
Clarahill *Laois*	36	R9
Clare *Suffolk*	13	T25
Clarecastle *Clare*	39	S6
Clareen *Offaly*	36	R8
Claregalway *Galway*	35	R6
Claremorris *Mayo*	35	Q5
Claretuam *Galway*	35	R6
Clarina *Limerick*	39	S6
Clarinbridge *Galway*	35	R6
Clash *Cork*	39	U7
Clashmore *Waterford*	39	T8
Clashmore *H'land*	28	G15
Claudy *Londonderry*	32	N9
Clavering *Essex*	12	U24
Claverley *Shrops*	10	S19
Clawton *Devon*	3	W15
Clay Cross *Derby*	11	R21
Claydon *Suffolk*	13	T26
Claypole *Lincs*	12	R22
Cleadale *H'land*	22	J11
Cleady *Kerry*	38	U4
Cleat *Orkney*	30	E18
Cleator Moor *Cumb*	14	N16
Cleethorpes *Humber*	17	Q23
Cleeve Prior *Warwick*	11	T20
Cleggan *Galway*	34	Q3
Clehonger		
Heref/Worcs	10	T18
Cleobury Mortimer		
Shrops	10	T19
Clevedon *Avon*	4	V18
Cleveleys *Lancs*	15	Q17
Cley *Norfolk*	13	S26
Clifden *Galway*	34	R3
Cliffe *Kent*	7	V25
Cliffony *Sligo*	32	P7
Clifford *Heref/Worcs*	10	T17
Clipston *Northants*	11	T22
Clitheroe *Lancs*	15	Q19
Clive *Shrops*	10	S18
Clogh *Antrim*	33	N11
Clogh *Kilkenny*	40	S9
Cloghan *Donegal*	32	N8
Cloghan *Offaly*	36	R8
Cloghan *Westmeath*	36	Q9
Cloghane *Kerry*	38	T3
Cloghaneely *Donegal*	32	M7
Cloghboy *Donegal*	32	N6
Clogheen *Tipperary*	39	T8
Clogher Head *Louth*	37	Q11
Clogher *Roscommon*	36	Q7
Clogher *Tyrone*	32	P9
Cloghjordan *Tipperary*	36	S7
Cloghran *Dublin*	37	R11
Cloghy *Down*	33	P13
Clomantagh *Kilkenny*	40	S9
Clonakilty *Cork*	39	U6
Clonaslee *Laois*	36	R8
Clonbulloge *Offaly*	36	R9
Clonbur *Galway*	34	Q5
Cloncurry *Kildare*	37	R10
Clondalkin *Dublin*	37	R11
Clonea *Waterford*	40	T9
Clonee *Meath*	37	R11
Cloneen *Tipperary*	39	T8
Clonelly *Fermanagh*	32	N8
Clones *Monaghan*	32	P9
Cloney *Kildare*	40	R9
Clonfert *Galway*	36	R7
Clonlee *Mayo*	35	Q6
Clonmacnoise *Offaly*	36	R8
Clonmany *Donegal*	32	M9
Clonmel *Tipperary*	39	T8
Clonmellon		
Westmeath	36	Q9
Clonmore *Carlow*	40	S10
Clonmore *Offaly*	36	R9
Clonmore *Tipperary*	39	S8
Clonord *Meath*	36	R9
Clonroche *Wexford*	40	T10
Clontarf *Dublin*	37	R11
Cloodara *Longford*	36	Q8
Cloonacool *Sligo*	35	P6
Cloonart *Longford*	36	Q8
Cloonbannin *Cork*	38	T5

Cloonboo Galway 35 R5
Cloone Leitrim 36 Q8
Cloonfad
  Roscommon 35 Q6
Cloonkeen Kerry 38 U5
Cloonlara Clare 39 S6
Cloonloogh Sligo 35 Q7
Cloonmore Mayo 35 Q6
Clophill Beds 12 T23
Clorbern Galway 35 Q6
Closeburn Dumf/Gal 19 M16
Clough Down 33 P12
Cloughton N Yorks 17 P23
Clova Angus 25 J17
Clovelly Devon 3 W15
Clovenfords Borders 20 L18
Clowne Derby 16 R21
Cloyne Cork 39 U7
Clun Shrops 10 T17
Clunbury Shrops 10 T18
Clunes H'land 23 J14
Clungunford Shrops 10 T18
Clutton Avon 4 V18
Clydach Swan 9 U16
Clydebank W Dunb 19 L15
Clynnog-fawr Gwyn 8 R15
Clyro Powys 10 T17
Côbh Cork 39 U7
Coachford Cork 39 U6
Coagh Tyrone 33 N10
Coalbrookdale
  Shrops 10 S18
Coalburn S Lanarks 19 L16
Coalisland Tyrone 33 N10
Coalville Leics 11 S21
Coatbridge N Lanarks 19 L15
Cobham Kent 7 V24
Cobham Surrey 6 V23
Cock Bridge Aberds 25 H17
Cockburnspath
  Borders 25 L19
Cockenzie E Loth 25 L18
Cockerham Lancs 15 Q18
Cockermouth Cumb 20 N17
Cockfield Durham 21 N20
Cockfield Suffolk 13 T25
Cockshutt Shrops 10 S18
Coddenham Suffolk 13 T26
Codford St. Mary
  Wilts 5 V19
Coggeshall Essex 7 U25
Coignafearn Lodge
  H'land 24 H15
Coille Mhorgil H'land 23 H13
Coillore H'land 26 H11
Colby I of Man 14 P14
Colchester Essex 13 U25
Cold Ashton Avon 5 V19
Coldingham Borders 21 L19
Coldstream Borders 21 L19
Colebrooke Devon 4 W16
Coleford Glos 4 U18
Colehill Longford 36 Q8
Coleraine
  Londonderry 33 M10
Coleshill Warwick 11 T20
Colinton C of Edinb 25 L17
Colintraive Arg/Bute 18 L13
Collin Dumf/Gal 20 M16
Collingbourne
  Kingston Wilts 5 V20
Collingham Notts 11 R22
Collingham W Yorks 16 Q21
Collinstown
  Westmeath 36 Q9
Collon Louth 37 Q11
Collooney Sligo 32 P7
Colmonel S Ayrs 18 M14
Colne Lancs 15 Q19
Colpy Aberds 29 H18
Colsterworth Lincs 12 S22
Coltishall Norfolk 13 S26
Colwell Northum 21 M19
Colwich Staffs 11 S20
Colwyn Bay
  Aber/Colw 8 R16
Colyton Devon 4 W17
Combe Martin Devon 3 V15
Comber Down 33 N12
Comberton Cambs 12 T24
Combwich Som'set 4 V17
Commeen Donegal 32 N8
Compton Martin Avon 4 V18
Compton Berks 5 U21
Compton W Sussex 6 W22
Comrie Perth/Kinr 24 K16
Condover Shrops 10 S18

Cong Mayo 34 Q5
Congleton Ches 10 R19
Congresbury Avon 4 V18
Coningsby Lincs 12 R23
Conisbrough S Yorks 16 R21
Coniston Cumb 15 P17
Conlig Down 33 N12
Conna Cork 39 T7
Connagh Galway 35 S7
Connah's Quay Flints 15 R17
Connel Park E Ayrs 19 M15
Connel Arg/Bute 23 K13
Connonagh Cork 38 U5
Connor Antrim 33 N11
Cononbridge H'land 28 G15
Consett Durham 21 N20
Contin H'land 28 G14
Convoy Donegal 32 N8
Conwy Aber/Colw 8 R16
Cookham Berks 6 U22
Cookstown Tyrone 33 N10
Coola Sligo 35 P7
Coolaney Sligo 32 P6
Coolbaun Tipperary 35 S7
Coolderg Galway 35 Q6
Coole Westmeath 36 Q9
Coolgreany Wexford 40 S11
Coolham W Sussex 6 W23
Coolmore Donegal 32 N7
Coolrain Laois 36 S8
Coombe Bissett Wilts 5 V20
Cooneen Fermanagh 32 P9
Cooraclare Clare 38 S5
Cootehill Cavan 36 P9
Copplestone Devon 4 W16
Coppull Lancs 15 Q18
Copthorne W Sussex 6 V23
Corbally Laois 40 S9
Corbally Sligo 35 P5
Corbridge Northum 21 N19
Corby Glen Lincs 12 S22
Corby Northants 12 T22
Cordal Kerry 38 T5
Corfe Castle Dorset 5 W19
Corfe Mullen Dorset 5 W19
Corgary Tyrone 32 N8
Cork Cork 39 U7
Corlea Longford 36 Q8
Corlogh Mayo 34 P3
Cornafulla
  Roscommon 36 R8
Cornamona Galway 35 Q5
Cornanagh Mayo 35 Q5
Cornhaw Cave 32 P8
Cornhill on Tweed
  Northum 21 L19
Corpach H'land 23 J13
Corran H'land 23 J13
Corranny Fermanagh 32 P9
Corrawalleen Leitrim 36 Q8
Corrie N Ayrs 18 L13
Corrigeenroe
  Roscommon 35 P7
Corringham Essex 7 U24
Corringham Lincs 17 R22
Corris Gwyn 8 S16
Corrofin Clare 35 S5
Corsham Wilts 5 V19
Corsley Wilts 5 V19
Corsock Dumf/Gal 19 M16
Corton Norfolk 13 S27
Corvally Monaghan 37 Q10
Corvoy Monaghan 37 P10
Corwen Denbs 8 S17
Coseley W Midlands 10 S19
Cosham Hants 6 W21
Costelloe Galway 34 R4
Costessey Norfolk 13 S26
Cotgrave Notts 11 S21
Cotherstone Durham 21 N20
Cottenham Cambs 12 T24
Cottered Herts 12 U23
Cottesmore Leics 12 S22
Cottingham Humber 17 Q23
Coulags H'land 27 H13
Coulport Arg/Bute 23 K14
Countesthorpe Leics 11 S21
Coupar Angus
  Perth/Kinr 24 J17
Courtmacsherry Cork 39 U6
Courtown Wexford 40 S11
Cove Bay Aberd C 25 H19
Cove Arg/Bute 23 L14
Cove H'land 27 G13
Coventry W Midlands 11 T21
Coverack Cornw'l 2 X13

Cowbit Lincs 12 S23
Cowbridge V of Glam 4 V17
Cowdenbeath Fife 24 K17
Cowes I of Wight 5 W21
Cowfold W Sussex 6 W23
Cowpen Northum 21 M20
Cowplain Hants 6 W21
Coxheath Kent 7 V25
Coylton S Ayrs 19 M14
Craanford Wexford 40 S11
Craggie H'land 28 H15
Crai Powys 9 U16
Craibstone Moray 29 G18
Craigavon Armagh 33 P11
Craigellachie Moray 29 H17
Craighouse Arg/Bute 18 L12
Craigmore Arg/Bute 18 L13
Craignure Arg/Bute 23 K12
Craigtown H'land 28 F16
Crail Fife 25 K18
Cramlington Northum 21 M20
Cranagh Tyrone 33 N9
Cranborne Dorset 5 W20
Cranbrook Kent 7 V25
Cranleigh Surrey 6 V23
Cranmore Som'set 5 V19
Cranwell Lincs 12 R23
Cratloe Limerick 38 T5
Crathie Aberds 25 H17
Craughwell Galway 35 R6
Craven Arms Shrops 10 T18
Crawford S Lanarks 20 M16
Crawfordjohn
  S Lanarks 19 L16
Crawley W Sussex 6 V23
Creag Ghoraidh
  W Isles 26 H9
Creaganhroe
  Monaghan 33 P10
Creake Norfolk 13 S25
Credenhill
  Heref/Worcs 10 T18
Crediton Devon 4 W16
Creegh Clare 38 S5
Creeragh Mayo 34 P5
Creeslough Donegal 32 M8
Creetown Dumf/Gal 19 N15
Creeve Tyrone 33 N10
Creeves Limerick 38 S5
Creggan Tyrone 33 N9
Cregganbaun Mayo 34 Q4
Creggs Galway 35 Q7
Cressage Shrops 10 S18
Cresselly Pembs 9 U14
Crewe Ches 10 R19
Crewkerne Som'set 4 W18
Crianlarich Stirl 24 K14
Criccieth Gwyn 8 S15
Crick Northants 11 T21
Crickhowell Powys 4 U17
Cricklade Wilts 5 U20
Crieff Perth/Kinr 24 K16
Crimond Aberds 29 G20
Crinan Arg/Bute 23 K12
Crindle Londonderry 33 M10
Crinkill Offaly 36 R8
Croagh Limerick 39 S6
Crocketford Dumf/Gal 19 M16
Crockets Town Mayo 35 P5
Croggan Arg/Bute 23 K12
Croghan Offaly 36 R9
Croghan Roscommon 35 Q7
Croglin Cumb 21 N18
Croick H'land 28 G14
Crolly Donegal 32 M7
Cromarty H'land 28 G15
Cromer Norfolk 13 S26
Cromor N Isles 26 F11
Crondall Hants 6 V22
Crook Durham 21 N20
Crookedwood
  Westmeath 36 Q9
Crookham Northum 21 L19
Crookhaven Cork 39 U4
Crooklands Cumb 15 P18
Crookstown Cork 39 U6
Croom Limerick 39 S6
Crosbost W Isles 26 F11
Crosby Ravensworth
  Cumb 21 N18
Crosby Cumb 20 N17
Crosby Mersey 15 R17
Cross Barry Cork 39 U6
Cross Keys Meath 37 Q10
Crossakiel Meath 36 Q9
Crossdoney Cavan 36 Q9

Crossgar Down 33 P12
Cross-Hands Carms 9 U15
Crosshaven Cork 39 U7
Crosshill S Ayrs 19 M14
Crossmaglen Armagh 37 P10
Crossmichael
  Dumf/Gal 19 N16
Crossmolina Mayo 34 P5
Croston Lancs 15 Q18
Crowborough
  E Sussex 6 V24
Crowland Lincs 12 S23
Crowle Humber 17 Q22
Crowthorne Berks 6 V22
Croxton Kerrial Leics 11 S22
Croyde Devon 3 V15
Croydon London 6 V23
Cruden Bay Aberds 29 H20
Crudgington Shrops 10 S18
Crumlin Antrim 33 N11
Crumlin Dublin 37 R11
Crusheen Clare 35 S6
Crymych Pembs 9 U14
Cuckfield W Sussex 6 V23
Cuddington Bucks 6 U22
Cuddington Ches 15 R18
Cudworth S Yorks 16 Q21
Cuffley Herts 6 U23
Culdaff Donegal 32 M9
Culgaith Cumb 21 N18
Culkein H'land 27 F13
Cullaville Armagh 37 P10
Cullen Tipperary 39 S7
Cullen Moray 29 G18
Cullicudden H'land 28 G15
Cullinane Antrim 33 N11
Cullion Tyrone 32 N9
Cullivoe Shetl'd 31 A21
Culloden H'land 28 H15
Cullompton Devon 4 W17
Cullyhanna Armagh 37 P10
Culmaize Dumf/Gal 19 N14
Culmington Shrops 10 T18
Culmstock Devon 4 W17
Culrain H'land 28 G15
Culross Fife 24 K16
Cults Aberd C 25 H19
Cumbernauld
  N Lanarks 19 L16
Cuminestown Aberds 29 G19
Cummertrees
  Dumf/Gal 20 N17
Cumnock E Ayrs 19 M15
Cumnor Oxon 5 U21
Cumwhinton Cumb 20 N18
Cupar Fife 25 K17
Curraglass Cork 39 T7
Currie C of Edinb 24 L17
Curry Sligo 35 Q6
Curry Rivel Som'set 4 V18
Curryglass Cork 38 U4
Cushendall Antrim 33 M11
Cushendun Antrim 33 M11
Cushina Offaly 36 R9
Cwmafan
  Neath P Talb 9 U16
Cwmann Carms 9 T15
Cwmbran Torf 4 U17
Cwrt Gwyn 8 S16
Cymmer Neath P Talb 9 U16
Cynwyl Elfed Carms 9 U15

D

Dacklin Roscommon 36 Q7
Dagenham London 6 U24
Dail bho Dheas
  W Isles 26 F11
Dailly S Ayrs 19 M14
Daingean Offaly 36 R9
Dalabrog W Isles 22 H9
Dalbeattie Dumf/Gal 19 N16
Dale Pembs 9 U13
Dale Shetl'd 31 B20
Dalguise Perth/Kinr 24 J16
Dalhalvaig H'land 28 F16
Dalkeith Midloth 25 L17
Dalkey Dublin 37 R11
Dallas Moray 28 G17
Dalleagles E Ayrs 19 M15
Dalmally Arg/Bute 23 K14
Dalmellington E Ayrs 19 M15
Dalnaspidal Perth/Kinr 24 J15

Dalnessie H'land 28 F15
Dalry Dumf/Gal 19 M15
Dalry N Ayrs 19 L14
Dalrymple E Ayrs 19 M14
Dalston Cumb 20 N18
Dalton Dumf/Gal 20 M17
Dalton N Yorks 16 P20
Dalton-in-Furness
  Cumb 15 P17
Dalwhinnie H'land 24 J15
Dalystown Galway 35 R7
Damerham Hants 5 W20
Damerstown Kilkenny 40 S9
Danbury Essex 7 U25
Darkley Armagh 33 P10
Darlington Durham 16 N21
Darragh Clare 38 S5
Dartford Kent 6 V24
Dartington Devon 3 X16
Dartmouth Devon 3 X16
Darton S Yorks 16 Q20
Darvel E Ayrs 19 L15
Darwen Lancs 15 Q19
Daventry Northants 11 T21
Davington Dumf/Gal 20 M17
Dawlish Devon 4 W17
Deal Kent 7 V26
Dearham Cumb 20 N17
Dearne S Yorks 16 Q21
Debenham Suffolk 13 T26
Deddington Oxon 11 T21
Deelish Cork 38 U5
Deeping St. Nicholas
  Lincs 12 S23
Deerness Orkney 30 E18
Deganwy Aber/Colw 8 R16
Delabole Cornw'l 2 W14
Delchirach Moray 28 H17
Delves Durham 21 N20
Delvin Westmeath 36 Q9
Denbigh Denbs 8 R17
Denby Dale W Yorks 16 Q20
Denholm Borders 21 M18
Denny Falk 24 K16
Dent Cumb 15 P19
Denton Gtr Man 15 R19
Denton Lincs 12 S22
Derby Derby 11 S21
Derry Sligo 35 P7
Derrybeg Donegal 32 M7
Derryboy Down 33 P12
Derrybrien Galway 35 R6
Derrycoosh Mayo 34 Q5
Derrygonnelly
  Fermanagh 32 P8
Derrygorry Monaghan 33 P9
Derrygrogan Offaly 36 R9
Derrykeighan Antrim 33 M10
Derrylin Fermanagh 32 P9
Derry W Yorks 32 BD
Derrymore Kerry 38 T4
Derrynacreeve Cavan 36 P8
Derrynane Kerry 38 U3
Derryrush Galway 34 R4
Derrytrasna Armagh 33 N11
Dersingham Norfolk 13 S24
Dervaig Arg/Bute 22 J11
Dervock Antrim 33 M11
Desborough
  Northants 11 T22
Desertmartin
  Londonderry 33 N10
Desford Leics 11 S21
Devil's Bridge Card 9 ST1
Devizes Wilts 5 V20
Devonport Devon 3 X15
Dewsbury W Yorks 16 Q20
Diabaig H'land 27 G12
Diamond Down 33 P11
Dibden Purlieu Hants 5 W21
Dickleborough
  Norfolk 13 T26
Didcot Oxon 5 U21
Digby Lincs 12 R23
Dinas Mawddwy
  Gwyn 8 S16
Dinas Powis
  V of Glam 4 V17
Dingle Kerry 38 T3
Dingwall H'land 28 G15
Dinnington S Yorks 16 R21
Dinton Wilts 5 V20
Dippen N Ayrs 18 M13
Dirleton E Loth 25 K18
Dirtagh Londonderry 33 M10
Diss Norfolk 13 T26

Distington *Cumb* 20 N16
Ditchingham *Norfolk* 13 T26
Ditchling *E Sussex* 6 W23
Dittisham *Devon* 3 X16
Ditton Priors *Shrops* 10 T18
Doagh *Antrim* 33 N11
Dobwalls *Cornw'l* 2 X14
Docking *Norfolk* 13 S25
Dockray *Cumb* 20 N18
Doddinghurst *Essex* 7 U24
Doddington *Cambs* 12 S24
Doddington *Northum* 21 L19
Dolanog *Powys* 8 S17
Dolfor *Powys* 8 T17
Dolgarrog *Aber/Colw* 8 R16
Dolgellau *Gwyn* 8 S16
Dolla *Tipperary* 39 S7
Dollar *Clack* 24 K16
Dolphinton *S Lanarks* 20 L17
Dolton *Devon* 3 W15
Dolwyddelan
  Aber/Colw 8 R16
Donabate *Dublin* 37 R11
Donadea *Kildare* 37 R10
Donagh *Fermanagh* 32 P9
Donaghadee *Down* 33 N12
Donaghmore *Laois* 39 S8
Donaghmore *Tyrone* 33 N10
Donard *Wicklow* 40 R10
Doncaster *S Yorks* 16 Q21
Donegal *Donegal* 32 N7
Doneraile *Cork* 39 T6
Donhead St. Andrew
  Wilts 5 V19
Donington *Lincs* 12 S23
Donnington *Shrops* 10 S19
Donohill *Tipperary* 39 S7
Donore *Meath* 37 Q11
Donoughmore *Cork* 39 U6
Dooagh *Mayo* 34 Q3
Doocharry *Donegal* 32 N7
Doogary *Cavan* 36 P8
Doogort *Mayo* 34 P3
Dooish *Tyrone* 32 N9
Doolin *Clare* 34 R5
Doon *Limerick* 39 S7
Doonaha *Clare* 38 S4
Doonbeg *Clare* 38 S4
Dorchester *Dorset* 5 W19
Dorchester *Oxon* 5 U21
Dores *H'land* 28 H15
Dorking *Surrey* 6 V23
Dornie *H'land* 27 H12
Dornoch *H'land* 28 G15
Dorridge *W Midlands* 11 T20
Dorstone *Heref/Worcs* 10 T18
Douglas *Cork* 39 U7
Douglas *I of Man* 14 P15
Douglas *S Lanarks* 19 L16
Dounby *Orkney* 30 D17
Doune *Stirl* 24 K15
Dounreay *H'land* 28 E16
Dove Holes *Derby* 15 R20
Dover *Kent* 7 V26
Doveridge *Derby* 11 S20
Downham Market
  Norfolk 12 S24
Downham *Cambs* 12 T24
Downhill *Londonderry* 33 M10
Downies *Donegal* 32 M8
Downpatrick *Down* 33 P12
Downton *Wilts* 5 W20
Dowra *Cavan* 32 P7
Drangan *Tipperary* 39 S8
Draperstown
  Londonderry 33 N10
Drayton *Norfolk* 13 S26
Dreenagh *Kerry* 38 T4
Dreghorn *N Ayrs* 19 L14
Drem *E Loth* 25 K18
Driffield *Humber* 17 P23
Drigg *Cumb* 14 P17
Drimnin *H'land* 23 J12
Drimoleague *Cork* 38 U5
Drinagh *Cork* 38 U5
Dripsey *Cork* 39 U6
Drogheda *Louth* 37 Q11
Droitwich
  Heref/Worcs 10 T19
Dromahair *Leitrim* 32 P7
Dromara *Down* 33 P11
Dromard *Sligo* 32 P6
Dromcolliher *Limerick* 39 T6
Dromin *Louth* 37 Q11
Dromina *Cork* 39 T6
Dromineer *Tipperary* 35 S7

Dromiskin *Louth* 37 Q11
Dromkeen *Limerick* 39 S7
Dromod *Leitrim* 36 Q8
Dromore *Down* 33 P11
Dromore *Tyrone* 32 N9
Dromore West *Sligo* 35 P6
Dronfield *Derby* 16 R21
Drongan *E Ayrs* 19 M15
Druid *Denbs* 8 S17
Drum *Monaghan* 36 P9
Drumaduff
  Londonderry 33 N10
Drumahoe
  Londonderry 32 N9
Drumakilly *Tyrone* 32 N9
Drumbad *Longford* 36 Q8
Drumbadmeen
  Fermanagh 32 P8
Drumbear *Monaghan* 33 P10
Drumbeg *Donegal* 32 N8
Drumbeg *Down* 33 N12
Drumbeg *H'land* 27 F13
Drumbilla *Louth* 37 P11
Drumbo *Monaghan* 37 Q10
Drumcard *Fermanagh* 32 P8
Drumcliff *Sligo* 32 P6
Drumcondra *Dublin* 37 R11
Drumcondra *Meath* 37 Q10
Drumcoo *Monaghan* 32 P9
Drumcree *Westmeath* 36 Q9
Drumdallagh *Antrim* 33 M11
Drumfin *Sligo* 35 P7
Drumfree *Donegal* 32 M9
Drumgask *H'land* 24 H15
Drumjohn *Dumf/Gal* 19 M15
Drumkeeran *Leitrim* 36 P7
Drumlegagh *Tyrone* 32 N9
Drumlish *Longford* 36 Q8
Drummore *Dumf/Gal* 18 N14
Drumnacross *Donegal* 32 N8
Drumnadrochit *H'land* 28 H15
Drumquin *Tyrone* 32 N9
Drumramer
  Londonderry 33 M10
Drumsallan *Armagh* 33 P10
Drumsaragh
  Londonderry 33 N10
Drumshanbo *Leitrim* 36 P7
Drumskinny
  Fermanagh 32 N8
Drumsna *Leitrim* 36 Q7
Drumsurn
  Londonderry 33 M10
Drymen *Stirl* 24 K15
Drynoch *H'land* 26 H11
Dublin *Dublin* 37 R11
Duchally *H'land* 27 F14
Duddington *Northants* 12 S22
Dudley *W Midlands* 10 S19
Duffield *Derby* 11 S21
Dufftown *Moray* 29 H17
Dukinfield *Gtr Man* 15 R19
Duleek *Meath* 37 Q11
Dullingham *Cambs* 12 T24
Dulnain Bridge *H'land* 28 H16
Duloe *Cornw'l* 3 X15
Dulverton *Som'set* 4 V16
Dumbarton *W Dunb* 19 L14
Dumfries *Dumf/Gal* 20 M16
Dun Laoghaire *Dublin* 37 R11
Dunaff *Donegal* 32 M9
Dunans *Arg/Bute* 23 K13
Dunbar *E Loth* 25 K18
Dunbeath *H'land* 28 F17
Dunblane *Stirl* 24 K16
Dunboyne *Meath* 37 R11
Duncansby *H'land* 29 E17
Dunchurch *Warwick* 11 T21
Duncormick *Wexford* 40 T10
Dundalk *Louth* 37 P11
Dundee *Dundee C* 25 K18
Dunderrow *Cork* 39 U6
Dunderry *Meath* 37 Q10
Dundonald *Down* 33 N12
Dundonald *S Ayrs* 19 L14
Dundrennan
  Dumf/Gal 19 N16
Dundrod *Antrim* 33 N11
Dundrum *Down* 33 P12
Dundrum *Dublin* 37 R11
Dundrum *Tipperary* 39 S7
Dunecht *Aberds* 25 H19
Dunfanaghy *Donegal* 32 M8
Dunfermline *Fife* 24 K17
Dungannon *Tyrone* 33 N10
Dungarvan *Waterford* 39 T8

Dungiven
  Londonderry 33 N10
Dunglow *Donegal* 32 N7
Dungourney *Cork* 39 U7
Dunheeda *Meath* 37 Q10
Dunino *Fife* 25 K18
Dunipace *Falk* 24 K16
Dunkeld *Perth/Kinr* 24 J16
Dunkerrin *Offaly* 39 S8
Dunkineely *Donegal* 32 N7
Dunlavin *Wicklow* 40 R10
Dunleer *Louth* 37 Q11
Dunlop *E Ayrs* 19 L14
Dunloy *Antrim* 33 M11
Dunmanway *Cork* 38 U5
Dunmore East
  Waterford 40 T10
Dunmore *Galway* 35 Q6
Dunmurry *Antrim* 33 N11
Dunnamanagh *Tyrone* 32 N9
Dunnet *H'land* 28 E17
Dunning *Perth/Kinr* 24 K16
Dunnington *N Yorks* 17 Q22
Dunoon *Arg/Bute* 18 L13
Dunragit *Dumf/Gal* 18 N14
Duns *Borders* 21 L19
Dunsany *Meath* 37 Q10
Dunsby *Lincs* 12 S23
Dunscore *Dumf/Gal* 19 M16
Dunsford *Devon* 4 W16
Dunshaughlin *Meath* 37 Q10
Dunstable *Beds* 6 U22
Dunster *Som'set* 4 V17
Dunston *Staffs* 10 S19
Dunsyre *S Lanarks* 20 L17
Dunure *S Ayrs* 19 M14
Dunvegan *H'land* 26 H10
Durham *Durham* 21 N20
Durness *H'land* 27 E14
Durrington *Wilts* 5 V20
Durrow Abbey *Offaly* 36 R8
Durrow *Laois* 40 S9
Durrus *Cork* 38 U4
Dursley *Glos* 5 U19
Dyan *Tyrone* 33 P10
Dyce *Aberd C* 25 H19
Dykehead *Angus* 25 J17
Dymchurch *Kent* 7 V26
Dymock *Glos* 10 U19
Dysart *Westmeath* 36 R9
Dysart *Fife* 25 K17
Dyserth *Denbs* 8 R17

E

Eaglescliffe *Clevl'd* 16 N21
Eaglesfield *Dumf/Gal* 20 M17
Eaglesham *E Renf* 19 L15
Eakring *Notts* 11 R22
Ealing *London* 6 U23
Earby *Lancs* 15 Q19
Eardisley *Heref/Worcs* 10 T17
Eargantea
  Londonderry 33 M10
Earith *Cambs* 12 T24
Earl Shilton *Leics* 11 S21
Earl Soham *Suffolk* 13 T26
Earls Barton
  Northants 12 T22
Earl's Colne *Essex* 13 U25
Earlsferry *Fife* 25 K18
Earlston *Borders* 21 L18
Earlstown *Galway* 35 R7
Earsdon *Tyne/Wear* 21 M21
Easebourne
  W Sussex 6 W22
Easington Colliery
  Durham 21 N21
Easington *Durham* 21 N21
Easington *Humber* 17 Q24
Easingwold *N Yorks* 16 P21
Easky *Sligo* 35 P6
East Bergholt *Suffolk* 13 U26
East Boldre *Hants* 5 W21
East Brent *Som'set* 4 V18
East Bridgford *Notts* 11 S22
East Calder *W Loth* 20 L17
East Cowes
  I of Wight 5 W21
East Cowton *N Yorks* 16 P20
East Dean *E Sussex* 6 W24
East Dereham *Norfolk* 13 S25
East Grinstead
  W Sussex 6 V24

East Harling *Norfolk* 13 T25
East Horsley *Surrey* 6 V23
East Ilsley *Berks* 5 U21
East Kilbride
  S Lanarks 19 L15
East Leake *Notts* 11 S21
East Linton *E Loth* 25 L18
East Looe *Cornw'l* 3 X15
East Markham *Notts* 17 R22
East Norton *Leics* 11 S22
East Oakley *Hants* 5 V21
East Wemyss *Fife* 25 K17
East Wittering
  W Sussex 6 W22
East Witton *N Yorks* 15 P20
East Woodhay *Hants* 5 V21
Eastbourne *E Sussex* 7 W24
Eastchurch *Kent* 7 V25
Easter Skeld *Shetl'd* 31 B21
Eastfield *N Yorks* 17 P23
Eastleigh *Hants* 5 W21
Eastnor *Heref/Worcs* 10 T19
Easton *Dorset* 5 W19
Easton *Leics* 12 S22
Easton *Northants* 12 S22
Easton-in-Gordano
  Avon 4 V18
Eastry *Kent* 7 V26
Eastwood *Notts* 11 R21
Eaton Socon *Cambs* 12 T23
Eaton *Leics* 11 S22
Ebberston *N Yorks* 17 P22
Ebbw Vale *Bl Gwent* 4 U17
Ecclaw *Borders* 25 L19
Ecclefechan *Dumf/Gal* 20 M17
Eccleshall *Staffs* 10 S19
Echt *Aberds* 25 H19
Eckington *Derby* 16 R21
Eckington
  Heref/Worcs 10 T19
Edderton *H'land* 28 G15
Eden *Antrim* 33 N12
Edenaveagh
  Fermanagh 32 N8
Edenbridge *Kent* 6 V24
Edenderry *Offaly* 36 R9
Ederny *Fermanagh* 32 N8
Edgeworthstown
  Longford 36 Q8
Edgmond *Shrops* 10 S19
Edinburgh *C of Edinb* 25 L17
Edington *Wilts* 5 V19
Edmondstown *Louth* 37 Q10
Edmundbyers
  Durham 21 N20
Edwinstowe *Notts* 11 R21
Edzell *Angus* 25 J18
Egham *Surrey* 6 V22
Eglinton *Londonderry* 32 M9
Eglish *Tyrone* 33 P10
Eglwyswrw *Pembs* 9 T14
Egremont *Cumb* 14 P16
Egton *N Yorks* 17 P22
Eighter *Cavan* 36 Q9
Eilean Iarmain *H'land* 23 H12
Elan Village *Powys* 9 T16
Elgin *Moray* 28 G17
Elgol *H'land* 22 H11
Elham *Kent* 7 V26
Elie *Fife* 25 K18
Elishaw *Northum* 21 M19
Elland *W Yorks* 15 Q20
Ellesmere Port *Ches* 15 R18
Ellesmere *Shrops* 10 S18
Ellington *Northum* 21 M20
Ellistrin *Donegal* 32 N8
Ellon *Aberds* 29 H19
Elmswell *Suffolk* 13 T25
Elphin *Roscommon* 35 Q7
Elphin *H'land* 27 F13
Elsdon *Northum* 21 M19
Eisenham *Essex* 12 U24
Elstead *Surrey* 6 V22
Elston *Notts* 11 R22
Elvanfoot *S Lanarks* 20 M16
Elveden *Suffolk* 13 T25
Elvington *N Yorks* 17 Q22
Elworth *Ches* 10 R19
Ely *Cambs* 12 T24
Embleton *Northum* 21 M20
Embo *H'land* 28 G15
Emly *Tipperary* 39 T7
Emmoo *Roscommon* 36 Q8
Empingham *Leics* 12 S22
Emsworth *Hants* 6 W22
Emyvale *Monaghan* 33 P10
Enderby *Leics* 11 S21

Endon *Staffs* 10 R19
Enfield *London* 6 U23
Ennis *Clare* 39 S6
Enniscorthy *Wexford* 40 S10
Enniskean *Cork* 39 U6
Enniskerry *Wicklow* 37 R11
Enniskillen
  Fermanagh 32 P8
Ennistimon *Clare* 34 S5
Enstone *Oxon* 11 U21
Enterkinfoot *Dumf/Gal* 19 M16
Epping *Essex* 6 U24
Epsom *Surrey* 6 V23
Epworth *Humber* 17 Q22
Eriboll *H'land* 28 F14
Errill *Laois* 39 S8
Errogie *H'land* 28 H15
Errol *Perth/Kinr* 25 K17
Erskine *Renf* 19 L15
Escrick *N Yorks* 16 Q21
Esh Winning *Durham* 21 N20
Esher *Surrey* 6 V23
Eskdalemuir
  Dumf/Gal 20 M17
Essexford *Monaghan* 37 Q10
Eston *Clevl'd* 21 N21
Etchingham *E Sussex* 7 V24
Eton *Berks* 6 V22
Ettington *Warwick* 11 T20
Etwall *Derby* 11 S20
Euxton *Lancs* 15 Q18
Evanton *H'land* 28 G15
Evercreech *Som'set* 5 V19
Everleigh *Wilts* 5 V20
Evershot *Dorset* 4 W18
Evesham *Heref/Worcs* 11 T20
Ewell *Surrey* 6 V23
Ewhurst *Surrey* 6 V23
Ewyas Harold
  Heref/Worcs 10 U18
Exbourne *Devon* 3 W16
Exeter *Devon* 4 W16
Exford *Som'set* 4 V16
Exminster *Devon* 4 W17
Exmouth *Devon* 4 W17
Exton *Leics* 12 S22
Eyam *Derby* 16 R20
Eye *Cambs* 12 S23
Eye *Suffolk* 13 T26
Eyemouth *Borders* 21 L19
Eynsford *Kent* 6 V24
Eynsham *Oxon* 5 U21
Eyrecourt *Galway* 36 R7

F

Faddiley *Ches* 10 R18
Fairbourne *Gwyn* 8 S15
Fairford *Glos* 5 U20
Fairlie *N Ayrs* 18 L14
Fairlight *E Sussex* 7 W25
Fakenham *Norfolk* 13 S25
Fala *Midloth* 20 L18
Falcarragh *Donegal* 32 M7
Faldingworth *Lincs* 17 R23
Falkirk *Falk* 24 K16
Falkland *Fife* 25 K17
Fallmore *Mayo* 34 P3
Falmer *E Sussex* 6 W23
Falmouth *Cornw'l* 2 X13
Falstone *Northum* 21 M19
Fardrum *Westmeath* 36 R8
Fareham *Hants* 5 W21
Faringdon *Oxon* 5 U20
Farnborough *Berks* 5 U21
Farnborough *Hants* 6 V22
Farndon *Ches* 10 R18
Farnham *Surrey* 6 V22
Farnworth *Gtr Man* 15 Q19
Farr *H'land* 28 H15
Farranfore *Kerry* 38 T4
Fasag *H'land* 27 G12
Faslane *Arg/Bute* 23 K14
Fauldhouse *W Loth* 20 L16
Faversham *Kent* 7 V25
Fawley *Hants* 5 W21
Fazeley *Staffs* 11 S20
Feakle *Clare* 35 S6
Fearn *H'land* 28 G16
Fearnan *Perth/Kinr* 24 J15
Feckenham
  Heref/Worcs 11 T20
Fedamore *Limerick* 39 S6

Feeard *Clare* 38 S4
Feenhanagh *Limerick* 39 T6
Feeny *Londonderry* 33 N9
Felinhelir *Gwyn* 8 R15
Felixstowe *Suffolk* 13 U26
Felton *Northum* 21 M20
Feltwell *Norfolk* 13 T25
Fenagh *Leitrim* 36 P8
Fenit *Kerry* 38 T4
Fennagh *Carlow* 40 S10
Ferndown *Dorset* 5 W20
Ferness *H'land* 28 H16
Fernhurst *W Sussex* 6 V22
Fernilea *H'land* 26 H11
Ferns *Wexford* 40 S11
Ferryhill *Durham* 21 N20
Ferryside *Carms* 9 U15
Fethard *Tipperary* 39 T8
Fethard *Wexford* 40 T10
Fettercairn *Aberds* 25 J18
Ffestiniog *Gwyn* 8 S16
Fiddown *Kilkenny* 40 T9
Filby *Norfolk* 13 S27
Filey *N Yorks* 17 P23
Fillongley *Warwick* 11 T20
Filton *Avon* 4 U18
Fincarn *Londonderry* 33 N10
Fincham *Norfolk* 12 S24
Finchingfield *Essex* 12 U24
Finchley *London* 6 U23
Findhorn *Moray* 28 G16
Findochty *Moray* 29 G18
Findon *W Sussex* 6 W23
Finedon *Northants* 12 T22
Finglas *Dublin* 37 R11
Finnea *Westmeath* 36 Q9
Finningley *S Yorks* 17 R22
Finnis *Down* 33 P11
Finstown *Orkney* 30 D17
Fintona *Tyrone* 32 P9
Fintown *Donegal* 32 N7
Fintry *Stirl* 24 K15
Finvoy *Antrim* 33 M11
Fionnphort *Arg/Bute* 22 K11
Fishbourne *I of Wight* 5 W21
Fishguard *Pembs* 9 U14
Fishnish *Arg/Bute* 23 J12
Fishtoft *Lincs* 12 S24
Five Alley *Offaly* 36 R8
Fivemiletown *Tyrone* 32 P9
Flagmount *Clare* 35 R6
Flamborough *Humber* 17 P23
Fleet *Hants* 6 V22
Fleetwood *Lancs* 15 Q17
Flimby *Cumb* 20 N17
Flint *Flints* 15 R17
Flitwick *Beds* 12 U22
Flodden *Northum* 21 L19
Flookburgh *Cumb* 15 P18
Fochabers *Moray* 29 G17
Foel *Powys* 8 S17
Folkestone *Kent* 7 V26
Fontmell Magna
 Dorset 5 W19
Fontstown *Kildare* 40 R10
Ford *Wexford* 40 S11
Ford *Arg/Bute* 23 K13
Forden *Powys* 10 S17
Fordham *Cambs* 12 T24
Fordingbridge *Hants* 5 W20
Fordstown *Meath* 37 Q10
Fordyce *Aberds* 29 G18
Fore *Westmeath* 36 Q9
Forest Row *E Sussex* 6 V24
Forfar *Angus* 25 J18
Forgney *Longford* 36 Q8
Forkill *Armagh* 37 P11
Formby *Mersey* 15 Q17
Forres *Moray* 28 G16
Forsinain *H'land* 28 F16
Forsinard *H'land* 28 F16
Fort Augustus *H'land* 24 H14
Fort William *H'land* 23 J13
Forth *S Lanarks* 20 L16
Fortrie *Aberds* 29 G18
Fortrose *H'land* 28 G15

Fortuneswell *Dorset* 5 W19
Fothergill *Cumb* 20 N17
Fotheringhay
 Northants 12 S23
Foulden *Borders* 21 L19
Foulkesmill *Wexford* 40 T10
Foulsham *Norfolk* 13 S25
Fountain Cross *Clare* 38 S5
Fountainhall *Borders* 20 L18
Four Mile House
 Roscommon 35 Q7
Fovant *Wilts* 5 V20
Fowey *Cornw'l* 2 X14
Fownhope
 Heref/Worcs 10 T18
Foxdale *I of Man* 14 P14
Foxford *Mayo* 35 Q5
Foyers *H'land* 24 H15
Foygh *Longford* 36 Q8
Foynes *Limerick* 38 S5
Fraddon *Cornw'l* 2 X14
Framlingham *Suffolk* 13 T26
Frampton on Severn
 Glos 5 U19
Frankville *Down* 33 P12
Frant *E Sussex* 7 V24
Fraserburgh *Aberds* 29 G19
Freckleton *Lancs* 15 Q18
Freemount *Cork* 39 T6
Freethorpe *Norfolk* 13 S27
Fremington *Devon* 3 V15
Frenchpark
 Roscommon 35 Q7
Frensham *Surrey* 6 V22
Freshford *Kilkenny* 40 S9
Freshwater *I of Wight* 5 W20
Fressingfield *Suffolk* 13 T26
Freswick *H'land* 29 E17
Freuchie *Fife* 25 K17
Friday Bridge *Cambs* 12 S24
Fridaythorpe *Humber* 17 P22
Frimley *Surrey* 6 V22
Frinton-on-Sea *Essex* 7 U26
Friockheim *Angus* 25 J18
Frizington *Cumb* 20 N17
Frodsham *Ches* 15 R18
Frome *Som'set* 5 V19
Frongoch *Gwyn* 8 S16
Froxfield *Wilts* 5 V20
Fuerty *Roscommon* 35 Q7
Fulbourn *Cambs* 12 T24
Fulford *N Yorks* 16 Q21
Fulwood *Lancs* 15 Q18
Funzie *Shetl'd* 31 A22
Furnace *Arg/Bute* 23 K13
Fybagh *Kerry* 38 T4
Fyfield *Essex* 7 U24
Fyvie *Aberds* 29 H19

G

Gaerwen *Angl* 8 R15
Gaick Lodge *H'land* 24 J15
Gailey *Staffs* 10 S19
Gainford *Durham* 21 N20
Gainsborough *Lincs* 17 R22
Gairloch *H'land* 27 G12
Gairlochy *H'land* 23 J14
Galashiels *Borders* 20 L18
Galbally *Limerick* 39 T7
Galgate *Lancs* 15 Q18
Galmisdale *H'land* 22 J11
Galmoy *Kilkenny* 39 S8
Galmpton *Devon* 3 X16
Galston *E Ayrs* 19 L15
Galway *Galway* 35 R5
Gamlingay *Cambs* 12 T23
Garbally *Galway* 35 R7
Garbhalt *Arg/Bute* 23 K13
Garboldisham *Norfolk* 13 S25
Gardenstown *Aberds* 29 G19
Garelochhead
 Arg/Bute 23 K14
Garforth *W Yorks* 16 Q21
Gargrave *N Yorks* 15 Q19
Gargunnock *Stirl* 24 K15
Garlieston *Dumf/Gal* 19 N15
Garmouth *Moray* 29 G17
Garrane *Cork* 38 T5
Garrison *Fermanagh* 32 P7
Garristown *Dublin* 37 Q11
Garrow *Perth/Kinr* 24 J16
Garryvoe *Cork* 39 U7

Garsdale Head *Cumb* 15 P19
Garstang *Lancs* 15 Q18
Garston *Mersey* 15 R18
Garton-on-the-Wolds
 Humber 17 P22
Garvagh *Londonderry* 33 N10
Garvaghy *Down* 33 P11
Garvaghy *Tyrone* 32 P9
Garvald *E Loth* 25 L18
Garvary *Fermanagh* 32 P8
Garve *H'land* 28 G14
Gatehouse of Fleet
 Dumf/Gal 19 N15
Gateshead *Tyne/Wear* 21 N20
Gatley *Gtr Man* 15 R19
Gattabaun *Kilkenny* 40 S9
Gawthwaite *Cumb* 15 P17
Gay Brook
 Westmeath 36 R9
Gaydon *Warwick* 11 T21
Gayton *Norfolk* 13 S25
Gaywood *Norfolk* 12 S24
Gearraidh na h-
 Aibhne *W Isles* 26 F10
Geary *H'land* 26 G10
Geashill *Offaly* 36 R9
Geddington *Northants* 12 T22
Gedney *Lincs* 12 S24
Georgeham *Devon* 3 V15
Gerrards Cross *Bucks* 6 U22
Gifford *E Loth* 25 L18
Giggleswick *N Yorks* 15 P19
Gilford *Down* 33 P11
Gillingham *Dorset* 5 V19
Gillingham *Kent* 7 V25
Gilmerton *Perth/Kinr* 24 K16
Gilsland *Northum* 21 N18
Gilwern *Monmouths* 4 U17
Giosla *W Isles* 26 F10
Girton *Cambs* 12 T24
Girvan *S Ayrs* 18 M14
Gisburn *Lancs* 15 Q19
Gladestry *Powys* 10 T17
Glamis *Angus* 25 J17
Glanaman *Carms* 9 U16
Glandore *Cork* 38 U5
Glanton *Northum* 21 M20
Glanworth *Cork* 39 T7
Glasbury *Powys* 10 T17
Glasdrumman *Down* 37 P12
Glasgow *C of Glasg* 19 L15
Glaslough *Monaghan* 33 P10
Glasnevin *Dublin* 37 R11
Glassan *Westmeath* 36 R8
Glasserton *Dumf/Gal* 19 N15
Glasson *Lancs* 15 Q18
Glastonbury *Som'set* 4 V18
Glastry *Down* 33 P13
Glemsford *Suffolk* 13 T25
Glen *Donegal* 32 M8
Glen *Fermanagh* 32 P7
Glenade *Leitrim* 32 P7
Glenamoy *Mayo* 34 P4
Glenariff *Antrim* 33 M11
Glenarm *Antrim* 33 N12
Glenavy *Antrim* 33 N11
Glenbarr *Arg/Bute* 18 L12
Glenbeigh *Kerry* 38 T4
Glenborrodale *H'land* 23 J12
Glenbrittle *H'land* 22 H11
Glencaple *Dumf/Gal* 20 N16
Glencar *Kerry* 38 T4
Glencarse *Perth/Kinr* 24 K17
Glencoe *H'land* 23 J13
Glencolumbkille
 Donegal 32 N6
Glendalough *Wicklow* 40 R11
Glendoll Lodge *Angus* 25 J17
Glendree *Clare* 39 S6
Gleneagles *Perth/Kinr* 24 K16
Glenealy *Wicklow* 40 S11
Gleneely *Donegal* 32 M9
Glenelg *H'land* 23 H12
Glenfarn *Leitrim* 32 P8
Glenfesk *Kerry* 38 T5
Glenfinnan *H'land* 23 J13
Glengarriff *Cork* 38 U4
Glengavlen *Cavan* 32 P8
Glengormly *Antrim* 33 N12
Glenluce *Dumf/Gal* 18 N14
Glenmaye *I of Man* 14 P14
Glenmore Lodge
 H'land 24 H16
Glennamaddy *Galway* 35 Q6
Glenoe *Antrim* 33 N12
Glenprosen Lodge
 Angus 25 J17

Glenrothes *Fife* 25 K17
Glenstal Abbey
 Limerick 39 S7
Glenstriven *Arg/Bute* 18 L13
Glentane *Galway* 35 R6
Glenties *Donegal* 32 N7
Glentrool Village
 Dumf/Gal 19 M14
Glenville *Cork* 39 T7
Glenwhilly *Dumf/Gal* 18 M14
Glin *Limerick* 38 S5
Glinsk *Galway* 34 R4
Glinsk *Galway* 35 Q7
Glinton *Cambs* 12 S23
Glossop *Derby* 15 R20
Gloucester *Glos* 10 U19
Glusburn *N Yorks* 15 Q20
Glyn Ceiriog *Wrex* 10 S17
Glyn Neath
 Neath P Talb 9 U16
Glyncorrwg
 Neath P Talb 9 U16
Glynde *E Sussex* 6 W24
Glyndyfrdwy *Denbs* 10 S17
Glynn *Antrim* 33 N12
Glynn *Carlow* 40 S10
Gnosall *Staffs* 10 S19
Goathland *N Yorks* 17 P22
Gobowen *Shrops* 10 S17
Godalming *Surrey* 6 V22
Godmanchester
 Cambs 12 T23
Godshill *I of Wight* 5 W21
Godstone *Surrey* 6 V23
Golden *Tipperary* 39 T8
Goldhanger *Essex* 7 U25
Goleen *Cork* 38 V4
Golspie *H'land* 28 G16
Goodrich
 Heref/Worcs 10 U18
Goodwick *Pembs* 9 T13
Goodwood *W Sussex* 6 W22
Goole *Humber* 17 Q22
Goonhavern *Cornw'l* 2 X13
Gordon *Borders* 21 L18
Gorebridge *Midloth* 20 L17
Goresbridge *Kilkenny* 40 S10
Gorey *Wexford* 40 S11
Gorey *Chan Is* 2 Z19
Goring *Oxon* 5 U21
Goring-by-Sea
 W Sussex 6 W23
Gorleston *Norfolk* 13 S27
Gormanstown *Meath* 37 Q11
Gorran Haven *Cornw'l* 2 X14
Gorseinon *Swan* 9 U15
Gorslas *Carms* 9 U15
Gort *Galway* 35 R6
Gortahork *Donegal* 32 M7
Gorteen *Galway* 35 Q6
Gorteen *Galway* 35 R6
Gorteen *Sligo* 35 Q6
Gorteen *Waterford* 39 T8
Gorteeng *Galway* 35 R7
Gortin *Tyrone* 32 N9
Gortnacross
 Londonderry 33 N10
Gortroe *Cork* 39 T6
Gortymadden *Galway* 35 R7
Gosberton *Lincs* 12 S23
Gosfield *Essex* 13 U25
Gosforth *Cumb* 14 P17
Gosport *Hants* 5 W21
Goswick *Northum* 21 L20
Gotham *Notts* 11 S21
Goudhurst *Kent* 7 V24
Gourdon *Aberds* 25 J19
Gourock *Invercl* 18 L14
Gowerton *Swan* 9 U15
Gowlaun *Galway* 34 Q4
Gowran *Kilkenny* 40 S9
Grabhair *W Isles* 26 F11
Graghil *Mayo* 34 P4
Graigue *Laois* 40 S10
Graiguenamanagh
 Kilkenny 40 S10
Grain *Kent* 7 V25
Grainthorpe *Lincs* 17 R24
Grampound *Cornw'l* 2 X14
Gramsdal *W Isles* 26 H9
Granard *Longford* 36 Q9
Grange *Kilkenny* 40 S9
Grange *Roscommon* 36 Q7
Grange *Sligo* 32 P6
Grangebellew *Louth* 37 Q11
Grangemouth *Falk* 24 K16

Grange-over-Sands
 Cumb 15 P18
Grantham *Lincs* 12 S22
Grantown-on-Spey
 H'land 28 H16
Grantshouse *Borders* 21 L19
Granville *Tyrone* 33 P10
Grasby *Lincs* 17 Q23
Grasmere *Cumb* 15 P17
Grassington *N Yorks* 15 P20
Grateley *Hants* 5 V20
Gravesend *Kent* 7 V24
Grayrigg *Cumb* 15 P18
Grays *Essex* 7 V24
Grayshott *Hants* 6 V22
Great Ayton *N Yorks* 16 N21
Great Baddow *Essex* 7 U25
Great Badminton
 Avon 5 U19
Great Barford *Beds* 12 T23
Great Bentley *Essex* 7 U26
Great Bridgeford
 Staffs 10 S19
Great Broughton
 N Yorks 16 P21
Great Chesterford
 Essex 12 T24
Great Clifton *Cumb* 20 N17
Great Dunmow *Essex* 7 U24
Great Eccleston
 Lancs 15 Q18
Great Ellingham
 Norfolk 13 S25
Great Gidding *Cambs* 12 T23
Great Harwood *Lancs* 15 Q19
Great Horwood
 Bucks 11 U22
Great Malvern
 Heref/Worcs 10 T19
Great Massingham
 Norfolk 13 S25
Great Missenden
 Bucks 6 U22
Great Oakley *Essex* 7 U26
Great Sampford
 Essex 12 U24
Great Shefford *Berks* 5 V21
Great Shelford
 Cambs 12 T24
Great Somerford
 Wilts 5 U19
Great Staunton
 Cambs 12 T23
Great Torrington
 Devon 3 W15
Great Wakering *Essex* 7 U25
Great Waltham *Essex* 7 U24
Great Witley
 Heref/Worcs 10 T19
Great Yarmouth
 Norfolk 13 S27
Greatham *Clevl'd* 21 N21
Greatstone-on-Sea
 Kent 7 W25
Green Hammerton
 N Yorks 16 P21
Greencastle *Donegal* 33 M10
Greencastle *Down* 37 P11
Greencastle *Tyrone* 33 N9
Greenhead *Northum* 21 N18
Greenholm *E Ayrs* 19 L15
Greenisland *Antrim* 33 N12
Greenlaw *Borders* 21 L18
Greenloaning
 Perth/Kinr 24 K16
Greenock *Invercl* 18 L14
Greenodd *Cumb* 15 P17
Greenore *Louth* 37 P11
Greenway *Pembs* 9 U14
Greenwich *London* 6 V24
Greevagh *Sligo* 35 P7
Gretna Green
 Dumf/Gal 20 M17
Gretna *Dumf/Gal* 20 N17
Gretton *Northants* 12 S22
Greyabbey *Down* 33 N12
Greysteel
 Londonderry 33 M9
Greystoke *Cumb* 20 N18
Greystones *Wicklow* 37 R11
Grimsby *Humber* 17 Q23
Gritley *Orkney* 30 E18
Grizebeck *Cumb* 15 P17
Groby *Leics* 11 S21
Groomsport *Down* 33 N12
Grove *Oxon* 5 U21

Grundisburgh *Suffolk* 13 T26
Guard Bridge *Fife* 25 K18
Gubaveeny *Cavan* 32 P8
Gudderstown *Louth* 37 Q10
Guestling Green
  E Sussex 7 W25
Guildford *Surrey* 6 V22
Guildtown *Perth/Kinr* 24 K17
Guilsfield *Powys* 10 S17
Guisborough *Clevl'd* 16 N21
Guiseley *W Yorks* 16 Q20
Gulladuff
  Londonderry 33 N10
Gullane *E Loth* 25 K18
Gunnerside *N Yorks* 15 P19
Gunnislake *Cornw'l* 3 W15
Gunnista *Shetl'd* 31 B21
Gutcher *Shetl'd* 31 A21
Gwalchmai *Angl* 8 R15
Gwaun-Cae-Gurwen
  Neath P Talb 9 U16
Gwbert-on-Sea *Card* 9 ST1
Gweedore *Donegal* 32 M7
Gweek *Cornw'l* 2 X13
Gwennap *Cornw'l* 2 X13
Gwessalia *Mayo* 34 P4
Gwydelwern *Denbs* 8 R17
Gwytherin *Aber/Colw* 8 R16

H

Hacketstown *Carlow* 40 S10
Hackney *London* 6 U23
Hackthorpe *Cumb* 21 N18
Haddenham *Bucks* 6 U22
Haddenham *Cambs* 12 T24
Haddington *E Loth* 25 L18
Haddiscoe *Norfolk* 13 S27
Hadleigh *Essex* 7 U25
Hadleigh *Suffolk* 13 T25
Hadlow *Kent* 7 V24
Hadnall *Shrops* 10 S18
Hagworthingham
  Lincs 17 R24
Hailsham *E Sussex* 7 W24
Hainton *Lincs* 17 R23
Halberton *Devon* 4 W17
Halesowen
  W Midlands 10 T19
Halesworth *Suffolk* 13 T27
Halford *Warwick* 11 T20
Halifax *W Yorks* 15 Q20
Halkirk *H'land* 28 E16
Halland *E Sussex* 6 W24
Hallow *Heref/Worcs* 10 T19
Hallworthy *Cornw'l* 2 W14
Halstead *Essex* 13 U25
Halton *Lancs* 15 P18
Haltwhistle *Northum* 21 N19
Halwill Junction
  Devon 3 W15
Hamble *Hants* 5 W21
Hambledon *Hants* 5 W21
Hambleton *Lancs* 15 Q18
Hambleton *N Yorks* 16 Q21
Hamerton *Cambs* 12 T23
Hamilstownbawn
  Armagh 33 P10
Hamilton *S Lanarks* 19 L15
Hammersmith &
  Fulham *London* 6 V23
Hamnavoe *Shetl'd* 31 B21
Hamnavoe *Shetl'd* 31 B21
Hampstead Norris
  Berks 5 V21
Hampton in Arden
  W Midlands 11 T20
Hamstreet *Kent* 7 V25
Handcross *W Sussex* 6 V23
Hannington *Hants* 5 V21
Harbury *Warwick* 11 T21
Harby *Leics* 11 S22
Hardingstone
  Northants 11 T22
Harewood *W Yorks* 16 Q20
Haringey *London* 6 U23
Harlech *Gwyn* 8 S15
Harleston *Norfolk* 13 T26
Harlow *Essex* 6 U24
Haroldswick *Shetl'd* 31 A22
Harrietfield *Perth/Kinr* 24 K16
Harrietsham *Kent* 7 V25

Harrington *Cumb* 20 N16
Harris *H'land* 22 J11
Harrogate *N Yorks* 16 P20
Harrold *Beds* 12 T22
Harrow *London* 6 U23
Harston *Cambs* 12 T24
Hartburn *Northum* 21 M20
Hartest *Suffolk* 13 T25
Hartfield *E Sussex* 6 V24
Harthill *N Lanarks* 19 L16
Hartington *Derby* 11 R20
Hartland *Devon* 3 W15
Hartlebury
  Heref/Worcs 10 T19
Hartlepool *Clevl'd* 21 N21
Hartley *Kent* 7 V24
Hartley *Northum* 21 M21
Hartley Wintney
  Hants 6 V22
Hartpury *Glos* 10 U19
Hartshill *Warwick* 11 S20
Harvington
  Heref/Worcs 11 T20
Harwell *Oxon* 5 U21
Harwich *Essex* 13 U26
Harworth *Notts* 16 R21
Haselbury Plucknett
  Som'set 4 W18
Haslemere *Surrey* 6 V22
Haslingden *Lancs* 15 Q19
Hassocks *W Sussex* 6 W23
Hastigrow *H'land* 29 E17
Hastings *E Sussex* 7 W25
Haswell *Durham* 21 N21
Hatch Beauchamp
  Som'set 4 W18
Hatfield Heath *Essex* 6 U24
Hatfield Peverel
  Essex 7 U25
Hatfield *Herts* 6 U23
Hatfield *S Yorks* 17 Q22
Hatherleigh *Devon* 3 W15
Hathersage *Derby* 16 R20
Hatton *Aberds* 29 H20
Hatton *Derby* 11 S20
Haugh of Urr
  Dumf/Gal 19 N16
Haughley *Suffolk* 13 T25
Haughton *Staffs* 10 S19
Havant *Hants* 6 W22
Haverfordwest *Pembs* 9 U14
Haverhill *Suffolk* 12 T24
Haverigg *Cumb* 14 P17
Havering *London* 6 U24
Hawarden *Flints* 10 R17
Hawes *N Yorks* 15 P19
Hawick *Borders* 20 M18
Hawkchurch *Devon* 4 W18
Hawkesbury Upton
  Avon 5 U19
Hawkhurst *Kent* 7 V25
Hawkinge *Kent* 7 V26
Hawkshead *Cumb* 15 P18
Hawnby *N Yorks* 16 P21
Haworth *W Yorks* 15 Q19
Hawsker *N Yorks* 17 P22
Haxby *N Yorks* 16 P21
Haxey *Humber* 17 R22
Haydon Bridge
  Northum 21 N19
Hayfield *Derby* 15 R20
Hayle *Cornw'l* 2 X13
Hay-on-Wye *Powys* 10 T17
Hayton *Cumb* 20 N18
Hayton *Humber* 17 Q22
Haywards Heath
  W Sussex 6 W23
Hazel Grove *Gtr Man* 15 R19
Hazlemere *Bucks* 6 U22
Heacham *Norfolk* 12 S24
Headcorn *Kent* 7 V25
Headford *Galway* 35 R5
Headley *Hants* 6 V22
Heanor *Derby* 11 R21
Heath End *Hants* 5 V21
Heathfield *E Sussex* 7 W24
Hebburn *Tyne/Wear* 21 N20
Hebden Bridge
  W Yorks 15 Q19
Heckington *Lincs* 12 S23
Hedge End *Hants* 5 W21
Hednesford *Staffs* 11 S20
Hedon *Humber* 17 Q23
Heighington *Durham* 21 N20
Heilam *H'land* 28 E14
Helensburgh *Arg/Bute* 24 K14

Hellifield *N Yorks* 15 P19
Helmsdale *H'land* 28 F16
Helmsley *N Yorks* 16 P21
Helperby *N Yorks* 16 P21
Helpringham *Lincs* 12 S23
Helsby *Ches* 15 R18
Helston *Cornw'l* 2 X13
Hemel Hempstead
  Herts 6 U23
Hemingbrough
  N Yorks 17 Q22
Hempnall *Norfolk* 13 S26
Hempton *Norfolk* 13 S25
Hemsby *Norfolk* 13 S27
Hemsworth *W Yorks* 16 Q21
Hemyock *Devon* 4 W17
Henfield *W Sussex* 6 W23
Hengoed *Caerph* 4 U17
Henley-in-Arden
  Warwick 11 T20
Henley-on-Thames
  Oxon 6 U22
Henllan *Denbs* 8 R17
Henlow *Beds* 12 T23
Henstridge *Som'set* 5 W19
Herbertstown
  Limerick 39 S7
Herbrandston *Pembs* 9 U13
Hereford *Heref/Worcs* 10 T18
Heriot *Borders* 20 L18
Hermitage *Berks* 5 V21
Herne Bay *Kent* 7 V26
Herstmonceux
  E Sussex 7 W24
Hertford *Herts* 6 U23
Hessle *Humber* 17 Q23
Heswall *Mersey* 15 R17
Hethersett *Norfolk* 13 S26
Hetton-le-Hole
  Tyne/Wear 21 N21
Hexham *Northum* 21 N19
Heybridge *Essex* 7 U25
Heysham *Lancs* 15 P18
Heytesbury *Wilts* 5 V19
Heywood *Gtr Man* 15 Q19
Hibaldstow *Humber* 17 Q22
High Bentham
  N Yorks 15 P19
High Bickington
  Devon 3 W15
High Ercall *Shrops* 10 S18
High Hesket *Cumb* 20 N18
High Legh *Ches* 15 R19
High Wycombe *Bucks* 6 U22
Higham Ferrers
  Northants 12 T22
Higham *Kent* 7 V24
Highbridge *Som'set* 4 V18
Highclere *Hants* 5 V21
Highley *Shrops* 10 T19
Hightae *Dumf/Gal* 20 M17
Highworth *Wilts* 5 U20
Hilborough *Norfolk* 13 S25
Hildenborough *Kent* 6 V24
Hilgay *Norfolk* 12 S24
Hillington *London* 6 U23
Hillington *Norfolk* 13 S25
Hillsborough *Down* 4 W17
Hillswick *Shetl'd* 31 B21
Hilltown *Down* 33 P11
Hilmarton *Wilts* 5 V20
Hilton *Derby* 11 S20
Hinckley *Leics* 11 S21
Hinderwell *N Yorks* 17 N22
Hindhead *Surrey* 6 V22
Hindley *Gtr Man* 15 Q18
Hindon *Wilts* 5 V19
Hingham *Norfolk* 13 S25
Hinstock *Shrops* 10 S19
Hirwaun *Rh Cyn Taff* 9 U17
Histon *Cambs* 12 T24
Hitchin *Herts* 12 U23
Hockley *Essex* 7 U25
Hockliffe *Beds* 12 U22
Hoddesdon *Herts* 6 U23
Hodnet *Shrops* 10 S18
Hoff *Cumb* 21 N18
Holbeach *Lincs* 12 S24
Holbrook *Suffolk* 13 U26
Holbury *Hants* 5 W21
Holford *Som'set* 4 V17
Holkham *Norfolk* 13 S25
Holland on Sea *Essex* 7 U26
Hollandstoun *Orkney* 30 D19
Hollym *Humber* 17 Q24
Hollymount *Mayo* 35 Q5

Hollywood *Wicklow* 37 R10
Holme-on-Spalding-
  moor *Humber* 17 Q22
Holmer *Heref/Worcs* 10 T18
Holmes Chapel *Ches* 10 R19
Holmfirth *W Yorks* 15 Q20
Holsworthy *Devon* 3 W15
Holt *Norfolk* 13 S26
Holt *Wrex* 10 R18
Holycross *Limerick* 39 S6
Holycross *Tipperary* 39 S8
Holyhead *Angl* 8 R14
Holywell *Flints* 15 R17
Holywood *Down* 33 N12
Honington *Lincs* 12 S22
Honiton *Devon* 4 W17
Hoo *Kent* 7 V25
Hook Norton *Oxon* 11 U21
Hook *Hants* 6 V22
Hope *Flints* 10 R17
Hope under Dinmore
  Heref/Worcs 10 T18
Hopeman *Moray* 28 G17
Horam *E Sussex* 7 W24
Horden *Durham* 21 N21
Horley *Surrey* 6 V23
Horncastle *Lincs* 17 R23
Horndean *Hants* 6 W21
Horninglow *Wilts* 5 V19
Hornsea *Humber* 17 Q23
Horrabridge *Devon* 3 X15
Horringer *Suffolk* 13 T25
Horseleap Crossroads
  Galway 35 R6
Horseleap *Offaly* 36 R8
Horsey *Norfolk* 13 S27
Horsford *Norfolk* 13 S26
Horsforth *W Yorks* 16 Q20
Horsham St. Faith
  Norfolk 13 S26
Horsham *W Sussex* 6 V23
Horsted Keynes
  W Sussex 6 V23
Horton in Ribblesdale
  N Yorks 15 P19
Horton *Northants* 11 T22
Horton *Som'set* 4 W18
Horwich *Gtr Man* 15 Q18
Hospital *Limerick* 39 T7
Hoswick *Shetl'd* 31 C21
Houghton Regis *Beds* 12 U22
Houghton *Cumb* 20 N18
Houghton-le-Spring
  Tyne/Wear 21 N21
Hounslow *London* 6 V23
Hove *E Sussex* 6 W23
Hoveton *Norfolk* 13 S26
Hovingham *N Yorks* 17 P22
Howden *Humber* 17 Q22
Howpasley *Borders* 20 M17
Howth *Dublin* 37 R11
Hoxne *Suffolk* 13 T26
Hoylake *Mersey* 15 R17
Hucknall *Notts* 11 R21
Huddersfield *W Yorks* 15 Q20
Hugh Town *I of Scilly* 2 Y11
Hulland Ward *Derby* 11 R20
Hullavington *Wilts* 5 U19
Hullbridge *Essex* 7 U25
Hulme End *Staffs* 11 R20
Humberston *Humber* 17 Q23
Humshaugh *Northum* 21 M19
Hundred House
  Powys 9 T17
Hungerford *Berks* 5 V20
Hunmanby *N Yorks* 17 P23
Hunstanton *Norfolk* 12 S24
Hunterston *N Ayrs* 18 L14
Huntford *Borders* 21 M19
Huntingdon *Cambs* 12 T23
Huntley *Glos* 10 U19
Huntly *Aberds* 29 H18
Hurlers Cross *Clare* 39 S6
Hurlford *E Ayrs* 19 L15
Hurliness *Orkney* 30 E17
Hurn *Dorset* 5 W20
Hursley *Hants* 5 V21
Hurstbourne Tarrant
  Hants 5 V21
Hurstpierpoint
  W Sussex 6 W23
Hurworth-on-Tees
  Durham 16 P20
Husbands Bosworth
  Leics 11 T21
Husinish *W Isles* 26 G9

Huttoft *Lincs* 17 R24
Hutton Cranswick
  Humber 17 Q23
Hutton Rudby
  N Yorks 16 P21
Hutton-le-Hole
  N Yorks 17 P22
Huyton *Mersey* 15 R18
Hyde *Gtr Man* 15 R19
Hynish *Arg/Bute* 22 K10
Hythe *Hants* 5 W21
Hythe *Kent* 7 V26

I

Ibsey *Hants* 5 W20
Ibstock *Leics* 11 S21
Icklingham *Suffolk* 13 T25
Idmiston *Wilts* 5 V20
Ilchester *Som'set* 4 W18
Ilderton *Northum* 21 M20
Ilfracombe *Devon* 3 V15
Ilkeston *Derby* 11 S21
Ilkley *W Yorks* 15 Q20
Illogan *Cornw'l* 2 X13
Ilminster *Som'set* 4 W18
Immingham *Humber* 17 Q23
Inagh *Clare* 38 S5
Inch *Cork* 39 U8
Inch *Kerry* 38 T4
Inchigeelagh *Cork* 38 U5
Inchnadamph *H'land* 27 F14
Ingatestone *Essex* 7 U24
Ingleton *N Yorks* 15 P19
Ingoldmells *Lincs* 12 R24
Ingram *Northum* 21 M20
Ingrave *Essex* 7 U24
Inishannon *Cork* 39 U6
Inishcrone *Sligo* 35 P5
Inishkeen *Monaghan* 37 P10
Inishrush
  Londonderry 33 N10
Inistioge *Kilkenny* 40 T9
Inkberrow
  Heref/Worcs 11 T20
Innellan *Arg/Bute* 18 L14
Innerleithen *Borders* 20 L17
Innermessan
  Dumf/Gal 18 N14
Infield *Meath* 37 R10
Insch *Aberds* 29 H18
Instow *Devon* 3 V15
Inver *Donegal* 32 N7
Inverallochy *Aberds* 29 G20
Inveran *Galway* 34 R5
Inveran *H'land* 28 G15
Inveraray *Arg/Bute* 23 K13
Inverarity *Angus* 25 J18
Inverbervie *Aberds* 25 J19
Invergarry *H'land* 24 H14
Invergordon *H'land* 28 G15
Invergowrie *Dundee C* 25 K17
Inverie *H'land* 23 H13
Inverinate *H'land* 23 H13
Inverkeilor *Angus* 25 J18
Inverkeithing *Fife* 24 K17
Inverkip *H'land* 27 F13
Inverlochlarig *Stirl* 24 K14
Invermoriston *H'land* 24 H14
Inverness *H'land* 28 H15
Inversnaid *Stirl* 24 K14
Inverurie *Aberds* 29 H19
Ipswich *Suffolk* 13 T26
Irchester *Northants* 12 T22
Irlam *Gtr Man* 15 R19
Ironbridge *Shrops* 10 S19
Irthlingborough
  Northants 12 T22
Irvine *N Ayrs* 19 L14
Irvinestown
  Fermanagh 32 P8
Isbister *Shetl'd* 31 A21
Islandtown *Antrim* 33 N11
Isle of Whithorn
  Dumf/Gal 19 N15
Isleham *Cambs* 12 T24
Islington *London* 6 U23
Islip *Oxon* 5 U21
Ivinghoe *Bucks* 6 U22
Ivybridge *Devon* 3 X16
Iwerne Minster *Dorset* 5 W19
Ixworth *Suffolk* 13 T25

J

Jamestown *W Dunb* 24 K14
Jarrow *Tyne/Wear* 21 N21
Jaywick *Essex* 7 U26
Jedburgh *Borders* 21 M18
Jervaulx *N Yorks* 16 P20
John o' Groats *H'land* 29 E17
Johnshaven *Aberds* 25 J19
Johnston *Pembs* 9 U13
Johnstone *Renf* 19 L15
Johnstown Bridge *Kildare* 37 R10
Johnstown *Kilkenny* 39 S8
Juliastown *Meath* 37 Q11

K

Kames *Arg/Bute* 18 L13
Kanturk *Cork* 39 T6
Katesbridge *Down* 33 P11
Kea *Cornw'l* 2 X13
Keadow *Roscommon* 36 P7
Keady *Armagh* 33 P10
Kealkill *Cork* 38 U5
Kedington *Suffolk* 12 T24
Keel *Mayo* 34 Q3
Keelby *Lincs* 17 Q23
Keele *Staffs* 10 R19
Keenagh *Longford* 36 Q8
Kegworth *Leics* 11 S21
Keighley *W Yorks* 15 Q20
Keillmore *Arg/Bute* 18 L12
Keiss *H'land* 29 E17
Keith *Moray* 29 G18
Keld *N Yorks* 15 P19
Kellas *Moray* 28 G17
Kells *Antrim* 33 N11
Kells *Kilkenny* 40 S9
Kells *Meath* 37 Q10
Kellystown *Louth* 37 Q11
Kelsale *Suffolk* 13 T27
Kelsall *Ches* 10 R18
Kelso *Borders* 21 L19
Keltneyburn *Perth/Kinr* 24 J15
Kelty *Fife* 24 K17
Kelvedon *Essex* 7 U25
Kelynack *Cornw'l* 2 X12
Kemble *Glos* 5 U20
Kemnay *Aberds* 25 H19
Kempsey *Heref/Worcs* 10 T19
Kempston *Beds* 12 T22
Kemsing *Kent* 6 V24
Kendal *Cumb* 15 P18
Kenilworth *Warwick* 11 T20
Kenmare *Kerry* 38 U4
Kenmore *Perth/Kinr* 24 J15
Kennacraig *Arg/Bute* 18 L13
Kennethmont *Aberds* 29 H18
Kennford *Devon* 4 W16
Kenninghall *Norfolk* 13 T25
Kennington *Oxon* 5 U21
Kensington & Chelsea *London* 6 V23
Kentford *Suffolk* 13 T25
Kentisbeare *Devon* 4 W17
Kentstown *Meath* 37 Q10
Kerry *Powys* 10 T17
Kerrysdale *H'land* 27 G12
Kershopefoot *Borders* 20 M18
Kesgrave *Suffolk* 13 T26
Kesh *Fermanagh* 32 N8
Keshcarrigan *Leitrim* 36 P8
Kessingland *Suffolk* 13 T27
Keswick *Cumb* 20 N17
Kettering *Northants* 12 T22
Kettletoft *Orkney* 30 D18
Kettlewell *N Yorks* 15 P19
Ketton *Leics* 12 S22
Kexby *Lincs* 17 R22
Keyingham *Humber* 17 Q23
Keymer *W Sussex* 6 W23
Keynsham *Avon* 4 V18
Keysoe *Beds* 12 T23
Keyworth *Notts* 11 S21
Kibworth Beauchamp *Leics* 11 S22
Kidderminster *Heref/Worcs* 10 T19

Kidlington *Oxon* 5 U21
Kidsgrove *Staffs* 10 R19
Kidstones *N Yorks* 15 P19
Kidwelly *Carms* 9 U15
Kielder *Northum* 21 M18
Kilamery *Kilkenny* 40 T9
Kilbaha *Clare* 38 S4
Kilbeggan *Westmeath* 36 R9
Kilbeheny *Limerick* 39 T7
Kilbennan Church *Galway* 35 Q6
Kilberry *Meath* 37 Q10
Kilberry *Arg/Bute* 18 L12
Kilbirnie *N Ayrs* 19 L14
Kilbrickan *Galway* 34 R4
Kilbride *Wicklow* 40 S11
Kilbride *Arg/Bute* 23 K13
Kilbrien *Waterford* 39 T8
Kilbrittain *Cork* 39 U6
Kilcadzow *S Lanarks* 19 L16
Kilcar *Donegal* 32 N6
Kilchattan *Arg/Bute* 18 M12
Kilchenzie *Arg/Bute* 18 M12
Kilchiaran *Arg/Bute* 18 L11
Kilchoan *H'land* 22 J11
Kilchreest *Galway* 35 R6
Kilchrenan *Arg/Bute* 23 K13
Kilclooney *Donegal* 32 N7
Kilcock *Kildare* 37 R10
Kilcoe *Cork* 38 U5
Kilcogy *Cavan* 36 Q9
Kilcolgan *Galway* 35 R6
Kilconly *Galway* 35 Q5
Kilconnell *Galway* 35 R7
Kilcoo *Down* 33 P11
Kilcoole *Wicklow* 37 R11
Kilcormac *Offaly* 36 R8
Kilcornan *Limerick* 39 S6
Kilcreggan *Arg/Bute* 23 L14
Kilcrohane *Cork* 38 U4
Kilcullen *Kildare* 37 R10
Kilcurry *Louth* 37 P11
Kildalkey *Meath* 37 Q10
Kildare *Kildare* 37 R10
Kildavin *Carlow* 40 S10
Kildimo *Limerick* 39 S6
Kildonan *H'land* 28 F16
Kildorrery *Cork* 39 T7
Kilfane *Kilkenny* 40 S9
Kilfeakle *Tipperary* 39 T7
Kilfearagh *Clare* 38 S4
Kilfenora *Clare* 35 S5
Kilfinan *Arg/Bute* 18 L13
Kilfinnane *Limerick* 39 T7
Kilflynn *Kerry* 38 T4
Kilgarrif *Galway* 35 R5
Kilgarvan *Kerry* 38 U5
Kilglass *Galway* 35 R7
Kilglass *Sligo* 35 P5
Kilgobnet *Kerry* 38 T4
Kilgolagh *Cavan* 36 Q9
Kilham *Humber* 17 P23
Kilkea *Kildare* 40 S10
Kilkee *Clare* 38 S4
Kilkeel *Down* 37 P11
Kilkelly *Mayo* 35 Q6
Kilkenny *Kilkenny* 40 S9
Kilkerrin *Galway* 35 Q6
Kilkhampton *Cornw'l* 2 W14
Kilkieran *Galway* 34 R4
Kilkinlea *Kerry* 38 T5
Kilkishen *Clare* 39 S6
Kill *Kildare* 37 R10
Kill *Waterford* 40 T9
Killadangan *Mayo* 34 Q4
Killadeas *Fermanagh* 32 P8
Killadoon *Mayo* 34 Q4
Killadysert *Clare* 38 S5
Killala *Mayo* 35 P5
Killaloe *Clare* 39 S7
Killaloo *Londonderry* 32 N9
Killamarsh *Derby* 16 R21
Killane *Offaly* 36 R9
Killarbran *Fermanagh* 32 P9
Killarga *Leitrim* 32 P7
Killargue *Leitrim* 32 P7
Killarney *Kerry* 38 T4
Killashandra *Cavan* 36 P8
Killashee *Longford* 36 Q8
Killavally *Mayo* 34 Q5
Killavullen *Cork* 39 T6
Killeagh *Cork* 39 U8
Killean *Arg/Bute* 18 L12
Killearn *Stirl* 24 K15
Killeen *Tipperary* 36 R8
Killeen *Tyrone* 33 N10
Killeevan *Monaghan* 36 P9

Killeglan *Roscommon* 36 R7
Killeigh *Offaly* 36 R9
Killen *Tyrone* 32 N8
Killenagh *Wexford* 40 S11
Killenaule *Tipperary* 39 S8
Killerig *Carlow* 40 S10
Killimor *Galway* 35 R7
Killin *Stirl* 24 K15
Killinaboy *Clare* 35 S5
Killinaspick *Kilkenny* 40 T9
Killiney *Dublin* 37 R11
Killinghall *N Yorks* 16 P20
Killinick *Wexford* 40 T11
Killorglin *Kerry* 38 T4
Killough *Down* 33 P12
Killowen *Down* 37 P11
Killsaran *Louth* 37 Q11
Killtullagh *Galway* 35 R6
Killucan *Westmeath* 36 Q9
Killurin *Wexford* 40 T10
Killybegs *Donegal* 32 N7
Killyfassy *Cavan* 36 Q9
Killygordon *Donegal* 32 N8
Killykergan *Londonderry* 33 M10
Killylea *Armagh* 33 P10
Killyleagh *Down* 33 P12
Killyon *Offaly* 36 R8
Kilmacolm *Invercl* 19 L14
Kilmacow *Kilkenny* 40 T9
Kilmacrenan *Donegal* 32 M8
Kilmacthomas *Waterford* 40 T9
Kilmaganny *Kilkenny* 40 T9
Kilmaine *Mayo* 35 Q5
Kilmaley *Clare* 38 S5
Kilmallock *Limerick* 39 T6
Kilmaluag *H'land* 26 G11
Kilmanagh *Kilkenny* 40 S8
Kilmany *Fife* 25 K18
Kilmarnock *E Ayrs* 19 L15
Kilmartin *Arg/Bute* 23 K13
Kilmaurs *E Ayrs* 19 L14
Kilmeadan *Waterford* 40 T9
Kilmeage *Kildare* 37 R10
Kilmeedy *Limerick* 39 T6
Kilmelford *Arg/Bute* 23 K13
Kilmichael *Cork* 38 U5
Kilmihil *Clare* 38 S5
Kilmore *Wexford* 40 T10
Kilmore Quay *Wexford* 40 T10
Kilmory *Arg/Bute* 18 L12
Kilmory *H'land* 22 H11
Kilmory *H'land* 22 J11
Kilmuckridge *Wexford* 40 S11
Kilmuir *H'land* 28 G15
Kilmurry *Clare* 38 S5
Kilmurry *Clare* 39 S6
Kilmurry *Galway* 34 R4
Kilnaleck *Cavan* 36 Q9
Kilninver *Arg/Bute* 23 K12
Kilnsea *Humber* 17 Q24
Kilpatrick *Cork* 39 U6
Kilrea *Londonderry* 33 N10
Kilreekil *Galway* 35 R7
Kilrenny *Fife* 25 K18
Kilronan *Galway* 34 R4
Kilronane *Cork* 38 U5
Kilross *Tipperary* 39 T7
Kilrush *Clare* 38 S5
Kilsallagh *Galway* 35 Q6
Kilsby *Northants* 11 T21
Kilshanny *Clare* 34 S5
Kilsheelan *Tipperary* 39 T8
Kilsyth *N Lanarks* 24 L15
Kiltamagh *Mayo* 35 Q5
Kiltartan *Galway* 35 R6
Kiltealy *Wexford* 40 S10
Kilteel *Kildare* 37 R10
Kilteely *Limerick* 39 S7
Kiltegan *Wicklow* 40 S10
Kiltiernan *Dublin* 37 R11
Kiltoom *Roscommon* 36 R7
Kiltormer *Galway* 35 R7
Kiltyclogher *Leitrim* 32 P7
Kilwinning *N Ayrs* 19 L14
Kilworth *Cork* 39 T7
Kimbolton *Cambs* 12 T23
Kimpton *Herts* 6 U23
Kinalag *Galway* 35 Q6
Kinawley *Fermanagh* 32 P8
Kinbrace *H'land* 28 F16
Kinbuck *Stirl* 24 K16
Kincardine *Fife* 24 K16
Kincardine *H'land* 28 G15

Kincaslough *Donegal* 32 M7
Kincraig *H'land* 24 H16
Kindrum *Donegal* 32 M8
Kineton *Warwick* 11 T20
Kingarrow *Donegal* 32 N7
Kingarth *Arg/Bute* 18 L13
Kinghorn *Fife* 25 K17
King's Cliffe *Northants* 12 S23
Kings Langley *Herts* 6 U23
King's Lynn *Norfolk* 12 S24
King's Somborne *Hants* 5 V21
King's Sutton *Northants* 11 T21
King's Thorn *Heref/Worcs* 10 U18
King's Worthy *Hants* 5 V21
Kingsbarns *Fife* 25 K18
Kingsbridge *Devon* 3 X16
Kingsbury *Warwick* 11 S20
Kingsclere *Hants* 5 V21
Kingscourt *Cavan* 37 Q10
Kingsdown *Kent* 7 V26
Kingskerswell *Devon* 3 X16
Kingsland *Heref/Worcs* 10 T18
Kingsley *Hants* 6 V22
Kingsley *Staffs* 11 R20
Kingsteignton *Devon* 4 W16
Kingston Bagpuize *Oxon* 5 U21
Kingston *Devon* 3 X16
Kingston *London* 6 V23
Kingston upon Hull *Humber* 17 Q23
Kingswear *Devon* 3 X16
Kingswood *Avon* 4 V18
Kington *Heref/Worcs* 10 T17
Kingussie *H'land* 24 H15
Kinloch Rannoch *Perth/Kinr* 24 J15
Kinloch *H'land* 22 H11
Kinloch *H'land* 27 F14
Kinlochbervie *H'land* 27 F13
Kinlocheil *H'land* 23 J13
Kinlochewe *H'land* 27 G13
Kinlochleven *H'land* 23 J14
Kinlochmoidart *H'land* 23 J12
Kinloss *Moray* 28 G16
Kinlough *Leitrim* 32 P7
Kinmel Bay *Aber/Colw* 8 R16
Kinnegad *Westmeath* 36 R9
Kinnitty *Offaly* 36 R8
Kinross *Perth/Kinr* 24 K17
Kinsale *Cork* 39 U6
Kintarvie *W Isles* 26 F10
Kintore *Aberds* 25 H19
Kinuachdrachd *Arg/Bute* 23 K12
Kinvarra *Galway* 35 R6
Kinver *Staffs* 10 T19
Kippax *W Yorks* 16 Q21
Kippen *Stirl* 24 K15
Kircubbin *Down* 33 P12
Kirk Michael *I of Man* 14 P14
Kirkabister *Shetl'd* 31 B21
Kirkbean *Dumf/Gal* 20 N16
Kirkbride *Cumb* 20 N17
Kirkburton *W Yorks* 16 Q20
Kirkby Lonsdale *Cumb* 15 P18
Kirkby Malzeard *N Yorks* 16 P20
Kirkby Stephen *Cumb* 15 P19
Kirkby Thore *Cumb* 21 N18
Kirkby *Mersey* 15 R18
Kirkby-in-Ashfield *Notts* 11 R21
Kirkby-in-Furness *Cumb* 15 P17
Kirkbymoorside *N Yorks* 17 P22
Kirkcaldy *Fife* 25 K17
Kirkcolm *Dumf/Gal* 18 N13
Kirkconnel *Dumf/Gal* 19 M15
Kirkcowan *Dumf/Gal* 19 N14
Kirkcudbright *Dumf/Gal* 19 N15
Kirkham *Lancs* 15 Q18
Kirkinner *Dumf/Gal* 19 N15
Kirkintilloch *E Dunb* 19 L15
Kirkland *Dumf/Gal* 19 M15
Kirkliston *C of Edinb* 24 L17
Kirkmichael *Perth/Kinr* 24 J16
Kirkmichael *S Ayrs* 19 M14

Kirknewton *Northum* 21 L19
Kirkoswald *Cumb* 21 N18
Kirkoswald *S Ayrs* 18 M14
Kirkpatrick Durham *Dumf/Gal* 19 M16
Kirkpatrick Fleming *Dumf/Gal* 20 M17
Kirkton of Glenisla *Angus* 24 J17
Kirkton of Largo *Fife* 25 K18
Kirkwall *Orkney* 30 E18
Kirkwhelpington *Northum* 21 M20
Kirriemuir *Angus* 25 J18
Kirtling *Cambs* 12 T24
Kirtlington *Oxon* 11 U21
Kirton in Lindsey *Humber* 17 R22
Kirton *Lincs* 12 S23
Kishkeam *Cork* 38 T5
Knaresborough *N Yorks* 16 P21
Knayton *N Yorks* 16 P21
Knebworth *Herts* 6 U23
Knighton *Powys* 10 T17
Knock *Clare* 38 S5
Knock *Mayo* 35 Q6
Knockaderry *Limerick* 39 T6
Knockagree *Cork* 38 T5
Knockalina *Mayo* 34 P4
Knockalough *Clare* 38 S5
Knockananna *Wicklow* 40 S11
Knockatallan *Monaghan* 32 P9
Knockbrit *Tipperary* 39 T8
Knockcroghery *Roscommon* 36 Q7
Knockfold *Donegal* 32 M7
Knocklofty *Tipperary* 39 T8
Knocklong *Limerick* 39 T7
Knocktopher *Kilkenny* 40 T9
Knott End-on-Sea *Lancs* 15 Q18
Knottingley *W Yorks* 16 Q21
Knowle *W Midlands* 11 T20
Knowsley *Mersey* 15 R18
Knutsford *Ches* 15 R19
Kyle of Lochalsh *H'land* 27 H12
Kyleakin *H'land* 27 H12
Kylerhea *H'land* 23 H12
Kylesa *Galway* 34 R4
Kylestrome *H'land* 27 F13

L

Laban *Galway* 35 R6
Labasheeda *Clare* 38 S5
Labby *Londonderry* 33 N10
Laceby *Humber* 17 Q23
Lack *Fermanagh* 32 N8
Lackamore *Tipperary* 39 S7
Lacock *Wilts* 5 V19
Ladock *Cornw'l* 2 X14
Ladybank *Fife* 25 K17
Ladysbridge *Cork* 39 U7
Lagg *Arg/Bute* 18 L12
Laggan *H'land* 24 H14
Laggan *H'land* 24 H15
Laggan *Moray* 29 H17
Laghtgeorge *Galway* 35 R6
Laghy *Donegal* 32 N7
Lahard *Cavan* 36 Q8
Lahardaun *Mayo* 34 P5
Laide *H'land* 27 G12
Lairg *H'land* 28 F15
Lakenheath *Suffolk* 13 T25
Lakyle *Clare* 38 S5
Lamberhurst *Kent* 7 V24
Lambeth *London* 6 V23
Lambley *Northum* 21 N18
Lambourn *Berks* 5 U20
Lamlash *N Ayrs* 18 L13
Lampeter *Card* 9 ST1
Lanark *S Lanarks* 19 L16
Lancaster *Lancs* 15 P18
Lanchester *Durham* 21 N20
Lancing *W Sussex* 6 W23
Landkey *Devon* 3 V15
Landrake *Cornw'l* 3 X15
Lanesborough *Longford* 36 Q8

Langford Budville
   Som'set 4 W17
Langham *Leics* 11 S22
Langholm *Dumf/Gal* 20 M18
Langport *Som'set* 4 V18
Langsett *S Yorks* 16 Q20
Langtoft *Humber* 17 P23
Langtoft *Lincs* 12 S23
Langton Matravers
   Dorset 5 W19
Langtree *Devon* 3 W15
Langwathby *Cumb* 21 N18
Langwell *H'land* 28 F15
Lanivet *Cornw'l* 2 X14
Lapford *Devon* 3 W16
Laracor *Meath* 37 Q10
Laragh *Wicklow* 40 R11
Larbert *Falk* 24 K16
Largan *Mayo* 34 P4
Largs *N Ayrs* 18 L14
Largy *Donegal* 32 N6
Larkhall *S Lanarks* 19 L16
Larkhill *Wilts* 5 V20
Larne *H'land* 33 N12
Lasswade *Midloth* 20 L17
Latchingdon *Essex* 7 U25
Latheron *H'land* 28 F17
Lattin *Tipperary* 39 T7
Lauder *Borders* 21 L18
Laugharne *Carms* 9 U15
Launceston *Cornw'l* 3 W15
Lauragh *Kerry* 38 U4
Laurencekirk *Aberds* 25 J19
Laurencetown *Galway* 36 R7
Laurieston *Dumf/Gal* 19 N15
Lavendon *Bucks* 12 T22
Lavenham *Suffolk* 13 T25
Lavey *Cavan* 36 Q9
Lawers *Perth/Kinr* 24 J15
Lawrencetown *Down* 33 P11
Laxey *I of Man* 14 P15
Laxfield *Suffolk* 13 T26
Laxford Bridge *H'land* 27 F13
Laxton *Notts* 11 R22
Layer de la Haye
   Essex 7 U25
Laytown *Meath* 37 Q11
Lazonby *Cumb* 21 N18
Lea *Lincs* 17 R22
Leadburn *Midloth* 20 L17
Leaden Roding *Essex* 7 U24
Leadgate *Durham* 21 N20
Leadhills *S Lanarks* 19 M16
Leap *Cork* 38 U5
Leasingham *Lincs* 12 R23
Leatherhead *Surrey* 6 V23
Lechlade *Glos* 5 U20
Leckanarainey *Leitrim* 32 P7
Leckaun *Leitrim* 32 P7
Leckemy *Donegal* 33 M9
Ledbury *Heref/Worcs* 10 T19
Ledmore *H'land* 27 F14
Leeds *W Yorks* 16 Q20
Leedstown *Cornw'l* 2 X13
Leek *Staffs* 10 R19
Leeming Bar *N Yorks* 16 P20
Leenaun *Galway* 34 Q4
Lee-on-the-Solent
   Hants 5 W21
Legbourne *Lincs* 17 R24
Legoniel *Antrim* 33 N12
Lehinch *Clare* 34 S5
Leicester *Leics* 11 S21
Leigh *Gtr Man* 15 Q18
Leigh *Heref/Worcs* 10 T19
Leighlinbridge *Carlow* 40 S10
Leighton Buzzard
   Beds 12 U22
Leintwardine
   Heref/Worcs 10 T18
Leiston *Suffolk* 13 T27
Leith *C of Edinb* 25 L17
Leitholm *Borders* 21 L19
Leitrim *Leitrim* 36 Q7
Leixlip *Kildare* 37 R11
Lelant *Cornw'l* 2 X13
Lemanaghan *Offaly* 36 R8
Lemybrien *Waterford* 39 T8
Lenadoot *S Ayrs* 18 M14
Lenham *Kent* 7 V25
Lennoxtown *E Dunb* 24 L15
Leominster
   Heref/Worcs 10 T18
Lephin *H'land* 26 H10
Lerrig *Kerry* 38 T4
Lerwick *Shetl'd* 31 B21

Lesbury *Northum* 21 M20
Leslie *Fife* 25 K17
Lesmahagow
   S Lanarks 19 L16
Leswalt *Dumf/Gal* 18 N13
Letchworth *Herts* 12 U23
Letterbreen
   Fermanagh 32 P8
Letterfrack *Galway* 34 Q4
Letterkenny *Donegal* 32 N8
Lettermacaward
   Donegal 32 N7
Lettermore *Galway* 34 R4
Lettermullan *Galway* 34 R4
Letterston *Pembs* 9 U14
Lettoch *H'land* 28 H17
Leuchars *Fife* 25 K18
Leumrabhagh *W Isles* 26 F11
Leven *Fife* 25 K18
Leven *Humber* 17 Q23
Lewes *E Sussex* 6 W24
Lewisham *London* 6 V23
Lewiston *H'land* 28 H15
Leyburn *N Yorks* 15 P20
Leyland *Lancs* 15 Q18
Leysdown on Sea
   Kent 7 V25
Lhanbryde *Moray* 29 G17
Liatrie *H'land* 27 H14
Lichfield *Staffs* 11 S20
Lidgate *Suffolk* 13 T25
Lifford *Donegal* 32 N9
Lifton *Devon* 3 W15
Ligfordrum *Tyrone* 32 N9
Lilleshall *Shrops* 10 S19
Limavady
   Londonderry 33 M10
Limerick *Limerick* 39 S6
Limerick Junction
   Tipperary 39 T7
Lincoln *Lincs* 17 R22
Lindale *Cumb* 15 P18
Lingfield *Surrey* 6 V23
Linkinhorne *Cornw'l* 3 W15
Linksness *Orkney* 30 E17
Linlithgow *W Loth* 24 L16
Linslade *Beds* 12 U22
Linton *Cambs* 12 T24
Liphook *Hants* 6 V22
Lisacul *Roscommon* 35 Q6
Lisbane *Down* 33 N12
Lisbellaw *Fermanagh* 32 P8
Lisburn *Antrim* 33 N11
Liscannor *Clare* 34 S5
Liscarroll *Cork* 39 T6
Lisdoonvarna *Clare* 34 R5
Lisgall *Monaghan* 37 P10
Lisgarode *Tipperary* 39 S7
Lisheen *Clare* 38 S5
Liskeard *Cornw'l* 3 X15
Lislap *Tyrone* 32 N9
Lislea *Armagh* 37 P11
Lismore *Waterford* 39 T8
Lisnacree *Down* 37 P11
Lisnagry *Limerick* 39 S6
Lisnamusk
   Londonderry 33 N10
Lisnarrick *Fermanagh* 32 P8
Lisnaskea *Fermanagh* 32 P9
Lisnaveane
   Monaghan 36 P9
Lispole *Kerry* 38 T3
Lisronagh *Tipperary* 39 T8
Liss *Hants* 6 V22
Lissatinnig Bridge
   Kerry 38 U4
Lisselton *Kerry* 38 T4
Lissett *Humber* 17 P23
Lissinagroagh *Leitrim* 32 P7
Lissycasey *Clare* 38 S5
Listerlin *Kilkenny* 40 T9
Listowel *Kerry* 38 T5
Litcham *Norfolk* 13 S25
Litherland *Mersey* 15 R18
Little Shelford *Cambs* 12 T24
Little Stukeley *Cambs* 12 T23
Little Walsingham
   Norfolk 13 S25
Littleborough *Gtr Man* 15 Q19
Littlehampton
   W Sussex 6 W22
Littlemill *H'land* 28 G16
Littleport *Cambs* 12 T24
Littlestone-on-Sea
   Kent 7 W25
Littleton *Tipperary* 39 S8
Liverpool *Mersey* 15 R18

Livingston *W Loth* 24 L17
Lixnaw *Kerry* 38 T4
Lizard *Cornw'l* 2 Y13
Llanaber *Gwyn* 8 S15
Llanaelhaiarn *Gwyn* 8 S15
Llanafan-fawr *Powys* 9 T16
Llanarmon Dyffryn
   Ceiriog *Wrex* 10 S17
Llanarmon *Denbs* 10 R17
Llanarth *Card* 9 ST1
Llanarthney *Carms* 9 U15
Llanbadarn Fynydd
   Powys 9 T17
Llanbedr *Gwyn* 8 S15
Llanbedrog *Gwyn* 8 S15
Llanberis *Gwyn* 8 R15
Llanbister *Powys* 9 T17
Llanbrynmair *Powys* 9 S16
Llanddewi-Brefi *Card* 9 ST1
Llanddulas *Aber/Colw* 8 R16
Llandeilo *Carms* 9 U16
Llandinam *Powys* 9 T17
Llandissilio *Pembs* 9 U14
Llandogo *Monmouths* 4 U18
Llandovery *Carms* 9 U16
Llandrillo *Denbs* 8 S17
Llandrindod Wells
   Powys 9 T17
Llandudno *Aber/Colw* 8 R16
Llandybie *Carms* 9 U15
Llandyfriog *Card* 9 ST1
Llandygwydd *Card* 9 ST1
Llandyrnog *Denbs* 8 R17
Llandysul *Card* 9 ST1
Llanelidan *Denbs* 8 R17
Llanelli *Carms* 9 U15
Llanelltyd *Gwyn* 8 S16
Llanenddwyn *Gwyn* 8 S15
Llanerchymedd *Angl* 8 R15
Llanerfyl *Powys* 8 S17
Llanfaethlu *Angl* 8 R14
Llanfair Caereinion
   Powys 8 S17
Llanfair Talhaiarn
   Aber/Colw 8 R16
Llanfairfechan
   Aber/Colw 8 R16
Llanfairpwlgwngyll
   Angl 8 R15
Llanfechain *Powys* 10 S17
Llanfechell *Angl* 8 R15
Llanfihangel-ar-arth
   Carms 9 T15
Llanfrynach *Powys* 9 U17
Llanfyllin *Powys* 10 S17
Llangadfan *Powys* 9 S16
Llangadog *Carms* 9 U16
Llangammarch Wells
   Powys 9 T16
Llangefni *Angl* 8 R15
Llangeitho *Card* 9 ST1
Llangelynin *Gwyn* 8 S15
Llangennech *Carms* 9 U15
Llangenyw
   Aber/Colw 8 R16
Llangoed *Angl* 8 R15
Llangollen *Denbs* 10 S17
Llangorse *Powys* 9 U17
Llangranog *Card* 9 ST1
Llangunllo *Powys* 9 T17
Llangurig *Powys* 9 T16
Llangwm *Aber/Colw* 8 S17
Llangwm *Monmouths* 4 U18
Llangybi *Card* 9 ST1
Llangynidr *Powys* 10 U17
Llangynog *Powys* 8 S17
Llanharan
   Rh Cyn Taff 4 U17
Llanidloes *Powys* 8 T16
Llanilar *Card* 9 ST1
Llanllyfni *Gwyn* 8 R15
Llannor *Gwyn* 8 S15
Llanon *Card* 9 ST1
Llanpumsaint *Carms* 9 U15
Llanrhaeadr-ym-
   Mochnant *Powys* 8 S17
Llanrhian *Pembs* 9 U13
Llanrhidian *Swan* 9 U15
Llanrhystyd *Card* 9 ST1
Llanrug *Gwyn* 8 R15
Llanrwst *Aber/Colw* 8 R16
Llansannan
   Aber/Colw 8 R16
Llansawel *Carms* 9 U16
Llanstephan *Carms* 9 U15
Llanthony *Monmouths* 10 U17

Llantrisant
   Rh Cyn Taff 4 U17
Llantwit-Major
   V of Glam 4 V17
Llanuwchllyn *Gwyn* 8 S16
Llanvihangel
   Crucorney
   Monmouths 10 U18
Llanwddyn *Powys* 8 S17
Llanwenog *Card* 9 ST1
Llanwrda *Carms* 9 U16
Llanwrtyd Wells
   Powys 9 T16
Llanyblodwel *Shrops* 10 S17
Llanybydder *Carms* 9 T15
Llanymynech *Powys* 10 S17
Llanystumdwy *Gwyn* 8 S15
Llay *Wrex* 10 R17
Lledrod *Card* 9 ST1
Llithfaen *Gwyn* 8 S15
Llwyngwril *Gwyn* 8 S15
Llyswen *Powys* 9 T17
Loanhead *Midloth* 20 L17
Lobinstown *Meath* 37 Q10
Loch Baghasdail
   W Isles 22 H9
Loch nam Madadh
   W Isles 26 G9
Lochailort *H'land* 23 J12
Lochaline *H'land* 23 J12
Lochans *Dumf/Gal* 18 N13
Locharbriggs
   Dumf/Gal 20 M16
Lochboisdale = Loch
   Baghasdail *W Isles* 22 H9
Lochbuie *Arg/Bute* 23 K12
Lochcarron *H'land* 27 H12
Lochdon *Arg/Bute* 23 K12
Lochearnhead *Stirl* 24 K15
Lochgair *Arg/Bute* 23 K13
Lochgelly *Fife* 24 K17
Lochgilphead
   Arg/Bute 23 K13
Lochgoilhead
   Arg/Bute 23 K14
Lochinver *H'land* 27 F13
Lochmaben *Dumf/Gal* 20 M17
Lochmaddy = Loch
   nam Madadh
   W Isles 26 G9
Lochranza *N Ayrs* 18 L13
Lochwinnoch *Renf* 19 L14
Lockerbie *Dumf/Gal* 20 M17
Lockton *N Yorks* 17 P22
Loddiswell *Devon* 3 X16
Loddon *Norfolk* 13 S27
Loftus *Clevl'd* 17 N22
Logan *E Ayrs* 19 M15
Loghill *Limerick* 38 S5
London Colney *Herts* 6 U23
London *London* 6 U23
Long Ashton *Avon* 4 V18
Long Bennington
   Lincs 11 S22
Long Clawson *Leics* 11 S22
Long Compton
   Warwick 11 T20
Long Crendon *Bucks* 6 U22
Long Eaton *Derby* 11 S21
Long Itchington
   Warwick 11 T21
Long Melford *Suffolk* 13 T25
Long Preston *N Yorks* 15 P19
Long Stratton *Norfolk* 13 T26
Long Sutton *Lincs* 12 S24
Longbenton
   Tyne/Wear 21 M20
Longbridge Deverill
   Wilts 5 V19
Longdon *Heref/Worcs* 10 T19
Longford *Longford* 36 Q8
Longford *Glos* 10 U19
Longforgan *Perth/Kinr* 25 K17
Longformacus
   Borders 21 L19
Longframlington
   Northum 21 M20
Longhope *Orkney* 30 E17
Longhorsley *Northum* 21 M20
Longhoughton
   Northum 21 M20
Longnor *Staffs* 11 R20
Longridge *Lancs* 15 Q18
Longside *Aberds* 29 G20
Longton *Lancs* 15 Q18
Longtown *Cumb* 20 M18

Longtown
   Heref/Worcs 10 U18
Longwood *Meath* 37 R10
Loose *Kent* 7 V25
Lossiemouth *Moray* 28 G17
Lostock Gralam *Ches* 15 R19
Lostwithiel *Cornw'l* 2 X14
Loughall *Armagh* 33 P10
Loughanavally
   Westmeath 36 R8
Loughanure *Donegal* 32 N7
Loughborough *Leics* 11 S21
Loughbrickland *Down* 33 P11
Loughglinn
   Roscommon 35 Q6
Loughguile *Antrim* 33 M11
Loughmoe *Tipperary* 39 S8
Loughor *Swan* 9 U15
Loughran *Antrim* 33 M11
Loughrea *Galway* 35 R6
Loughton *Essex* 6 U24
Louisburgh *Mayo* 34 Q4
Louth *Louth* 37 Q10
Louth *Lincs* 17 R23
Lowdham *Notts* 11 R22
Lower Beeding
   W Sussex 6 V23
Lower Killeyan
   Arg/Bute 18 L11
Lower Langford *Avon* 4 V18
Lower Mayland *Essex* 7 U25
Lower Shiplake *Oxon* 6 U22
Lowestoft *Suffolk* 13 T27
Lowick *Northum* 21 L20
Loxwood *W Sussex* 6 V22
Lubcroy *H'land* 27 G14
Lucan *Dublin* 37 R11
Lucker *Northum* 21 L20
Ludborough *Lincs* 17 R23
Ludford *Lincs* 17 R23
Ludgershall *Wilts* 5 V20
Ludgvan *Cornw'l* 2 X12
Ludham *Norfolk* 13 S27
Ludlow *Shrops* 10 T18
Lugatemple *Mayo* 35 Q5
Lugton *E Ayrs* 19 L14
Lugwardine
   Heref/Worcs 10 T18
Lukeswell *Kilkenny* 40 T9
Lumphanan *Aberds* 25 H18
Lumsden *Aberds* 29 H18
Lurgan *Armagh* 33 P11
Lurgangreen *Louth* 37 Q11
Lusk *Dublin* 37 Q11
Luss *Arg/Bute* 24 K14
Lusta *H'land* 26 G10
Luton *Beds* 6 U23
Lutterworth *Leics* 11 T21
Lutton *Northants* 12 T23
Lybster *H'land* 28 F17
Lydd *Kent* 7 W25
Lydford *Devon* 3 W15
Lydham *Shrops* 10 S18
Lydney *Glos* 4 U18
Lyme Regis *Dorset* 4 W18
Lyminge *Kent* 7 V26
Lymington *Hants* 5 W20
Lymm *Ches* 15 R19
Lympne *Kent* 7 V26
Lympstone *Devon* 4 W17
Lyndhurst *Hants* 5 W20
Lyneham *Wilts* 5 U20
Lyness *Orkney* 30 E17
Lynmouth *Devon* 3 V16
Lynton *Devon* 3 V16
Lyracrumpane *Kerry* 38 T5
Lytchett Minster
   Dorset 5 W19
Lytham St. Anne's
   Lancs 15 Q17
Lythe *N Yorks* 17 N22

M

Maam Cross *Galway* 34 R4
Maas *Donegal* 32 N7
Mablethorpe *Lincs* 17 R24
Macclesfield *Ches* 15 R19
Macduff *Aberds* 29 G18
Machen *Caerph* 4 U17
Machrihanish
   Arg/Bute 18 M12
Machynlleth *Powys* 8 S16
Mackan *Fermanagh* 32 P8

Macmerry *E Loth* 25 L18
Macosquin
  Londonderry 33 M10
Macroom *Cork* 39 U6
Madeley *Staffs* 10 S19
Madley *Heref/Worcs* 10 T18
Maentwrog *Gwyn* 8 S16
Maesteg *Brigd* 9 U16
Maghera *Londonderry* 33 N10
Magherafelt
  Londonderry 33 N10
Magheragall *Antrim* 33 N11
Magheraveely
  Fermanagh 32 P9
Maghery *Armagh* 33 N10
Maghery *Donegal* 32 N7
Maghull *Mersey* 15 Q18
Magor *Monmouths* 4 U18
Maguiresbridge
  Fermanagh 32 P9
Maiden Bradley *Wilts* 5 V19
Maiden Newton
  Dorset 4 W18
Maidenhead *Berks* 6 U22
Maidstone *Kent* 7 V25
Malahide *Dublin* 37 R11
Maldon *Essex* 7 U25
Malham *N Yorks* 15 P19
Malin *Donegal* 32 M9
Malin More *Donegal* 32 N6
Mallaig *H'land* 23 H12
Mallaranny *Mayo* 34 Q4
Mallow *Cork* 39 T6
Mallwyd *Gwyn* 8 S16
Malmesbury *Wilts* 5 U19
Malpas *Ches* 10 R18
Maltby le Marsh *Lincs* 17 R24
Maltby *S Yorks* 16 R21
Malton *N Yorks* 17 P22
Manafon *Powys* 8 S17
Manby *Lincs* 17 R24
Manchester *Gtr Man* 15 R19
Manea *Cambs* 12 T24
Manfieldstown *Louth* 37 Q11
Mangotsfield *Avon* 5 V19
Manningtree *Essex* 13 U26
Manorbier *Pembs* 9 U14
Manorhamilton
  Leitrim 32 P7
Manselstown
  Tipperary 39 S8
Mansfield *Notts* 11 R21
Mansfield Woodhouse
  Notts 11 R21
Manton *Leics* 12 S22
Manulla *Mayo* 35 Q5
Marazion *Cornw'l* 2 X13
March *Cambs* 12 S24
Marden *Heref/Worcs* 10 T18
Marden *Kent* 7 V24
Mareham le Fen *Lincs* 12 R23
Maresfield *E Sussex* 6 W24
Marfleet *Humber* 17 Q23
Margam *Neath P Talb* 9 U16
Margate *Kent* 7 V26
Marham *Norfolk* 13 S25
Market Bosworth
  Leics 11 S21
Market Deeping *Lincs* 12 S23
Market Drayton
  Shrops 10 S19
Market Harborough
  Leics 11 T22
Market Lavington
  Wilts 5 V20
Market Rasen *Lincs* 17 R23
Market Weighton
  Humber 17 Q22
Markethill *Armagh* 33 P10
Markfield *Leics* 11 S21
Markinch *Fife* 25 K17
Marks Tey *Essex* 7 U25
Markyate *Herts* 6 U23
Marlborough *Devon* 3 X16
Marlborough *Wilts* 5 V20
Marlow *Bucks* 6 U22
Marnhull *Dorset* 5 W19
Marple *Gtr Man* 15 R19
Marshchapel *Lincs* 17 R24
Marshfield *Avon* 5 V19
Marske by the Sea
  Clevl'd 16 N21
Marston Magna
  Som'set 4 W18
Martham *Norfolk* 13 S27
Martin *Hants* 5 W20
Martley *Heref/Worcs* 10 T19

Martock *Som'set* 4 W18
Marton *Lincs* 17 R22
Marykirk *Aberds* 25 J18
Marypark *Moray* 28 H17
Maryport *Cumb* 20 N17
Marytavy *Devon* 3 W15
Marywell *Aberds* 25 H18
Marywell *Angus* 25 J18
Masham *N Yorks* 16 P20
Mathry *Pembs* 9 U13
Matlock *Derby* 11 R20
Mattishall *Norfolk* 13 S26
Mauchline *E Ayrs* 19 L15
Maud *Aberds* 29 G19
Maughold *I of Man* 14 P15
Maulyneill *Kerry* 38 U4
Maum *Galway* 34 Q4
Mawgan *Cornw'l* 2 X13
Maxwellheugh
  Borders 21 L19
Maybole *S Ayrs* 19 M14
Mayfield *E Sussex* 7 V24
Mayfield *Staffs* 11 R20
Maylough *Galway* 35 R6
Maynooth *Kildare* 37 R10
Mayo Bridge *Down* 33 P11
Mayo *Mayo* 35 Q5
Mealabost *W Isles* 31 A10
Mealsgate *Cumb* 20 N17
Measham *Leics* 11 S20
Medstead *Hants* 6 V21
Meenaneary *Donegal* 32 N6
Meidrim *Carms* 9 U15
Meifod *Powys* 10 S17
Meigh *Armagh* 37 P11
Meigle *Perth/Kinr* 25 J17
Melbourn *Cambs* 12 T24
Melbourne *Derby* 11 S21
Melksham *Wilts* 5 V19
Mell *Louth* 37 Q11
Mellon Charles *H'land* 27 G12
Mellor *Lancs* 15 Q18
Melmerby *Cumb* 21 N18
Melrose *Borders* 21 L18
Melsonby *N Yorks* 16 P20
Meltham *W Yorks* 15 Q20
Melton Constable
  Norfolk 13 S26
Melton Mowbray
  Leics 11 S22
Melton *Suffolk* 13 T26
Melvaig *H'land* 27 G12
Melvich *H'land* 28 E16
Menai Bridge *Angl* 8 R15
Mendlesham *Suffolk* 13 T26
Menlough *Galway* 35 R5
Mennock *Dumf/Gal* 19 M16
Menston *W Yorks* 15 Q20
Menstrie *Clack* 24 K16
Meonstoke *Hants* 5 W21
Meopham *Kent* 7 V24
Mere Brow *Lancs* 15 Q18
Mere *Wilts* 5 V19
Meriden *W Midlands* 11 T20
Merriott *Som'set* 4 W18
Merthyr Tydfil
  Merth Tyd 9 U17
Merton *London* 6 V23
Meshaw *Devon* 3 W16
Messingham *Humber* 17 Q22
Metfield *Suffolk* 13 T26
Metheringham *Lincs* 12 R23
Methil *Fife* 25 K17
Methlick *Aberds* 29 H19
Methven *Perth/Kinr* 24 K16
Methwold *Norfolk* 13 S25
Mevagissey *Cornw'l* 2 X14
Mexborough *S Yorks* 16 R21
Mey *H'land* 29 E17
Micheldever *Hants* 5 V20
Michelmersh *Hants* 5 W20
Mickleover *Derby* 11 S20
Mickleton *Durham* 21 N19
Mickleton *Glos* 11 T20
Mid Lavant *W Sussex* 6 W22
Mid Yell *Shetl'd* 31 A21
Midbea *Orkney* 30 D18
Middle Barton *Oxon* 11 U21
Middleham *N Yorks* 15 P20
Middlemarsh *Dorset* 5 W19
Middlesbrough
  Clevl'd 21 N21
Middleton Cheney
  Northants 11 T21
Middleton in Teesdale
  Durham 21 N19

Middleton on the
  Wolds *Humber* 17 Q22
Middleton *Arg/Bute* 22 K10
Middleton *Gtr Man* 15 Q19
Middleton *Norfolk* 12 S24
Middleton-on-Sea
  W Sussex 6 W22
Middletown *Armagh* 33 P10
Middlewich *Ches* 10 R19
Middlezoy *Som'set* 4 V18
Midhurst *W Sussex* 6 W22
Midleton *Cork* 39 U7
Midsomer Norton
  Avon 5 V19
Milborne Port
  Som'set 5 W19
Mildenhall *Suffolk* 13 T25
Milestone *Tipperary* 39 S7
Milford Haven *Pembs* 9 U13
Milford *Cork* 39 T6
Milford *Donegal* 32 M8
Milford on Sea *Hants* 5 W20
Milford *Surrey* 6 V22
Millbrook *Beds* 36 Q9
Millbrook *Cornw'l* 3 X15
Milford *Armagh* 33 P10
Millisle *Down* 33 N12
Millom *Cumb* 14 P17
Millport *N Ayrs* 18 L14
Millstreet *Cork* 38 T5
Millstreet *Waterford* 39 T8
Milltown *Antrim* 33 N12
Milltown *Cavan* 36 P9
Milltown *Galway* 35 Q6
Milltown *Kerry* 38 T3
Milltown *Kerry* 38 T4
Milltown *Londonderry* 33 M10
Milltown *Monaghan* 33 P10
Milltown Malbay *Clare* 38 S5
Milnathort *Perth/Kinr* 24 K17
Milngavie *E Dunb* 19 L15
Milnthorpe *Cumb* 15 P18
Milovaig *H'land* 26 H10
Milton Abbot *Devon* 3 W15
Milton Keynes *Bucks* 12 T22
Milton *H'land* 27 G14
Miltown *Kildare* 37 R10
Milverton *Som'set* 4 V17
Minane Bridge *Cork* 39 U7
Minchinhampton *Glos* 5 U19
Minehead *Som'set* 4 V17
Minera *Wrex* 10 R17
Minety *Wilts* 5 U20
Mingary *H'land* 22 J11
Minnigaff *Dumf/Gal* 19 N15
Minstead *Hants* 5 W20
Minster *Kent* 7 V25
Minster *Kent* 7 V26
Minsterley *Shrops* 10 S18
Mirfield *W Yorks* 16 Q20
Misterton *Notts* 17 R22
Misterton *Som'set* 4 W18
Mistley *Essex* 13 U26
Mitchel Troy
  Monmouths 4 U18
Mitcheldean *Glos* 5 U19
Mitchelstown *Cork* 39 T7
Moate *Westmeath* 36 R8
Modbury *Devon* 3 X16
Modreeny *Tipperary* 36 S7
Moelfre *Angl* 8 R15
Mohill *Leitrim* 36 Q8
Moira *Down* 33 P11
Mold *Flints* 10 R17
Monaghan *Monaghan* 33 P10
Monar Lodge *H'land* 27 H13
Monasterevin *Kildare* 36 R9
Moneygall *Offaly* 39 S8
Moneyglass *Antrim* 33 N11
Moneymore
  Londonderry 33 N10
Moneyneany
  Londonderry 33 N10
Moniaive *Dumf/Gal* 19 M16
Monifieth *Angus* 25 K18
Monikie *Angus* 25 J18
Moniva *Galway* 35 R6
Monkland
  Heref/Worcs 10 T18
Monkokehampton
  Devon 3 W15
Monkstown *Cork* 39 U7
Monkton *S Ayrs* 19 L14
Monmouth
  Monmouths 4 U18

Montacute *Som'set* 4 W18
Montgomery *Powys* 10 S17
Montrose *Angus* 25 J19
Monymusk *Aberds* 25 H18
Mooncoin *Kilkenny* 40 T9
Moone *Kildare* 40 S10
Moorfields *Antrim* 33 N11
Morar *H'land* 23 J12
Morchard Bishop
  Devon 4 W16
Mordiford
  Heref/Worcs 10 T18
Morebattle *Borders* 21 L19
Morecambe *Lancs* 15 P18
Moretonhampstead
  Devon 3 W16
Moreton-in-Marsh
  Glos 11 U20
Morley *W Yorks* 16 Q20
Mornington *Meath* 37 Q11
Morpeth *Northum* 21 M20
Mortehoe *Devon* 3 V15
Mortimer's Cross
  Heref/Worcs 10 T18
Morwenstow *Cornw'l* 2 W14
Mossley *Antrim* 33 N12
Mossley *Gtr Man* 15 Q19
Moss-side *Antrim* 33 M11
Mostyn *Flints* 15 R17
Motcombe *Dorset* 5 V19
Motherwell *N Lanarks* 19 L16
Mottisfont *Hants* 5 V20
Moulton *Lincs* 12 S23
Moulton *Northants* 11 T22
Moulton *Suffolk* 13 T25
Mount Bellew Bridge
  Galway 35 R7
Mount Ida *Down* 33 P11
Mount Nugent *Cavan* 36 Q9
Mount Talbot
  Roscommon 35 Q7
Mountain Ash
  Rh Cyn Taff 9 U17
Mountcharles
  Donegal 32 N7
Mountfield *Tyrone* 32 N9
Mountjoy *Tyrone* 32 N9
Mountmellick *Laois* 36 R9
Mountnorris *Armagh* 33 P11
Mountrath *Laois* 40 R9
Mountshannon *Clare* 35 S7
Mountsorrel *Leics* 11 S21
Mousehole *Cornw'l* 2 X12
Mouswald *Dumf/Gal* 20 M17
Moville *Donegal* 33 M9
Moy *Tyrone* 33 P10
Moy *H'land* 28 H15
Moyad *Down* 37 P11
Moyard *Galway* 34 Q3
Moyasta *Clare* 38 S4
Moycullen *Galway* 35 R5
Moymore *Clare* 39 S6
Moynalty *Meath* 37 Q10
Moyne *Longford* 36 Q8
Moyne *Tipperary* 39 S8
Moyroughly
  Westmeath 36 R8
Moyvally *Kildare* 37 R10
Moyvore *Westmeath* 36 Q8
Much Dewchurch
  Heref/Worcs 10 U18
Much Marcle
  Heref/Worcs 10 U19
Much Wenlock
  Shrops 10 S18
Muchalls *Aberds* 25 H19
Muckross *Kerry* 38 T5
Muff *Donegal* 32 M9
Muine Bheag *Carlow* 40 S10
Muineagh *Donegal* 32 M8
Muir of Ord *H'land* 28 G15
Muirdrum *Angus* 25 J18
Muirhead *N Lanarks* 19 L15
Muirkirk *E Ayrs* 19 L15
Muker *N Yorks* 15 P19
Mulben *Moray* 29 G17
Mullagh *Cavan* 37 Q10
Mullagh *Galway* 35 R7
Mullagh *Meath* 37 R10
Mullaghnaneane *Sligo* 32 P8
Mullan *Fermanagh* 32 P8
Mullans Town *Tyrone* 33 N9
Mullanys Cross *Sligo* 35 P6
Mullarts *Antrim* 33 M11
Mulldonagh
  Londonderry 32 N9
Mullinahone *Tipperary* 39 S8

Mullinavat *Kilkenny* 40 T9
Mullingar *Westmeath* 36 Q9
Mullion *Cornw'l* 2 X13
Mullughmore *Sligo* 32 P7
Mundesley *Norfolk* 13 S26
Mundford *Norfolk* 13 S25
Mungret *Limerick* 39 S6
Munlochy *H'land* 28 G15
Murlaggan *H'land* 23 J13
Murroogh *Clare* 34 R5
Murton *Durham* 21 N21
Musbury *Devon* 4 W17
Musselburgh *E Loth* 25 L17
Muthill *Perth/Kinr* 24 K16
Mybster *H'land* 28 F17
Myddfai *Carms* 9 U16
Myddle *Shrops* 10 S18
Mydroilyn *Card* 9 ST1
Mynydd Isa *Flints* 10 R17
Myshall *Carlow* 40 S10

N

Naas *Kildare* 37 R10
Nad *Cork* 39 T6
Nafferton *Humber* 17 P23
Nailsea *Avon* 4 V18
Nailsworth *Glos* 5 U19
Nairn *H'land* 28 G16
Nannerch *Flints* 14 R17
Nantwich *Ches* 10 R18
Nappa *N Yorks* 15 Q19
Naran *Donegal* 32 N7
Narberth *Pembs* 9 U14
Narborough *Leics* 11 S21
Naseby *Northants* 11 T22
Naul *Dublin* 37 Q11
Navan *Meath* 37 Q10
Navenby *Lincs* 12 R22
Neale *Mayo* 35 Q5
Neap *Shetl'd* 31 B21
Neath *Neath P Talb* 9 U16
Necton *Norfolk* 13 S25
Needham Market
  Suffolk 13 T26
Needingworth *Cambs* 12 T23
Nefyn *Gwyn* 8 S14
Neilston *E Renf* 19 L15
Nelson *Lancs* 15 Q19
Nenagh *Tipperary* 39 S7
Nenthead *Cumb* 21 N19
Neston *Ches* 15 R17
Nether Stowey
  Som'set 4 V17
Netheravon *Wilts* 5 V20
Netherbury *Dorset* 4 W18
Netherton *Northum* 21 M19
Nethy Bridge *H'land* 28 H16
Netley *Hants* 5 W21
Nettlebed *Oxon* 6 U22
Nettleham *Lincs* 17 R23
Nettleton *Lincs* 17 R23
Nevern *Pembs* 9 T14
New Abbey *Dumf/Gal* 20 N16
New Aberdour *Aberds* 29 G19
New Alresford *Hants* 5 V21
New Birmingham
  Tipperary 39 S8
New Buckenham
  Norfolk 13 T26
New Buildings
  Londonderry 32 N9
New Chapel Cross
  Kerry 38 U3
New Clipstone *Notts* 11 R21
New Costessey
  Norfolk 13 S26
New Cumnock *E Ayrs* 19 M15
New Deer *Aberds* 29 G19
New Earswick
  N Yorks 16 Q21
New Edlington
  S Yorks 16 R21
New Galloway
  Dumf/Gal 19 M15
New Holland *Humber* 17 Q23
New Inn *Cavan* 36 Q9
New Inn *Galway* 35 R7
New Inn *Laois* 36 R9
New Luce *Dumf/Gal* 18 N14
New Mills *Derby* 15 R20
New Milton *Hants* 5 W20
New Pitsligo *Aberds* 29 G19
New Quay *Card* 9 ST1

New Radnor *Powys* 10 T17
New Romney *Kent* 7 W25
New Ross *Wexford* 40 T10
New Rossington
  S Yorks 16 R21
New Scone *Perth/Kinr* 24 K17
New Tredegar *Caerph* 4 U17
New Waltham
  Humber 17 Q23
Newark-on-Trent
  Notts 11 R22
Newbiggin-by-the-
  Sea *Northum* 21 M20
Newbigging
  S Lanarks 20 L16
Newbliss *Monaghan* 36 P9
Newborough *Angl* 8 R15
Newbridge *Galway* 35 Q7
Newbridge *Kildare* 37 R10
Newbridge *Limerick* 39 S6
Newbridge on Wye
  Powys 9 T17
Newbridge *Caerph* 4 U17
Newbrough *Northum* 21 M19
Newburgh *Aberds* 29 H19
Newburgh *Fife* 25 K17
Newburn *Tyne/Wear* 21 N20
Newbury *Berks* 5 V21
Newby Bridge *Cumb* 15 P18
Newbyth *Aberds* 29 G19
Newcastle Emlyn
  Carms 9 T15
Newcastle *Down* 33 P12
Newcastle *Tipperary* 39 T8
Newcastle *Wicklow* 37 R11
Newcastle *Shrops* 10 T17
Newcastle West
  Limerick 38 T5
Newcastleton *Borders* 20 M18
Newcastle-under-
  Lyme *Staffs* 10 R19
Newcastle-upon-Tyne
  Tyne/Wear 21 N20
Newchurch *Powys* 10 T17
Newdigate *Surrey* 6 V23
Newent *Glos* 10 U19
Newgale *Pembs* 9 U13
Newham *London* 6 U24
Newhaven *E Sussex* 6 W24
Newick *E Sussex* 6 W24
Newington *Kent* 7 V25
Newington *Kent* 7 V26
Newinn *Tipperary* 39 T8
Newlyn East *Cornw'l* 2 X13
Newlyn *Cornw'l* 2 X12
Newmachar *Aberds* 29 H19
Newmarket *Cork* 39 T6
Newmarket *Suffolk* 12 T24
Newmarket *W Isles* 26 F11
Newmarket-on-
  Fergus *Clare* 39 S6
Newmill *Moray* 29 G18
Newmills *Donegal* 32 N8
Newmilns *E Ayrs* 19 L15
Newnham *Glos* 5 U19
Newport *Mayo* 34 Q4
Newport *Tipperary* 39 S7
Newport Pagnell
  Bucks 12 T22
Newport *Essex* 12 U24
Newport *I of Wight* 5 W21
Newport *Newp* 4 U18
Newport *Pembs* 9 T14
Newport *Shrops* 10 S19
Newport-on-Tay *Fife* 25 K18
Newquay *Cornw'l* 2 X13
Newry *Down* 33 P11
Newton Abbot *Devon* 4 W16
Newton Arlosh *Cumb* 20 N17
Newton Aycliffe
  Durham 21 N20
Newton Ferrers
  Devon 3 X15
Newton le Willows
  Mersey 15 R18
Newton Mearns
  E Renf 19 L15
Newton Poppleford
  Devon 4 W17
Newton St. Cyres
  Devon 4 W16
Newton Stewart
  Dumf/Gal 19 N15
Newton *Lancs* 15 Q19
Newtongrange
  Midloth 20 L17
Newtonhill *Aberds* 25 H19

Newtonmore *H'land* 24 H15
Newtown Crommelin
  Antrim 33 N11
Newtown
  Cunningham
  Donegal 32 N8
Newtown Forbes
  Longford 36 Q8
Newtown Gore
  Leitrim 36 P8
Newtown Hamilton
  Armagh 33 P10
Newtown *Laois* 40 S9
Newtown *Longford* 36 Q8
Newtown *Tipperary* 39 T7
Newtown
  Monasterboice
  Louth 37 Q10
Newtown Mount
  Kennedy *Wicklow* 37 R11
Newtown St.
  Boswells *Borders* 21 L18
Newtown Sands
  Kerry 38 S5
Newtown
  Heref/Worcs 10 T19
Newtown *Powys* 8 S17
Newtownabbey
  Antrim 33 N12
Newtownards *Down* 33 N12
Newtownbreda *Down* 33 N12
Newtownbutler
  Fermanagh 32 P9
Newtownshandrum
  Cork 39 T6
Newtownstewart
  Tyrone 32 N9
Neyland *Pembs* 9 U14
Ninemilehouse
  Tipperary 40 T9
Ninfield *E Sussex* 7 W24
Niton *I of Wight* 5 W21
Nobber *Meath* 37 Q10
Nohaval *Cork* 39 U7
Nordelph *Norfolk* 12 S24
Norham *Northum* 21 L19
Normanby le Wold
  Lincs 17 R23
Normanton *W Yorks* 16 Q21
North Baddesley
  Hants 5 W21
North Berwick *E Loth* 25 K18
North Cerney *Glos* 5 U20
North Charlton
  Northum 21 M20
North Elmham *Norfolk* 13 S25
North Ferriby *Humber* 17 Q22
North Frodingham
  Humber 17 Q22
North Hill *Cornw'l* 3 W15
North Hykeham *Lincs* 12 R22
North Kessock *H'land* 28 G15
North Molton *Devon* 3 V16
North Newbald
  Humber 17 Q22
North Petherton
  Som'set 4 V17
North Queensferry
  Fife 24 K17
North Somercotes
  Lincs 17 R24
North Sunderland
  Northum 21 L20
North Tawton *Devon* 3 W16
North Thoresby *Lincs* 17 R23
North Tidworth *Wilts* 5 V20
North Walsham
  Norfolk 13 S25
North Wingfield *Derby* 11 R21
Northallerton *N Yorks* 16 P21
Northam *Devon* 3 V15
Northampton
  Northants 11 T22
Northchapel
  W Sussex 6 V22
Northfleet *Kent* 7 V24
Northiam *E Sussex* 7 W25
Northleach *Glos* 5 U20
Northop *Flints* 10 R17
Northpunds *Shetl'd* 31 C21
Northrepps *Norfolk* 13 S26
Northwich *Ches* 15 R18
Northwold *Norfolk* 13 S25
Northwood *I of Wight* 5 W21
Northwood *London* 6 U23
Norton Fitzwarren
  Som'set 4 V17

Norton *Glos* 10 U19
Norton *Heref/Worcs* 10 T19
Norton *N Yorks* 17 P22
Norton *Suffolk* 13 T25
Norwich *Norfolk* 13 S26
Norwick *Shetl'd* 31 A22
Nottingham *Notts* 11 S21
Nuneaton *Warwick* 11 S21
Nunney *Som'set* 5 V19
Nurney *Carlow* 40 S10
Nutley *E Sussex* 6 V24
Nutts Corner *Antrim* 33 N11
Nybster *H'land* 29 E17

O

Oadby *Leics* 11 S21
Oakdale *Caerph* 4 U17
Oakengates *Shrops* 10 S19
Oakham *Leics* 12 S22
Oban *Arg/Bute* 22 J11
O'Briensbridge *Clare* 39 S7
Ochiltree *E Ayrs* 19 M15
Ockley *Surrey* 6 V23
Odie *Orkney* 30 D18
Odiham *Hants* 6 V22
Offord D'Arcy *Cambs* 12 T23
Ogbourne St. George
  Wilts 5 V20
Oghill *Londonderry* 32 N9
Oilgate *Wexford* 40 T10
Okehampton *Devon* 3 W15
Old Basing *Hants* 6 V22
Old Bolingbroke *Lincs* 12 R24
Old Colwyn
  Aber/Colw 8 R16
Old Deer *Aberds* 29 G19
Old Fletton *Cambs* 12 S23
Old Leake *Lincs* 12 R24
Old Radnor *Powys* 10 T17
Old Ross *Wexford* 40 T10
Oldbury *Avon* 4 U18
Oldcastle *Meath* 36 Q9
Oldham *Gtr Man* 15 Q19
Oldleighlin *Carlow* 40 S9
Oldmeldrum *Aberds* 29 H19
Oldtown *Laois* 40 S9
Olgrinmore *H'land* 28 F16
Ollerton *Notts* 11 R21
Olney *Bucks* 12 T22
Omagh *Tyrone* 32 N9
Ombersley
  Heref/Worcs 10 T19
Omeath *Louth* 37 P11
Onchan *Isle of Man* 14 P15
Onich *H'land* 23 J13
Oola *Limerick* 39 S7
Oran *Roscommon* 35 Q7
Oranmore *Galway* 35 R6
Ordhead *Aberds* 25 H18
Ordie *Aberds* 25 H18
Orford *Suffolk* 13 T27
Oristown *Meath* 37 Q10
Orleton *Heref/Worcs* 10 T18
Ormesby St. Margaret
  Norfolk 13 S27
Ormiston *E Loth* 25 L18
Ormskirk *Lancs* 15 Q18
Orphir *Orkney* 30 E17
Orpington *London* 6 V24
Orton *Cumb* 15 P18
Osbournby *Lincs* 12 S23
Oskamull *Arg/Bute* 22 J10
Osmotherley *N Yorks* 16 P21
Ossett *W Yorks* 16 Q20
Oswaldtwistle *Lancs* 15 Q19
Oswestry *Shrops* 10 S17
Otford *Kent* 6 V24
Othery *Som'set* 4 V18
Otley *W Yorks* 16 Q20
Otter Ferry *Arg/Bute* 23 K13
Otterburn *Northum* 21 M19
Otterton *Devon* 4 W17
Ottery St. Mary
  Devon 4 W17
Oughterard *Galway* 34 R5
Oulton Broad *Suffolk* 13 S27
Oulton *Norfolk* 13 S27
Oundle *Northants* 12 T23
Ousdale *H'land* 28 F16
Outwell *Norfolk* 12 S24
Over *Cambs* 12 T24
Over Wallop *Hants* 5 V20
Overbister *Orkney* 30 D18

Overseal *Derby* 11 S20
Overstrand *Norfolk* 13 S26
Overton *Hants* 5 V21
Overton *Wrex* 10 S18
Owston Ferry *Humber* 17 R22
Oxenholme *Cumb* 15 P18
Oxford *Oxon* 5 U21
Oxnam *Borders* 21 M19
Oxted *Surrey* 6 V24
Oykel Bridge *H'land* 27 G14

P

Pabail *W Isles* 27 F11
Paddock Wood *Kent* 7 V24
Padiham *Lancs* 15 Q19
Padstow *Cornw'l* 2 W14
Paibeil *W Isles* 26 G9
Paignton *Devon* 3 X16
Pailton *Warwick* 11 T21
Painscastle *Powys* 10 T17
Painshawfield
  Northum 21 N20
Painswick *Glos* 5 U19
Paisley *Renf* 19 L15
Palgrave *Suffolk* 13 T26
Pallas Green *Limerick* 39 S7
Pallaskenry *Limerick* 39 S6
Palnackie *Dumf/Gal* 19 N16
Pangbourne *Berks* 5 V21
Papworth Everard
  Cambs 12 T23
Park *Galway* 35 R6
Park *Londonderry* 33 N9
Parkeston *Essex* 13 U26
Parkhurst *I of Wight* 5 W21
Parknasilla *Kerry* 38 U4
Parkview *Antrim* 33 N12
Parracombe *Devon* 3 V16
Partney *Lincs* 12 R24
Parton *Cumb* 20 N16
Partry *Mayo* 34 Q5
Passage East
  Waterford 40 T10
Passage West *Cork* 39 U7
Pateley Bridge
  N Yorks 15 P20
Pathhead *Midloth* 20 L18
Patna *E Ayrs* 19 M15
Patrick Brompton
  N Yorks 16 P20
Patrickswell *Limerick* 39 S6
Patrington *Humber* 17 Q23
Patterdale *Cumb* 15 N18
Paull *Humber* 17 Q23
Paulstown *Kilkenny* 40 S9
Paulton *Avon* 4 V18
Peacehaven *E Sussex* 6 W24
Peak Forest *Derby* 15 R20
Peasedown St. John
  Avon 5 V19
Peasenhall *Suffolk* 13 T26
Peasmarsh *E Sussex* 7 W25
Peebles *Borders* 20 L17
Peel *I of Man* 14 P14
Pegswood *Northum* 21 M20
Pembrey *Carms* 9 U15
Pembridge
  Heref/Worcs 10 T18
Pembroke Dock
  Pembs 9 U14
Pembroke *Pembs* 9 U14
Pembury *Kent* 7 V24
Penally *Pembs* 9 U14
Penarth *V of Glam* 4 V17
Pencader *Carms* 9 T15
Pencoed *Bridg* 4 U16
Pendeen *Cornw'l* 2 X12
Penderyn *Rh Cyn Taff* 9 U16
Pendine *Carms* 9 U14
Penicuik *Midloth* 20 L17
Penistone *S Yorks* 16 Q20
Penkridge *Staffs* 10 S19
Penmachno
  Aber/Colw 8 R16
Penmaenmawr
  Aber/Colw 8 R16
Pennan *Aberds* 29 G19
Pennyghael *Arg/Bute* 22 K11
Penpont *Dumf/Gal* 19 M16
Penrhyndeudraeth
  Gwyn 8 S15
Penrith *Cumb* 21 N18
Penryn *Cornw'l* 2 X13

Pensford *Avon* 4 V18
Penshaw *Tyne/Wear* 21 N21
Penshurst *Kent* 6 V24
Pensilva *Cornw'l* 3 X15
Pentraeth *Angl* 8 R15
Pentrefoelas
  Aber/Colw 8 R16
Penwortham *Lancs* 15 Q18
Penybont *Powys* 9 T17
Penybontfawr *Powys* 8 S17
Penygroes *Carms* 9 U15
Penygroes *Gwyn* 8 R15
Penysarn *Angl* 8 R15
Penzance *Cornw'l* 2 X12
Perranporth *Cornw'l* 2 X13
Perranzabuloe
  Cornw'l 2 X13
Pershore *Heref/Worcs* 10 T19
Perth *Perth/Kinr* 24 K17
Peterborough *Cambs* 12 S23
Peterchurch
  Heref/Worcs 10 T18
Peterculter *Aberd C* 25 H19
Peterhead *Aberds* 29 G20
Peterlee *Durham* 21 N21
Petersfield *Hants* 6 V22
Peterswell *Galway* 35 R6
Petham *Kent* 7 V26
Pettigo *Donegal* 32 N8
Petworth *W Sussex* 6 W22
Pevensey *E Sussex* 7 W24
Pewsey *Wilts* 5 V20
Pickering *N Yorks* 17 P22
Piddletrenthide
  Dorset 5 W19
Pidley *Cambs* 12 T23
Pierowall *Orkney* 30 D18
Pilling *Lancs* 15 Q18
Pilton *Som'set* 4 V18
Piltown *Kilkenny* 40 T9
Pinchbeck *Lincs* 12 S23
Pinhoe *Devon* 4 W17
Pinmore Mains *S Ayrs* 18 M14
Pinwherry *S Ayrs* 18 M14
Pirbright *Surrey* 6 V22
Pirnmill *N Ayrs* 18 L13
Pitlochry *Perth/Kinr* 24 J16
Pittenweem *Fife* 25 K18
Plean *Stirl* 24 K16
Plockton *H'land* 27 H12
Pluck *Donegal* 32 N8
Pluckley *Kent* 7 V25
Plumbridge *Tyrone* 32 N9
Plumpton *Cumb* 20 N18
Plymouth *Devon* 3 X15
Plympton *Devon* 3 X15
Plymstock *Devon* 3 X15
Pocklington *Humber* 17 Q22
Polegate *E Sussex* 7 W24
Polesworth *Warwick* 11 S20
Polloch *H'land* 23 J12
Pollremon *Galway* 35 Q6
Polperro *Cornw'l* 2 X14
Polruan *Cornw'l* 2 X14
Polwarth *Borders* 21 L19
Polzeath *Cornw'l* 2 W14
Pomeroy *Tyrone* 33 N10
Pontardawe
  Neath P Talb 9 U16
Pontardulais *Swan* 9 U16
Pontefract *W Yorks* 16 Q21
Ponteland *Northum* 21 M20
Ponterwyd *Card* 9 ST1
Pontesbury *Shrops* 10 S18
Pontoon *Mayo* 35 Q5
Pontrhydfendigaid
  Card 9 ST1
Pontrilas *Heref/Worcs* 10 U18
Pontyates *Carms* 9 U15
Pontyberem *Carms* 9 U15
Pontycymer *Bridg* 9 U16
Pontypool *Torf* 4 U17
Pontypridd
  Rh Cyn Taff 9 U17
Pool *Cornw'l* 2 X13
Poole *Dorset* 5 W20
Poolewe *H'land* 27 G12
Pooley Bridge *Cumb* 20 N18
Porlock *Som'set* 4 V16
Port Askaig *Arg/Bute* 18 L11
Port Bannatyne
  Arg/Bute 18 L13
Port Carlisle *Cumb* 20 N17
Port Charlotte
  Arg/Bute 18 L11
Port Ellen *Arg/Bute* 18 L11
Port Erin *I of Man* 14 P14

Port Eynon Swan 9 U15
Port Glasgow Invercl 19 L14
Port Henderson H'land 27 G12
Port Isaac Cornw'l 2 W14
Port Logan Dumf/Gal 18 N14
Port Nan Giuran W Isles 27 F11
Port Nis W Isles 27 F11
Port St. Mary I of Man 14 P14
Port Talbot Neath P Talb 9 U16
Port William Dumf/Gal 19 N14
Portacloy Mayo 34 P4
Portadown Armagh 33 P11
Portaferry Down 33 P12
Portarlington Offaly 36 R9
Portavadie Arg/Bute 18 L13
Portavogie Down 33 P13
Portballintrae Antrim 33 M10
Portglenone Antrim 33 N11
Portgordon Moray 29 G17
Porth Rh Cyn Taff 9 U17
Porthcawl Bridg 4 V16
Porthleven Cornw'l 2 X13
Porthmadog Gwyn 8 S15
Portishead Avon 4 V18
Portknockie Moray 29 G18
Portlaoise Laois 40 R9
Portlaw Waterford 40 T9
Portlethen Aberds 25 H19
Portmagee Kerry 38 U3
Portmahomack H'land 28 G16
Portmarnock Dublin 37 R11
Portnacroish Arg/Bute 23 J13
Portnahaven Arg/Bute 18 L10
Porton Wilts 5 V20
Portpatrick Dumf/Gal 18 N13
Portrane Dublin 37 R11
Portreath Cornw'l 2 X13
Portree H'land 27 H11
Portroe Tipperary 39 S7
Portrush Antrim 33 M10
Portsalon Donegal 32 M8
Portskerra H'land 28 E16
Portslade E Sussex 6 W23
Portsmouth Hants 5 W21
Portsoy Aberds 29 G18
Portstewart Londonderry 33 M10
Portumna Galway 35 R7
Postbridge Devon 3 W16
Potter Heigham Norfolk 13 S27
Potterne Wilts 5 V19
Potters Bar Herts 6 U23
Potterspury Northants 11 T22
Potton Beds 12 T23
Poulton-le-Fylde Lancs 15 Q18
Poundstock Cornw'l 2 W14
Powick Heref/Worcs 10 T19
Poynton Ches 15 R19
Poyntz Pass Armagh 33 P11
Praa Sands Cornw'l 2 X13
Prees Shrops 10 S18
Preesall Lancs 15 Q18
Presbury Ches 15 R19
Prescot Mersey 15 R18
Prestatyn Denbs 8 R17
Prestbury Glos 10 U19
Presteigne Powys 10 T17
Preston Candover Hants 5 V21
Preston Borders 21 L19
Preston Dorset 5 W19
Preston Humber 17 Q23
Preston Kent 7 V26
Preston Lancs 15 Q18
Prestonpans E Loth 25 L18
Prestwich Gtr Man 15 Q19
Prestwick S Ayrs 19 M14
Prestwood Bucks 6 U22
Princes Risborough Bucks 6 U22
Princetown Devon 3 W15
Probus Cornw'l 2 X14
Prosperous Kildare 37 R10
Prudhoe Northum 21 N20
Puckaun Tipperary 35 S7
Pucklechurch Avon 5 V19
Puddletown Dorset 5 W19
Pudsey W Yorks 16 Q20
Pulborough W Sussex 6 W22

Pulham Market Norfolk 13 T26
Pulham St. Mary Norfolk 13 T26
Pumpsaint Carms 9 T16
Purfleet Essex 7 V24
Purley Berks 6 V21
Purley London 6 V23
Purton Wilts 5 U20
Puttenham Surrey 6 V22
Pwllheli Gwyn 8 S15
Pyle Bridg 4 U16

Q

Quadring Lincs 12 S23
Quainton Bucks 6 U22
Quarryfield Sligo 35 P6
Quedgeley Glos 5 U19
Queenborough Kent 7 V25
Queensbury W Yorks 15 Q20
Queensferry Flints 10 R17
Quilty Clare 38 S5
Quin Clare 39 S6
Quorndon Leics 11 S21

R

Rackenford Devon 4 W16
Rackheath Norfolk 13 S26
Rackwick Orkney 30 E17
Radcliffe Gtr Man 15 Q19
Radcliffe-on-Trent Notts 11 S21
Radlett Herts 6 U23
Radley Oxon 5 U21
Radstock Avon 5 V19
Radyr Card 4 U17
Raglan Monmouths 4 U18
Rahan Offaly 36 R8
Rahara Roscommon 36 Q7
Raharney Westmeath 36 Q9
Raheen Tipperary 39 T8
Rainham Kent 7 V25
Rainworth Notts 11 R21
Rampark Louth 37 P11
Rampside Cumb 14 P16
Ramsbottom Gtr Man 15 Q19
Ramsbury Wilts 5 V20
Ramsey Cambs 12 T23
Ramsey Essex 13 U26
Ramsey I of Man 14 P15
Ramseycleuch Borders 20 M17
Ramsgate Kent 7 V27
Randalstown Antrim 33 N11
Rannoch Station Perth/Kinr 24 J14
Raphoe Donegal 32 N8
Rapness Orkney 30 D18
Rasharkin Antrim 33 N11
Rath Offaly 36 R8
Rathangan Kildare 37 R10
Ratharney Longford 36 Q8
Rathclogh Tipperary 39 S8
Rathconrath Westmeath 36 Q8
Rathcool Cork 39 T6
Rathcoole Dublin 37 R11
Rathcor Louth 37 P11
Rathcormack Cork 39 T7
Rathdowney Laois 39 S8
Rathdrum Wicklow 40 S11
Rathduff Cork 39 T6
Rathen Aberds 29 G20
Rathfriland Down 33 P11
Rathgormuck Waterford 39 T9
Rathkeale Limerick 39 S6
Rathkenny Meath 37 Q10
Rathlacken Mayo 34 P5
Rathmelton Donegal 32 M8
Rathmolyon Meath 37 R10
Rathmore Kerry 38 T5
Rathmore Kildare 37 R10
Rathmore Longford 36 Q8
Rathmullan Donegal 32 M8
Rathnew Wicklow 40 S11
Rathnure Wexford 40 T10
Rathowen Westmeath 36 Q8
Rathvilla Offaly 36 R9

Rathvilly Carlow 40 S10
Ratoath Meath 37 Q11
Rattray Perth/Kinr 24 J17
Raunds Northants 12 T22
Ravenglass Cumb 14 P17
Ravensdale Louth 37 P11
Ravenshead Notts 11 R21
Ravenstonedale Cumb 15 P19
Rawcliffe N Yorks 16 Q21
Rawmarsh S Yorks 16 R21
Rawtenstall Lancs 15 Q19
Rayleigh Essex 7 U25
Reading Berks 6 V22
Rear Cross Tipperary 39 S7
Reay H'land 28 E16
Recess Galway 34 R4
Red Castle Donegal 32 M9
Red Dial Cumb 20 N17
Red Point H'land 27 G12
Redbourn Herts 6 U23
Redbridge London 6 U24
Redcar Clevl'd 16 N21
Redditch Heref/Worcs 11 T20
Redesmouth Northum 21 M19
Redhill Surrey 6 V23
Redland Orkney 30 D17
Redlynch Wilts 5 W20
Redmile Leics 11 S22
Redmire N Yorks 15 P20
Redruth Cornw'l 2 X13
Reedham Norfolk 13 S27
Reepham Norfolk 13 S26
Reeth N Yorks 15 P20
Reiff H'land 27 F13
Reigate Surrey 6 V23
Reiss H'land 29 F17
Renfrew Renf 19 L15
Rennington Northum 21 M20
Repton Derby 11 S20
Resolven Neath P Talb 9 U16
Reston Borders 21 L19
Retford Notts 17 R22
Reydon Suffolk 13 T27
Rhayader Powys 9 T17
Rhewl Denbs 8 R17
Rhiconich H'land 27 F14
Rhiw Gwyn 8 S14
Rhode Offaly 36 R9
Rhondda Rh Cyn Taff 9 U17
Rhoose V of Glam 4 V17
Rhoslan Gwyn 8 S15
Rhoslanerchrugog Wrex 10 R17
Rhosneigr Angl 8 R14
Rhos-on-Sea Aber/Colw 8 R16
Rhossili Swan 9 U15
Rhostryfan Gwyn 8 S15
Rhubodach Arg/Bute 18 L13
Rhuddlan Denbs 8 R17
Rhyd-Ddu Gwyn 8 S15
Rhyl Denbs 8 R17
Rhymney Caerph 9 U17
Rhynie Aberds 29 H18
Riccall N Yorks 16 Q21
Rich Hill Armagh 33 P10
Richmond London 6 V23
Richmond N Yorks 16 P20
Rickmansworth Herts 6 U23
Ridsdale Northum 21 M19
Rievaulx N Yorks 16 P21
Rigside S Lanarks 19 L16
Rillington N Yorks 17 P22
Ringaskiddy Cork 39 U7
Ringford Dumf/Gal 19 N15
Ringmer E Sussex 6 W24
Ringsend Londonderry 33 M10
Ringville Waterford 39 T8
Ringwood Hants 5 W20
Ripley Derby 11 R21
Ripley N Yorks 16 P20
Ripley Surrey 6 V23
Ripon N Yorks 16 P20
Ripponden W Yorks 15 Q20
Risca Caerph 4 U17
Rishton Lancs 15 Q19
Riverchapel Wexford 40 S11
Riverstick Cork 39 U7
Riverstown Cork 39 U7
Riverstown Sligo 35 P7
Roade Northants 11 T22
Roadhead Cumb 20 M18
Roberton Borders 20 M18

Robertsbridge E Sussex 7 W24
Robertstown Kildare 37 R10
Robin Hood's Bay N Yorks 17 P22
Rocester Staffs 11 S20
Rochdale Gtr Man 15 Q19
Roche Cornw'l 2 X14
Rochester Kent 7 V25
Rochester Northum 21 M19
Rochford Essex 7 U25
Rochfortbridge Westmeath 36 R9
Rockchapel Cork 38 T5
Rockcliffe Cumb 20 N18
Rockcliffe Dumf/Gal 19 N16
Rockcorry Monaghan 36 P9
Rockhill Limerick 39 T6
Rockingham Northants 11 S22
Rockmills Cork 39 T7
Rogart H'land 28 F15
Rogate W Sussex 6 V22
Roghadal W Isles 26 G10
Rolvenden Kent 7 V25
Romford London 6 U24
Romsey Hants 5 W21
Roosky Leitrim 36 Q8
Ropsley Lincs 12 S22
Roscommon Roscommon 35 Q7
Roscrea Tipperary 36 S8
Rosedale Abbey N Yorks 17 P22
Rosegreen Tipperary 39 T8
Rosehall H'land 28 G14
Rosehearty Aberds 29 G19
Rosemarket Pembs 9 U14
Rosemarkie H'land 28 G15
Rosenallis Laois 36 R9
Roskhill H'land 26 H10
Roslin Midloth 20 L17
Rosmult Tipperary 39 S8
Rosneath Arg/Bute 23 K14
Ross Carbery Cork 38 U5
Ross Northum 21 L20
Rossaveel Galway 34 R4
Rosscahill Galway 35 R5
Rosses Point Sligo 32 P6
Rossett Wrex 10 R18
Rossinver Leitrim 32 P7
Rosslare Harbour Wexford 40 T11
Rosslare Wexford 40 T11
Rosslea Fermanagh 32 P9
Rossnowlagh Donegal 32 N7
Ross-on-Wye Heref/Worcs 10 U18
Rostellan Cork 39 U7
Rostrevor Down 37 P11
Rosturk Mayo 34 Q4
Rosyth Fife 24 K17
Rothbury Northum 21 M20
Rotherham S Yorks 16 R21
Rothes Moray 29 G17
Rothesay Arg/Bute 18 L13
Rothienorman Aberds 29 H19
Rothiesholm Orkney 30 D18
Rothwell Northants 11 T22
Rothwell W Yorks 16 Q21
Rottal Angus 25 J17
Rottingdean E Sussex 6 W23
Roundstone Galway 34 R4
Roundwood Wicklow 40 R11
Rousky Tyrone 32 N9
Rowanburn Dumf/Gal 20 M18
Rowlands Gill Tyne/Wear 21 N20
Roxburgh Borders 21 L19
Roxby Humber 17 Q22
Royal Leamington Spa Warwick 11 T20
Royal Tunbridge Wells Kent 7 V24
Roybridge H'land 23 J14
Royston Herts 12 T23
Royston S Yorks 16 Q21
Royton Gtr Man 15 Q19
Rozel Chan Is 2 Z19
Ruabon Wrex 10 S17
Ruan Clare 35 S6
Ruan Minor Cornw'l 2 Y13
Ruardean Glos 4 U18
Rubery Heref/Worcs 10 T19
Rudston Humber 17 P23
Rufford Lancs 15 Q18

Rugby Warwick 11 T21
Rugeley Staffs 11 S20
Ruislip London 6 U23
Rumburgh Suffolk 13 T26
Rumney Card 4 U17
Runcorn Ches 15 R18
Rushden Northants 12 T22
Rushwick Heref/Worcs 10 T19
Ruskington Lincs 12 R23
Rutherglen S Lanarks 19 L15
Ruthin Denbs 8 R17
Ruthven H'land 24 H15
Ruthwell Dumf/Gal 20 N17
Ryal Northum 21 M20
Rydal Cumb 15 P18
Ryde I of Wight 5 W21
Rye E Sussex 7 W25
Ryhall Leics 12 S23
Ryhope Tyne/Wear 21 N21
Ryton Warwick 11 T21

S

Sacriston Durham 21 N20
Saddell Arg/Bute 18 L12
Saffron Walden Essex 12 T24
Sageston Pembs 9 U14
Saggart Dublin 37 R11
St. Abb's Borders 25 L19
St. Agnes Cornw'l 2 X13
St. Albans Herts 6 U23
St. Andrews Fife 25 K18
St. Ann's Dumf/Gal 20 M17
St. Arvans Monmouths 4 U18
St. Asaph Denbs 8 R17
St. Athan V of Glam 4 V17
St. Aubin Chan Is 2 Z19
St. Austell Cornw'l 2 X14
St. Bees Cumb 14 N16
St. Blazey Cornw'l 2 X14
St. Brelade Chan Is 2 Z19
St. Breward Cornw'l 2 W14
St. Briavels Glos 4 U18
St. Bride's Major V of Glam 4 V16
St. Buryan Cornw'l 2 X12
St. Clears Carms 9 U14
St. Columb Major Cornw'l 2 X14
St. Columb Minor Cornw'l 2 X13
St. Combs Aberds 29 G20
St. Cyrus Aberds 25 J19
St. David's Pembs 9 U13
St. Day Cornw'l 2 X13
St. Dennis Cornw'l 2 X14
St. Dogmaels Card 9 ST1
St. Dominick Cornw'l 3 X15
St. Enoder Cornw'l 2 X14
St. Erth Cornw'l 2 X13
St. Fergus Aberds 29 G20
St. Fillans Perth/Kinr 24 K15
St. Germans Cornw'l 3 X15
St. Harmon Powys 9 T17
St. Helens Mersey 15 R18
St. Helier Chan Is 2 Z19
St. Issey Cornw'l 2 W14
St. Ives Cambs 12 T23
St. Ives Cornw'l 2 X13
St. Johns Chapel Durham 21 N19
St. John's I of Man 14 P14
St. Johnstown Donegal 32 N9
St. Just Cornw'l 2 X12
St. Keverne Cornw'l 2 X13
St. Leonards E Sussex 7 W25
St. Levan Cornw'l 2 X12
St. Mabyn Cornw'l 2 W14
St. Margaret's Hope Orkney 30 E18
St. Margaret's-at-Cliffe Kent 7 V26
St. Martin Chan Is 2 Z18
St. Martin Chan Is 2 Z19
St. Mary Bourne Hants 5 V21
St. Mary's Bay Kent 7 V25
St. Mary's Orkney 30 E18
St. Mawes Cornw'l 2 X13

St. Mellons *Card*	4	U17
St. Merryn *Cornw'l*	2	W13
St. Minver *Cornw'l*	2	W14
St. Neots *Cambs*	12	T23
St. Olaves *Norfolk*	13	S27
St. Osyth *Essex*	7	U26
St. Peter Port *Chan Is*	2	Z18
St. Peter *Chan Is*	2	Z19
St. Sampson *Chan Is*	2	Z18
St. Stephen *Cornw'l*	2	X14
St. Teath *Cornw'l*	2	W14
St. Tudy *Cornw'l*	2	W14
Saintfield *Down*	33	P12
Salcombe *Devon*	3	X16
Sale *Gtr Man*	15	R19
Salen *Arg/Bute*	23	J12
Salen *H'land*	23	J12
Salford Priors *Warwick*	11	T20
Salford *Gtr Man*	15	R19
Saline *Fife*	24	K16
Salisbury *Wilts*	5	V20
Sallachy *H'land*	28	F15
Sallahig *Kerry*	38	U3
Sallins *Kildare*	37	R10
Sally Gap *Wicklow*	37	R11
Sallybrook *Cork*	39	U7
Saltash *Cornw'l*	3	X15
Saltburn by the Sea *Clevl'd*	17	N22
Saltcoats *N Ayrs*	18	L14
Salterstown *Louth*	37	Q11
Saltfleet *Lincs*	17	R24
Saltfleetby *Lincs*	17	R24
Salthill *Galway*	35	R5
Saltpans *Donegal*	32	M8
Saltwood *Kent*	7	V26
Sampford Courtenay *Devon*	3	W16
Sanaigmore *Arg/Bute*	18	L11
Sandbach *Ches*	10	R18
Sandbank *Arg/Bute*	23	L14
Sandgate *Kent*	7	V26
Sandhead *Dumf/Gal*	18	N14
Sandhurst *Berks*	6	V22
Sandleigh *Oxon*	5	U21
Sandness *Shetl'd*	31	B20
Sandown *I of Wight*	5	W21
Sandringham *Norfolk*	13	S25
Sandwich *Kent*	7	V26
Sandy *Beds*	12	T23
Sanquhar *Dumf/Gal*	19	M16
Sarnau *Card*	9	ST1
Sarnesfield *Heref/Worcs*	10	T18
Sarre *Kent*	7	V26
Satterthwaite *Cumb*	15	P17
Saundersfoot *Pembs*	9	U14
Sawbridgeworth *Herts*	6	U24
Sawston *Cambs*	12	T24
Sawtry *Cambs*	12	T23
Saxilby *Lincs*	17	R22
Saxlingham Nethergate *Norfolk*	13	S26
Saxmundham *Suffolk*	13	T27
Saxthorpe *Norfolk*	13	S26
Scalasaig *Arg/Bute*	22	K11
Scalby *N Yorks*	17	P23
Scalloway *Shetl'd*	31	B21
Scamblesby *Lincs*	17	R23
Scarborough *N Yorks*	17	P23
Scardoy *H'land*	27	G14
Scarinish *Arg/Bute*	22	J10
Scarning *Norfolk*	13	S25
Scarriff *Clare*	39	S6
Scarva *Down*	33	P11
Scogh *Kilkenny*	40	T9
Scole *Norfolk*	13	T26
Sconser *H'land*	27	H11
Scopwick *Lincs*	12	R23
Scorton *N Yorks*	16	P20
Scotch Corner *Monaghan*	33	P10
Scotch Corner *N Yorks*	16	P20
Scotstown *Monaghan*	33	P9
Scotter *Lincs*	17	Q22
Scourie *H'land*	27	F13
Scousburgh *Shetl'd*	31	C21
Scrabster *H'land*	28	E16
Scraghy *Tyrone*	32	N8
Scramoge *Roscommon*	36	Q7
Screeb *Galway*	34	R4
Screggan *Offaly*	36	R8
Scremerston *Northum*	21	L20
Scribbagh *Fermanagh*	32	P7
Scunthorpe *Humber*	17	Q22
Sea Palling *Norfolk*	13	S27
Seaford *E Sussex*	6	W24
Seaham *Durham*	21	N21
Seahouses *Northum*	21	L20
Seamer *N Yorks*	17	P23
Seascale *Cumb*	14	P17
Seaton Delaval *Northum*	21	M20
Seaton *Cumb*	20	N16
Seaton *Devon*	4	W17
Sebergham *Cumb*	20	N18
Sedbergh *Cumb*	15	P18
Sedgefield *Durham*	21	N21
Seend *Wilts*	5	V19
Selborne *Hants*	6	V22
Selby *N Yorks*	16	Q21
Sellafield *Cumb*	14	P17
Selsey *W Sussex*	6	W22
Sennen *Cornw'l*	2	X12
Sennybridge *Powys*	9	U16
Seskinore *Tyrone*	32	N9
Settle *N Yorks*	15	P19
Seven Sisters *Neath P Talb*	9	U16
Sevenoaks *Kent*	6	V24
Severn Beach *Avon*	4	U18
Severn Stoke *Heref/Worcs*	10	T19
Sgarasta Mhor *W Isles*	26	G9
Shaftesbury *Dorset*	5	V19
Shalcombe *I of Wight*	5	W21
Shaldon *Devon*	4	W16
Shalford *Surrey*	6	V22
Shanagolden *Limerick*	38	S5
Shankill *Roscommon*	35	Q7
Shanklin *I of Wight*	5	W21
Shanlaragh *Cork*	38	U5
Shannonbridge *Offaly*	36	R7
Shannow *Cavan*	36	Q9
Shanovogh *Clare*	38	S5
Shantonagh *Monaghan*	37	P10
Shap *Cumb*	15	N18
Sharavogue *Offaly*	36	R8
Sharnbrook *Beds*	12	T22
Sharpness *Glos*	5	U19
Shawbury *Shrops*	10	S18
Shawford *Hants*	5	V21
Shebbear *Devon*	3	W15
Sheerness *Kent*	7	V25
Sheffield *S Yorks*	16	R21
Shefford *Beds*	12	T23
Sheigra *H'land*	27	F13
Shenfield *Essex*	7	U24
Shepherdswell *Kent*	7	V26
Shepley *W Yorks*	16	Q20
Shepshed *Leics*	11	S21
Shepton Mallet *Som'set*	4	V18
Sherborne St. John *Hants*	5	V21
Sherborne *Dorset*	4	W18
Sherburn in Elmet *N Yorks*	16	Q21
Sherburn *N Yorks*	17	P22
Shercock *Cavan*	37	Q10
Shere *Surrey*	6	V23
Sherfield English *Hants*	5	V20
Sherfield on Lodden *Hants*	6	V21
Sheriff Hutton *N Yorks*	16	P21
Sheringham *Norfolk*	13	S26
Sherston *Wilts*	5	U19
Shiel Bridge *H'land*	23	H13
Shieldaig *H'land*	27	G12
Shifnal *Shrops*	10	S19
Shilbottle *Northum*	21	M20
Shildon *Durham*	21	N20
Shillelagh *Wicklow*	40	S10
Shillingstone *Dorset*	5	W19
Shillington *Beds*	12	T23
Shinfield *Berks*	6	V22
Shinrone *Offaly*	36	S8
Shipdham *Norfolk*	13	S25
Shipley *W Yorks*	15	Q20
Shipston-on-Stour *Warwick*	11	T20
Shipton under Wychwood *Oxon*	5	U20
Shirebrook *Notts*	11	R21
Shoeburyness *Essex*	7	U25
Shoreham by Sea *W Sussex*	6	W23
Shorwell *I of Wight*	5	W21
Shotley Gate *Suffolk*	13	U26
Shottermill *Surrey*	6	V22
Shottisham *Suffolk*	13	T26
Shotts *N Lanarks*	19	L16
Shrewsbury *Shrops*	10	S18
Shrewton *Wilts*	5	V20
Shrigley *Down*	33	P12
Shrivenham *Oxon*	5	U20
Shrule *Mayo*	35	Q5
Siabost *W Isles*	26	F10
Sible Hedingham *Essex*	13	U25
Sibsey *Lincs*	12	R24
Sidbury *Devon*	4	W17
Sidford *Devon*	4	W17
Sidlesham *W Sussex*	6	W22
Sidmouth *Devon*	4	W17
Silloth *Cumb*	20	N17
Silsden *W Yorks*	15	Q20
Silver End *Essex*	7	U25
Silverdale *Lancs*	15	P18
Silvermines *Tipperary*	39	S7
Silverstone *Northants*	11	T21
Silverstream *Monaghan*	33	P10
Silverton *Devon*	4	W17
Simonsbath *Som'set*	4	V16
Single Street *Donegal*	32	P7
Singleton *W Sussex*	6	W22
Sion Mills *Tyrone*	32	N9
Sittingbourne *Kent*	7	V25
Six Crosses *Kerry*	38	T4
Sixmilebridge *Clare*	39	S6
Sixmilecross *Tyrone*	32	N9
Sixpenny Handley *Dorset*	5	W20
Sizewell *Suffolk*	13	T27
Skeagh *Westmeath*	36	Q8
Skegness *Lincs*	12	R24
Skellingthorpe *Lincs*	17	R22
Skelmersdale *Lancs*	15	Q18
Skelmorlie *N Ayrs*	18	L14
Skelton *Clevl'd*	17	N22
Skelton *Cumb*	20	N18
Skerries *Dublin*	37	Q11
Skibbereen *Cork*	38	U5
Skinburness *Cumb*	20	N17
Skipness *Arg/Bute*	18	L13
Skipsea *Humber*	17	Q23
Skipton *N Yorks*	15	Q19
Skull *Cork*	38	U4
Slaidburn *Lancs*	15	Q19
Slaithwaite *W Yorks*	15	Q20
Slaley *Northum*	21	N19
Slamannan *Falk*	19	L16
Slane *Meath*	37	Q10
Sleaford *Lincs*	12	S23
Sledmere *Humber*	17	P22
Sleights *N Yorks*	17	P22
Sligachan *H'land*	27	H11
Sligo *Sligo*	32	P7
Slisgarrow *Fermanagh*	32	P8
Slough *Berks*	6	U22
Smailholm *Borders*	21	L18
Smarden *Kent*	7	V25
Smethwick *W Midlands*	11	S20
Smithborough *Monaghan*	32	P9
Smithfield *Cumb*	20	N18
Snainton *N Yorks*	17	P22
Snaith *Humber*	16	Q21
Snape *Suffolk*	13	T27
Sneaton *N Yorks*	17	P22
Sneem *Kerry*	38	U4
Snettisham *Norfolk*	13	S25
Snodland *Kent*	7	V24
Soham *Cambs*	12	T24
Solas *W Isles*	26	G9
Solihull *W Midlands*	11	T20
Solva *Pembs*	9	U13
Somerby *Leics*	11	S22
Somercotes *Derby*	11	R21
Somersham *Cambs*	12	T23
Somerton *Som'set*	4	V18
Sonning Common *Oxon*	6	U22
Sonning *Berks*	6	V22
Sopley *Hants*	5	W20
Sorbie *Dumf/Gal*	19	N15
Sordale *H'land*	28	E17
Sorisdale *Arg/Bute*	22	J11
Sorn *E Ayrs*	19	L15
Sortat *H'land*	29	E17
Soulby *Cumb*	15	P19
South Anston *S Yorks*	16	R21
South Benfleet *Essex*	7	U25
South Brent *Devon*	3	X16
South Cave *Humber*	17	Q22
South Cerney *Glos*	5	U20
South Elkington *Lincs*	17	R23
South Harting *W Sussex*	6	W22
South Hayling *Hants*	6	W22
South Kelsey *Lincs*	17	R22
South Kirkby *W Yorks*	16	Q21
South Molton *Devon*	3	V16
South Ockendon *Essex*	7	U24
South Otterington *N Yorks*	16	P21
South Petherton *Som'set*	4	W18
South Petherwin *Cornw'l*	3	W15
South Queensferry *C of Edinb*	24	L17
South Shields *Tyne/Wear*	21	N21
South Skirlaugh *Humber*	17	Q23
South Tawton *Devon*	3	W16
South Tidworth *Hants*	5	V20
South Walsham *Norfolk*	13	S26
South Warnborough *Hants*	6	V22
South Woodham Ferrers *Essex*	7	U25
South Wootton *Norfolk*	12	S24
South Zeal *Devon*	3	W16
Southam *Warwick*	11	T21
Southampton *Hants*	5	W21
Southborough *Kent*	7	V24
Southend *Arg/Bute*	18	M12
Southend-on-Sea *Essex*	7	U25
Southery *Norfolk*	12	S24
Southminster *Essex*	7	U25
Southport *Mersey*	15	Q17
Southwark *London*	6	V23
Southwell *Notts*	11	R22
Southwick *W Sussex*	6	W23
Southwold *Suffolk*	13	T27
Sowerby Bridge *W Yorks*	15	Q20
Sowerby *N Yorks*	16	P21
Spa *Kerry*	38	T4
Spalding *Lincs*	12	S23
Spaldwick *Cambs*	12	T23
Spancelhill *Clare*	39	S6
Sparkford *Som'set*	4	V18
Spean Bridge *H'land*	23	J14
Speenoge *Donegal*	32	M9
Speke *Mersey*	15	R18
Spennymoor *Durham*	21	N20
Sperrin *Tyrone*	33	N9
Spiddle *Galway*	34	R5
Spilsby *Lincs*	12	R24
Spittal of Glenmuick *Aberds*	25	J17
Spittal *Pembs*	9	U14
Spittle of Glenshee *Perth/Kinr*	24	J17
Spixworth *Norfolk*	13	S26
Spofforth *N Yorks*	16	Q21
Spott *E Loth*	25	L18
Spreyton *Devon*	4	W16
Springfield *Fermanagh*	32	P8
Sproatley *Humber*	17	Q23
Square *Down*	33	P11
Srahmore *Mayo*	34	P4
Srahnalong *Mayo*	34	Q5
Stadhampton *Oxon*	5	U21
Staffin *H'land*	27	G11
Stafford *Staffs*	10	S19
Staindrop *Durham*	21	N20
Staines *Surrey*	6	V23
Stainforth *N Yorks*	15	P19
Stainforth *S Yorks*	16	Q21
Stainton *Clevl'd*	16	N21
Stainton *Lincs*	17	R23
Staintondale *N Yorks*	17	P23
Staithes *N Yorks*	17	N22
Stalbridge *Dorset*	5	W19
Stalham *Norfolk*	13	S27
Stallingborough *Humber*	17	Q23
Stalybridge *Gtr Man*	15	R19
Stamford Bridge *Humber*	17	Q22
Stamford *Lincs*	12	S23
Stamfordham *Northum*	21	M20
Standish *Gtr Man*	15	Q18
Standlake *Oxon*	5	U21
Stanford le Hope *Essex*	7	U24
Stanford on Teme *Heref/Worcs*	10	T19
Stanhope *Durham*	21	N19
Stanley *Durham*	21	N20
Stanley *Perth/Kinr*	24	K17
Stannington *Northum*	21	M20
Stansted Mountfitchet *Essex*	12	U24
Stanton Harcourt *Oxon*	5	U21
Stanton St. John *Oxon*	5	U21
Stanton *Suffolk*	13	T25
Stanway *Glos*	11	U20
Stanwix *Cumb*	20	N18
Stapleford *Notts*	11	S21
Staplehurst *Kent*	7	V25
Starcross *Devon*	4	W17
Staunton on Wye *Heref/Worcs*	10	T18
Staunton *Glos*	10	U19
Staveley *Cumb*	15	P18
Staveley *Derby*	16	R21
Staxigoe *H'land*	29	F17
Staxton *N Yorks*	17	P23
Steeple Bumpstead *Essex*	12	T24
Steeple Claydon *Bucks*	11	U22
Stein *H'land*	26	G10
Stenhousemuir *Falk*	24	K16
Stevenage *Herts*	12	U23
Steventon *N Ayrs*	19	L14
Stewarton *E Ayrs*	19	L14
Stewartstown *Tyrone*	33	N10
Steyning *W Sussex*	6	W23
Stibb Cross *Devon*	3	W15
Stichill *Borders*	21	L19
Stickford *Lincs*	12	R24
Stickney *Lincs*	12	R24
Stillington *N Yorks*	16	P21
Stillorgan *Dublin*	37	R11
Stilton *Cambs*	12	T23
Stirling *Stirl*	24	K16
Stobbs *Borders*	20	M18
Stobo *Borders*	20	L17
Stock *Essex*	7	U24
Stockbridge *Hants*	5	V21
Stockport *Gtr Man*	15	R19
Stocksbridge *S Yorks*	16	R20
Stockton *Warwick*	11	T21
Stockton-on-Tees *Clevl'd*	21	N21
Stoer *H'land*	27	F13
Stoke Albany *Northants*	11	T22
Stoke Ferry *Norfolk*	13	S25
Stoke Fleming *Devon*	3	X16
Stoke Gabriel *Devon*	3	X16
Stoke Mandeville *Bucks*	6	U22
Stoke Poges *Bucks*	6	U22
Stoke Prior *Heref/Worcs*	10	T19
Stoke *Kent*	7	V25
Stokenchurch *Bucks*	6	U22
Stoke-on-Trent *Staffs*	10	R19
Stokesley *N Yorks*	16	P21
Stone *Bucks*	6	U22
Stone *Glos*	5	U19
Stone *Staffs*	10	S19
Stonehaven *Aberds*	25	J19
Stonehouse *Glos*	5	U19
Stonehouse *S Lanarks*	19	L16
Stoneykirk *Dumf/Gal*	18	N14
Stonham Aspal *Suffolk*	13	T26
Stony Stratford *Bucks*	11	T22
Stonyford *Kilkenny*	40	S9
Store *Orkney*	30	D18
Stornoway *W Isles*	26	F11
Storrington *W Sussex*	6	W23
Stotfold *Beds*	12	T23
Stourbridge *W Midlands*	10	T19
Stourpaine *Dorset*	5	W19
Stourport-on-Severn *Heref/Worcs*	10	T19

Stow Bardolph *Norfolk* 12 S24
Stow *Borders* 20 L18
Stowmarket *Suffolk* 13 T26
Stow-on-the-Wold *Glos* 11 U20
Strabane *Tyrone* 32 N9
Strachan *Aberds* 25 H18
Strachur *Arg/Bute* 23 K13
Stradbally *Kerry* 38 T3
Stradbally *Laois* 40 R9
Stradbally *Waterford* 40 T9
Stradbroke *Suffolk* 13 T26
Strade Friary *Mayo* 35 Q5
Stradone *Cavan* 36 Q9
Straffan *Kildare* 37 R10
Straiton *S Ayrs* 19 M14
Strandhill *Sligo* 32 P6
Strangford *Down* 33 P12
Stranorlar *Donegal* 32 N8
Stranraer *Dumf/Gal* 18 N13
Stratford St. Mary *Suffolk* 13 U25
Stratford-upon-Avon *Warwick* 11 T20
Strathan *H'land* 28 E15
Strathaven *S Lanarks* 19 L15
Strathblane *Stirl* 24 L15
Strathdon *Aberds* 25 H17
Strathkanaird *H'land* 27 G13
Strathpeffer *H'land* 28 G14
Strathy *H'land* 28 E16
Strathyre *Stirl* 24 K15
Stratmiglo *Fife* 24 K17
Stratton St. Margaret *Wilts* 5 U20
Stratton *Cornw'l* 2 W14
Stratton *Glos* 5 U20
Streamstown *Galway* 34 Q3
Streatley *Berks* 5 U21
Street *Som'set* 4 V18
Strensall *N Yorks* 16 P21
Stretford *Gtr Man* 15 R19
Stretham *Cambs* 12 T24
Stretton *Ches* 15 R18
Stretton *Leics* 12 S22
Stretton *Staffs* 11 S20
Strichen *Aberds* 29 G19
Strokestown *Roscommon* 36 Q7
Stromeferry *H'land* 27 H12
Stromemore *H'land* 27 H12
Stromness *Orkney* 30 E17
Stronachlachar *Stirl* 24 K14
Strone *Arg/Bute* 23 L14
Strontian *H'land* 23 J12
Stroove *Donegal* 33 M10
Stroud *Glos* 5 U19
Struy *H'land* 28 H14
Stubbington *Hants* 5 W21
Studland *Dorset* 5 W20
Studley *Warwick* 11 T20
Sturminster Marshall *Dorset* 5 W19
Sturminster Newton *Dorset* 5 W19
Sturry *Kent* 7 V26
Sturton *Lincs* 17 R22
Sudbury *Derby* 11 S20
Sudbury *Suffolk* 13 T25
Sulby *I of Man* 14 P15
Sullom *Shetl'd* 31 B21
Sully *V of Glam* 4 V17
Summerhill *Meath* 37 R10
Sunderland *Tyne/Wear* 21 N21
Sunk Island *Humber* 17 Q23
Sunninghill *Berks* 6 V22
Sutterton *Lincs* 12 S23
Sutton Bridge *Lincs* 12 S24
Sutton Coldfield *W Midlands* 11 S20
Sutton Courtenay *Oxon* 5 U21
Sutton Lane Ends *Ches* 15 R19
Sutton Scotney *Hants* 5 V21
Sutton *Cambs* 12 T24
Sutton *London* 6 V23
Sutton Valence *Kent* 7 V25
Sutton-in-Ashfield *Notts* 11 R21
Sutton-on-Sea *Lincs* 17 R24
Sutton-on-Trent *Notts* 11 R22
Sutton-under-Whitestonecliffe *N Yorks* 16 P21
Swadlincote *Derby* 11 S20
Swaffham *Norfolk* 13 S25
Swalcliffe *Oxon* 11 T21
Swalecliffe *Kent* 7 V26
Swan *Laois* 40 S9
Swanage *Dorset* 5 W20
Swanley *Kent* 6 V24
Swanlinbar *Cavan* 32 P8
Swansea *Swan* 9 U16
Swatragh *Londonderry* 33 N10
Sway *Hants* 5 W20
Swindon *Wilts* 5 U20
Swinefleet *Humber* 17 Q22
Swineshead *Lincs* 12 S23
Swinford *Mayo* 35 Q6
Swinton *Borders* 21 L19
Swinton *Gtr Man* 15 Q19
Swinton *S Yorks* 16 R21
Swords *Dublin* 37 R11
Symbister *Shetl'd* 31 B21
Symington *S Lanarks* 20 L16
Symonds Yat *Heref/Worcs* 4 U18
Syresham *Northants* 11 T21
Syston *Leics* 11 S21

T

Tadcaster *N Yorks* 16 Q21
Tadley *Hants* 5 V21
Taghmon *Wexford* 40 T10
Tain *H'land* 28 G15
Talgarth *Powys* 10 U17
Talladale *H'land* 27 G12
Tallaght *Dublin* 37 R11
Tallanstown *Louth* 37 Q10
Talley *Carms* 9 U15
Tallow *Waterford* 39 T7
Tallowbridge *Waterford* 39 T7
Talsarnau *Gwyn* 8 S15
Talybont *Card* 8 ST1
Tal-y-llyn *Gwyn* 8 S16
Talysarn *Gwyn* 8 R15
Tamerton Foliot *Devon* 3 X15
Tamworth *Staffs* 11 S20
Tandragee *Armagh* 33 P11
Tang *Westmeath* 36 Q8
Tangmere *W Sussex* 6 W22
Tannadice *Angus* 25 J18
Tanworth *Warwick* 11 T20
Taobh Tuath *W Isles* 26 G9
Tara *Meath* 37 Q10
Tarbert = Aird Asaig Tairbeart *W Isles* 26 G10
Tarbert *Kerry* 38 S5
Tarbert *Arg/Bute* 18 L13
Tarbet *Arg/Bute* 24 K14
Tarbet *H'land* 23 J12
Tarbolton *S Ayrs* 19 L15
Tarland *Aberds* 25 H18
Tarleton *Lancs* 15 Q18
Tarporley *Ches* 10 R18
Tarrant Hinton *Dorset* 5 W19
Tarskavaig *H'land* 23 H12
Tarves *Aberds* 29 H19
Tarvin *Ches* 10 R18
Tattenhall *Ches* 10 R18
Tattersett *Norfolk* 13 S25
Taunton *Som'set* 4 V17
Taur *Cork* 38 T5
Tavistock *Devon* 3 W15
Tawnyinah *Mayo* 35 Q6
Tayinloan *Arg/Bute* 18 L12
Taynuilt *Arg/Bute* 23 K13
Tayport *Fife* 25 K18
Teangue *H'land* 23 H12
Tebay *Cumb* 15 P18
Tedavnet *Monaghan* 33 P9
Tedburn St. Mary *Devon* 4 W16
Teeshan *Antrim* 33 N11
Teesside *Clevl'd* 21 N21
Teignmouth *Devon* 4 W16
Telford *Shrops* 10 S19
Temple Combe *Som'set* 5 W19
Temple Ewell *Kent* 7 V26
Temple Sowerby *Cumb* 21 N18
Templeboy *Sligo* 35 P6
Templederry *Tipperary* 39 S7
Templemore *Tipperary* 39 S8
Templenoe *Kerry* 38 U4
Templepatrick *Antrim* 33 N11
Templeton *Pembs* 9 U14
Templetouhy *Tipperary* 39 S8
Tempo *Fermanagh* 32 P9
Tenbury Wells *Heref/Worcs* 10 T18
Tenby *Pembs* 9 U14
Tenterden *Kent* 7 V25
Termon *Cavan* 32 P8
Termon *Donegal* 32 M8
Termonfeckin *Louth* 37 Q11
Terrington St. Clement *Norfolk* 12 S24
Terrington *N Yorks* 17 P22
Terryglass *Tipperary* 36 R7
Tetbury *Glos* 5 U19
Tetney *Lincs* 17 R23
Tetsworth *Oxon* 6 U22
Teviothead *Borders* 20 M18
Tewkesbury *Glos* 10 U19
Teynham *Kent* 7 V25
Thame *Oxon* 6 U22
Thatcham *Berks* 5 V21
Thaxted *Essex* 12 U24
The Barony *Orkney* 30 D17
The Downs *Westmeath* 36 Q9
The Loup *Londonderry* 33 N10
The Mumbles *Swan* 9 U16
The Sheddings *Antrim* 33 N11
The Temple *Down* 33 P12
Theale *Berks* 6 V21
Thetford *Norfolk* 13 T25
Thirsk *N Yorks* 16 P21
Thomas Street *Roscommon* 35 R7
Thomastown *Kilkenny* 40 S9
Thornaby on Tees *Clevl'd* 21 N21
Thornbury *Avon* 4 U18
Thorndon *Suffolk* 13 T26
Thorne *S Yorks* 17 Q22
Thorney *Cambs* 12 S23
Thornham *Norfolk* 13 S25
Thornhill *Dumf/Gal* 19 M16
Thornhill *Stirl* 24 K15
Thornthwaite *Cumb* 20 N17
Thornton Dale *N Yorks* 17 P22
Thornton *Lancs* 15 Q17
Thorpe le Soken *Essex* 7 U26
Thorpe *Norfolk* 13 S26
Thorverton *Devon* 4 W16
Thrapston *Northants* 12 T22
Three Legged Cross *Dorset* 5 W20
Threlkeld *Cumb* 20 N17
Threshfield *N Yorks* 15 P19
Thrumster *H'land* 29 F17
Thurcroft *S Yorks* 16 R21
Thurlby *Lincs* 12 S23
Thurles *Tipperary* 39 S8
Thurlestone *Devon* 3 X16
Thurmaston *Leics* 11 S21
Thursby *Cumb* 20 N17
Thurso *H'land* 28 E16
Ticehurst *E Sussex* 7 V24
Tickhill *S Yorks* 16 R21
Tideswell *Derby* 15 R20
Tighnabruaich *Arg/Bute* 18 L13
Tilbury *Essex* 7 V24
Tillicoultry *Clack* 24 K16
Tillingham *Essex* 7 U25
Tilmanstone *Kent* 7 V26
Timahoe *Kildare* 37 R10
Timahoe *Laois* 40 S9
Timberscombe *Som'set* 4 V16
Timoleague *Cork* 39 U6
Timolin *Kildare* 40 S10
Timsbury *Avon* 5 V19
Tinahely *Wicklow* 40 S11
Tingewick *Bucks* 11 U21
Tintagel *Cornw'l* 2 W14
Tintern Abbey *Wexford* 40 T10
Tintern *Monmouths* 4 U18
Tipperary *Tipperary* 39 T7
Tipton *W Midlands* 10 S19
Tiptree *Essex* 7 U25
Tisbury *Wilts* 5 V19
Titchfield *Hants* 5 W21
Tiverton *Devon* 4 W17
Tobercurry *Sligo* 35 P6
Tobermoney *Down* 33 P12
Tobermore *Londonderry* 33 N10
Tobermory *Arg/Bute* 22 J11
Toberonochy *Arg/Bute* 23 K12
Toberroe *Galway* 35 R6
Tobha Mor *W Isles* 26 H9
Toddington *Beds* 12 U22
Todmorden *W Yorks* 15 Q19
Togher *Cork* 38 U5
Togher *Louth* 37 Q11
Tolastadh bho Thuath *W Isles* 27 F11
Tollesbury *Essex* 7 U25
Tolob *Shetl'd* 31 C21
Tolpuddle *Dorset* 5 W19
Tomatin *H'land* 28 H16
Tomdoun *H'land* 23 H13
Tomintoul *Moray* 24 H17
Tomnavoulin *Moray* 28 H17
Tonbridge *Kent* 7 V24
Tondu *Bridg* 4 U16
Tong *Shrops* 10 S19
Tongue *H'land* 28 F15
Tonyrefail *Rh Cyn Taff* 9 U17
Toomakeady *Mayo* 34 Q5
Toombeola *Galway* 34 R4
Toome *Antrim* 33 N11
Toomyvara *Tipperary* 39 S7
Toormore *Cork* 38 U4
Topcliffe *N Yorks* 16 P21
Topsham *Devon* 4 W17
Torbay *Devon* 3 X16
Torcross *Devon* 3 X16
Torness *H'land* 28 H15
Torphins *Aberds* 25 H18
Torpoint *Cornw'l* 3 X15
Torquay *Devon* 3 X16
Torridon *H'land* 27 G12
Torroble *H'land* 28 F15
Torteval *Chan Is* 2 Z18
Torthorwald *Dumf/Gal* 20 M16
Torver *Cumb* 15 P17
Toscaig *H'land* 27 H12
Totland *I of Wight* 5 W20
Totley *S Yorks* 16 R20
Totnes *Devon* 3 X16
Totton *Hants* 5 W20
Tow Law *Durham* 21 N20
Towcester *Northants* 11 T22
Tower Hamlets *London* 6 U23
Town Yetholm *Borders* 21 L19
Trafford Park *Gtr Man* 15 R19
Tralee *Kerry* 38 T4
Tramore *Waterford* 40 T9
Tranent *E Loth* 25 L18
Trawsfynydd *Gwyn* 8 S16
Trecastle *Powys* 9 U16
Tredegar *Bl Gwent* 4 U17
Trefeglwys *Powys* 8 S16
Trefnant *Denbs* 8 R17
Trefriw *Aber/Colw* 8 R16
Tregaron *Card* 9 ST1
Tregony *Cornw'l* 2 X14
Tregynon *Powys* 8 S17
Treharris *Merth Tyd* 9 U17
Trelech *Carms* 9 U15
Tremadog *Gwyn* 8 S15
Trenance *Cornw'l* 2 X13
Trentham *Staffs* 10 S19
Treorchy *Rh Cyn Taff* 9 U16
Tresilian *Cornw'l* 2 X13
Tretower *Powys* 10 U17
Treuddyn *Flints* 10 R17
Trillick *Tyrone* 32 P9
Trim *Meath* 37 Q10
Trimdon *Durham* 21 N21
Trimley *Suffolk* 13 U26
Tring *Herts* 6 U22
Trinity *Chan Is* 2 Z19
Troon *S Ayrs* 19 L14
Troutbeck *Cumb* 15 P18
Trowbridge *Wilts* 5 V19
Trull *Som'set* 4 W17
Trumpington *Cambs* 12 T24
Trunch *Norfolk* 13 S26
Truro *Cornw'l* 2 X13
Tuam *Galway* 35 Q6
Tuamgraney *Clare* 39 S6
Tubber *Galway* 35 R6
Tuddenham *Suffolk* 13 T25
Tudweiliog *Gwyn* 8 S14
Tulla *Clare* 39 S6
Tullaghan *Leitrim* 32 P7
Tullaghoge *Tyrone* 33 N10
Tullaghought *Kilkenny* 40 T9
Tullagower *Clare* 38 S5
Tullamore *Offaly* 36 R9
Tullaroan *Kilkenny* 40 S9
Tullow *Carlow* 40 S10
Tully Cross *Galway* 34 Q4
Tully *Roscommon* 36 Q7
Tullybeg *Galway* 35 Q6
Tullycrossmearan *Fermanagh* 32 P8
Tullymacreeve *Armagh* 37 P11
Tullynessle *Aberds* 29 H18
Tullyverry *Londonderry* 32 M9
Tullyvin *Cavan* 36 P9
Tulsk *Roscommon* 35 Q7
Tummel Bridge *Perth/Kinr* 24 J15
Tummery *Tyrone* 32 P8
Tunstall *Suffolk* 13 T26
Turloughmore *Galway* 35 R6
Turnberry *S Ayrs* 18 M14
Turreen *Longford* 36 Q8
Turriff *Aberds* 29 G19
Turvey *Beds* 12 T22
Tutbury *Staffs* 11 S20
Tuxford *Notts* 17 R22
Twatt *Orkney* 30 D17
Tweedmouth *Northum* 21 L19
Tweedshaws *Borders* 20 M16
Tweedsmuir *Borders* 20 L17
Twenty *Lincs* 12 S23
Twomileborris *Tipperary* 39 S8
Twyford *Berks* 6 V22
Twyford *Hants* 5 V21
Twyford *Leics* 11 S22
Tydd St. Giles *Cambs* 12 S24
Tydd St. Mary *Lincs* 12 S24
Tylorstown *Rh Cyn Taff* 9 U17
Tynagh *Galway* 35 R7
Tynan *Armagh* 33 P10
Tyndrum *Stirl* 24 K14
Tynemouth *Tyne/Wear* 21 M21
Ty'n-y-groes *Aber/Colw* 8 R16
Tyrrellspass *Westmeath* 36 R9
Tywardreath *Cornw'l* 2 X14
Tywyn *Gwyn* 8 S15

U

Uckfield *E Sussex* 6 W24
Uddingston *S Lanarks* 19 L15
Uffculme *Devon* 4 W17
Uffington *Oxon* 5 U20
Ufford *Suffolk* 13 T26
Ugborough *Devon* 3 X16
Uig *H'land* 26 G11
Ulbster *H'land* 29 F17
Ulceby Cross *Lincs* 17 R24
Ulceby *Humber* 17 Q23
Uley *Glos* 5 U19
Ullapool *H'land* 27 G13
Ulsta *Shetl'd* 31 A21
Ulverston *Cumb* 15 P17
Unapool *H'land* 27 F13
Upavon *Wilts* 5 V20
Uphill *Avon* 4 V18
Upper Chapel *Powys* 9 T17
Upper Heyford *Oxon* 11 U21
Upper Hindhope *Borders* 21 M19
Upper Poppleton *N Yorks* 16 Q21
Upper Tean *Staffs* 11 S20
Upperchurch *Tipperary* 39 S7
Uppingham *Leics* 12 S22
Upton Snodsbury *Heref/Worcs* 10 T19
Upton *Ches* 15 R18
Upton-upon-Severn *Heref/Worcs* 10 T19
Upwey *Dorset* 5 W19

Urchfont *Wilts*	5	V20
Urlingford *Kilkenny*	39	S8
Urmston *Gtr Man*	15	R19
Usk *Monmouths*	4	U18
Usselby *Lincs*	17	R23
Uttoxeter *Staffs*	11	S20
Uyeasound *Shetl'd*	31	A22

V

Valley *Angl*	8	R14
Veness *Orkney*	30	D18
Ventnor *I of Wight*	5	W21
Ventry *Kerry*	38	T3
Verwood *Dorset*	5	W20
Veryan *Cornw'l*	2	X14
Vicarstown *Laois*	40	R9
Vickerstown *Cumb*	14	P17
Vidlin *Shetl'd*	31	B21
Virginia *Cavan*	36	Q9
Virginia Water *Surrey*	6	V22
Voe *Shetl'd*	31	B21
Voy *Orkney*	30	D17

W

Waddesdon *Bucks*	6	U22
Waddingham *Lincs*	17	R22
Waddington *Wexford*	40	T10
Waddington *Lincs*	12	R22
Wadebridge *Cornw'l*	2	W14
Wadhurst *E Sussex*	7	V24
Wainfleet All Saints *Lincs*	12	R24
Wakefield *W Yorks*	16	Q21
Walberswick *Suffolk*	13	T27
Walcott *Lincs*	12	R23
Walderslade *Kent*	7	V25
Waldron *E Sussex*	6	W24
Walford *Heref/Worcs*	10	T18
Walkerburn *Borders*	20	L18
Walkeringham *Notts*	17	R22
Wallasey *Mersey*	15	R17
Wallingford *Oxon*	5	U21
Walls *Shetl'd*	31	B21
Wallsend *Tyne/Wear*	21	N20
Walmer *Kent*	7	V26
Walpole *Norfolk*	12	S24
Walsall *W Midlands*	11	S20
Walsham le Willows *Suffolk*	13	T25
Walsoken *Cambs*	12	S24
Waltham Abbey *Essex*	6	U24
Waltham Forest *London*	6	U24
Waltham on the Wolds *Leics*	11	S22
Walton *Cumb*	21	N18
Walton-on-Thames *Surrey*	6	V23
Walton-on-the-Naze *Essex*	7	U26
Wanborough *Wilts*	5	U20
Wandsworth *London*	6	V23
Wangford *Suffolk*	13	T27
Wansford *Cambs*	12	S23
Wantage *Oxon*	5	U21
Warboys *Cambs*	12	T23
Ward *Dublin*	37	R11
Wardington *Oxon*	11	T21
Wardle *Ches*	10	R18
Ware *Herts*	6	U23
Wareham *Dorset*	5	W19
Wargrave *Berks*	6	V22
Waringstown Down	33	P11
Wark *Northum*	21	M19
Warkworth *Northum*	21	M20
Warley *W Midlands*	11	T20
Warminster *Wilts*	5	V19
Warrenpoint *Down*	37	P11
Warrington *Ches*	15	R18
Warsop *Notts*	11	R21
Warton *Lancs*	15	P18
Warwick *Warwick*	11	T20
Wasbister *Orkney*	30	D17
Washaway *Cornw'l*	2	X14
Washford *Som'set*	4	V17
Washingborough *Lincs*	17	R23
Washington *Tyne/Wear*	21	N20

Washington *W Sussex*	6	W23
Watchet *Som'set*	4	V17
Watchfield *Oxon*	5	U20
Waterbeach *Cambs*	12	T24
Waterford *Waterford*	40	T9
Watergrasshill *Cork*	39	T7
Waterhead *Angus*	25	J18
Waterhouses *Staffs*	11	R20
Wateringbury *Kent*	7	V24
Waterlooville *Hants*	6	W21
Waterside Londonderry	32	N9
Waterville *Kerry*	38	U3
Watford *Herts*	6	U23
Wath upon Dearne *S Yorks*	16	R21
Watlington *Norfolk*	12	S24
Watlington *Oxon*	6	U22
Watten *H'land*	28	F17
Watton *Norfolk*	13	S25
Waunfawr *Gwyn*	8	R15
Weachyburn *Aberds*	29	G18
Wearhead *Durham*	21	N19
Weasenham *Norfolk*	13	S25
Weaverham *Ches*	15	R18
Weaverthorpe *N Yorks*	17	P22
Wedmore *Som'set*	4	V18
Wednesbury *W Midlands*	10	S19
Wednesfield *W Midlands*	10	S19
Weedon Bec *Northants*	11	T21
Weeley *Essex*	7	U26
Welbourn *Lincs*	12	R22
Weldon *Northants*	12	T22
Weldon *Northum*	21	M20
Welford *Berks*	5	V21
Welford *Northants*	11	T21
Wellesbourne *Warwick*	11	T20
Wellingborough *Northants*	12	T22
Wellington *Shrops*	10	S18
Wellington *Som'set*	4	W17
Wellingtonbridge *Wexford*	40	T10
Wellow *Avon*	5	V19
Wells *Som'set*	4	V18
Wells-next-the-Sea *Norfolk*	13	S25
Welney *Norfolk*	12	S24
Welshampton *Shrops*	10	S18
Welshpool *Powys*	10	S17
Welton *Lincs*	17	R23
Welwyn Garden City *Herts*	6	U23
Wem *Shrops*	10	S18
Wembury *Devon*	3	X15
Wemyss Bay *Invercl*	18	L14
Wendover *Bucks*	6	U22
Wensley *N Yorks*	15	P20
Wenvoe *V of Glam*	4	V17
Weobley *Heref/Worcs*	10	T18
Werrington *Cornw'l*	3	W15
West Auckland *Durham*	21	N20
West Bergholt *Essex*	13	U25
West Bridgford *Notts*	11	S21
West Bromwich *W Midlands*	11	S20
West Burton *N Yorks*	15	P20
West Calder *W Loth*	20	L16
West Coker *Som'set*	4	W18
West Dean *Wilts*	5	V20
West End *Hants*	5	W21
West Felton *Shrops*	10	S18
West Grinstead *W Sussex*	6	W23
West Haddon *Northants*	11	T21
West Kilbride *N Ayrs*	18	L14
West Kingsdown *Kent*	7	V24
West Kirby *Mersey*	15	R17
West Linton *Borders*	20	L17
West Looe *Cornw'l*	3	X15
West Lulworth *Dorset*	5	W19
West Malling *Kent*	7	V24
West Meon *Hants*	5	V21
West Mersea *Essex*	7	U25
West Moors *Dorset*	5	W20
West Rasen *Lincs*	17	R23
West Thorney *W Sussex*	6	W22
West Wellow *Hants*	5	W20
West Woodburn *Northum*	21	M19

Westbourne *W Sussex*	6	W22
Westbury *Shrops*	10	S18
Westbury *Wilts*	5	V19
Westbury-on-Severn *Glos*	5	U19
Westbury-sub-Mendip *Som'set*	4	V18
Westcott *Surrey*	6	V23
Westerham *Kent*	6	V24
Westfield *E Sussex*	7	W25
Westhill *Aberds*	25	H19
Westhoughton *Gtr Man*	15	Q18
Westleton *Suffolk*	13	T27
Westminster *London*	6	U23
Weston *Staffs*	10	S19
Weston-Super-Mare *Avon*	4	V18
Westonzoyland *Som'set*	4	V18
Westport *Mayo*	34	Q4
Westruther *Borders*	21	L18
Westward Ho! *Devon*	3	V15
Wetheral *Cumb*	20	N18
Wetherby *W Yorks*	16	Q21
Wetwang *Humber*	17	P22
Wexford *Wexford*	40	T11
Weybourne *Norfolk*	13	S26
Weybridge *Surrey*	6	V23
Weyhill *Hants*	5	V20
Weymouth *Dorset*	5	W19
Whaley Bridge *Derby*	15	R20
Whalley *Lancs*	15	Q19
Whalton *Northum*	21	M20
Whaplode *Lincs*	12	S23
Whatton *Notts*	11	S22
Whauphill *Dumf/Gal*	19	N15
Wheathampstead *Herts*	6	U23
Wheathill *Fermanagh*	32	P8
Wheatley Hill *Durham*	21	N21
Wheatley *Notts*	17	R22
Wheatley *Oxon*	5	U21
Wheaton Aston *Staffs*	10	S19
Wheldrake *N Yorks*	17	Q22
Whicham *Cumb*	14	P17
Whickham *Tyne/Wear*	21	N20
Whimple *Devon*	4	W17
Whipsnade *Beds*	6	U22
Whissendine *Leics*	11	S22
Whitburn *W Loth*	20	L16
Whitby *N Yorks*	17	P22
Whitchurch *Avon*	4	V18
Whitchurch *Bucks*	6	U22
Whitchurch *Devon*	3	W15
Whitchurch *Hants*	5	V21
Whitchurch *Heref/Worcs*	4	U18
Whitchurch *Shrops*	10	S18
White Bridge *H'land*	24	H14
White Castle *Donegal*	32	M9
Whitecross *Armagh*	33	P11
Whitegate *Clare*	35	S7
Whitegate *Cork*	39	U7
Whitehall *Orkney*	30	D18
Whitehaven *Cumb*	20	N16
Whitehead *Antrim*	33	N12
Whitehill *Fermanagh*	32	P8
Whitehouse *Arg/Bute*	18	L13
Whitekirk *E Loth*	25	K18
Whiteparish *Wilts*	5	V20
Whitfield *Kent*	7	V26
Whithorn *Dumf/Gal*	19	N15
Whitland *Carms*	9	U14
Whitley Bay *Tyne/Wear*	21	M21
Whitsome *Borders*	21	L19
Whitstable *Kent*	7	V26
Whitstone *Cornw'l*	3	W15
Whittington *Derby*	16	R21
Whittington *Lancs*	15	P18
Whittington *Shrops*	10	S18
Whittington *Staffs*	11	S20
Whittlebury *Northants*	11	T22
Whittlesey *Cambs*	12	S23
Whittlesford *Cambs*	12	T24
Whitwell *Derby*	16	R21
Whitwell *I of Wight*	5	W21
Whitwick *Leics*	11	S21
Whitworth *Lancs*	15	Q19
Whixley *N Yorks*	16	P21
Wick *Avon*	5	V19
Wick *H'land*	29	F17
Wick *V of Glam*	4	V16
Wick *Wilts*	5	W20
Wicken *Cambs*	12	T24
Wickford *Essex*	7	U25

Wickham Market *Suffolk*	13	T26
Wickham *Hants*	5	W21
Wicklow *Wicklow*	40	S11
Wickwar *Avon*	5	U19
Widdrington *Northum*	21	M20
Wide Open *Tyne/Wear*	21	M20
Widecombe *Devon*	3	W16
Widemouth *Cornw'l*	2	W14
Widnes *Ches*	15	R18
Wigan *Gtr Man*	15	Q18
Wigmore *Heref/Worcs*	10	T18
Wigmore *Kent*	7	V25
Wigston *Leics*	11	S21
Wigton *Cumb*	20	N17
Wigtown *Dumf/Gal*	19	N15
Willand *Devon*	4	W17
Willaston *Ches*	15	R17
Willenhall *W Midlands*	10	S19
Willersley *Heref/Worcs*	10	T17
Willesborough *Kent*	7	V25
Williamstown *Galway*	35	Q6
Willingdon *E Sussex*	7	W24
Willington *Beds*	12	T23
Willington *Durham*	21	N20
Williton *Som'set*	4	V17
Willoughby *Lincs*	17	R24
Wilmington *Devon*	4	W17
Wilmslow *Ches*	15	R19
Wilnecote *Staffs*	11	S20
Wilton *Wilts*	5	V20
Wimbledon *Cambs*	12	S24
Wimborne Minster *Dorset*	5	W20
Wincanton *Som'set*	5	V19
Winchcombe *Glos*	11	U20
Winchelsea *E Sussex*	7	W25
Winchester *Hants*	5	V21
Windermere *Cumb*	15	P18
Windgap *Kilkenny*	40	T9
Windsor *Berks*	6	V22
Windygates *Fife*	25	K17
Wing *Bucks*	6	U22
Wingate *Durham*	21	N21
Wingham *Kent*	7	V26
Winkleigh *Devon*	3	W16
Winscombe *Avon*	4	V18
Winsford *Ches*	10	R18
Winslow *Bucks*	11	U22
Winster *Derby*	11	R20
Winston *Durham*	21	N20
Winterborne Abbas *Dorset*	4	W18
Winterborne Stickland *Dorset*	5	W19
Winterton *Humber*	17	Q22
Winterton *Norfolk*	13	S27
Wirksworth *Derby*	11	R20
Wisbech St. Mary *Cambs*	12	S24
Wisbech *Cambs*	12	S24
Wisborough Green *W Sussex*	6	V23
Wishaw *N Lanarks*	19	L16
Witchampton *Dorset*	5	W19
Witchford *Cambs*	12	T24
Witham *Essex*	7	U25
Witheridge *Devon*	4	W16
Withern *Lincs*	17	R24
Withernsea *Humber*	17	Q24
Withington *Glos*	5	U20
Witley *Surrey*	6	V22
Witnesham *Suffolk*	13	T26
Witney *Oxon*	5	U21
Wittersham *Kent*	7	V25
Wiveliscombe *Som'set*	4	V17
Wivelsfield *E Sussex*	6	W23
Wivenhoe *Essex*	7	U25
Wix *Essex*	13	U26
Woburn Sands *Bucks*	12	T22
Woburn *Beds*	12	U22
Woking *Surrey*	6	V22
Wokingham *Berks*	6	V22
Wolf's Castle *Pembs*	9	U14
Wollaston *Northants*	12	T22
Wolsingham *Durham*	21	N20
Wolverhampton *W Midlands*	10	S19
Wolverton *Bucks*	11	T22
Wolviston *Clevl'd*	21	N21
Wombwell *S Yorks*	16	Q21
Wonersh *Surrey*	6	V22
Wonston *Hants*	5	V21
Woodbridge *Suffolk*	13	T26
Woodbury *Devon*	4	W17

Woodchester *Glos*	5	U19
Woodchurch *Kent*	7	V25
Woodcote *Oxon*	6	U21
Woodenbridge *Wicklow*	40	S11
Woodford *Galway*	35	R7
Woodgreen *Hants*	5	W20
Woodhall Spa *Lincs*	12	R23
Woodhouse Eaves *Leics*	11	S21
Woodhouse *S Yorks*	16	R21
Woodlawn *Galway*	35	R7
Woodley *Berks*	6	V22
Woodstock *Oxon*	5	U21
Woodtown *Meath*	37	Q10
Woofferton *Shrops*	10	T18
Wookey Hole *Som'set*	4	V18
Wookey *Som'set*	4	V18
Wool *Dorset*	5	W19
Woolacombe *Devon*	3	V15
Woolavington *Som'set*	4	V18
Wooler *Northum*	21	L19
Woolwich *London*	6	V24
Wooperton *Northum*	21	M20
Woore *Shrops*	10	S19
Wootton Bassett *Wilts*	5	U20
Wootton Bridge *I of Wight*	5	W21
Wootton Wawen *Warwick*	11	T20
Worcester *Heref/Worcs*	10	T19
Worfield *Shrops*	10	S19
Workington *Cumb*	20	N16
Worksop *Notts*	16	R21
Wormit *Fife*	25	K18
Worsbrough *S Yorks*	16	Q21
Wortham *Suffolk*	13	T26
Worthing *W Sussex*	6	W23
Wotton under Edge *Glos*	5	U19
Wragby *Lincs*	17	R23
Wrangle *Lincs*	12	R24
Wrea Green *Lancs*	15	Q18
Wrentham *Suffolk*	13	T27
Wretham *Norfolk*	13	T25
Wrexham *Wrex*	10	R17
Writtle *Essex*	7	U24
Wroughton *Wilts*	5	U20
Wroxham *Norfolk*	13	S26
Wroxton *Oxon*	11	T21
Wyberton *Lincs*	12	S23
Wye *Kent*	7	V25
Wylye *Wilts*	5	V20
Wymondham *Leics*	12	S22
Wymondham *Norfolk*	13	S26

Y

Yalding *Kent*	7	V24
Yarcombe *Devon*	4	W17
Yardley Hastings *Northants*	12	T22
Yarm *Clevl'd*	16	N21
Yarmouth *I of Wight*	5	W21
Yarnton *Oxon*	5	U21
Yarrow *Borders*	20	L17
Yate *Avon*	5	U19
Yatton *Avon*	4	V18
Yaxley *Cambs*	12	S23
Yeadon *W Yorks*	16	Q20
Yealmpton *Devon*	3	X16
Yelverton *Devon*	3	X15
Yeovil *Som'set*	4	W18
Yetminster *Dorset*	4	W18
York *N Yorks*	16	Q21
Youghal *Cork*	39	U8
Youlgreave *Derby*	11	R20
Yoxall *Staffs*	11	S20
Yoxford *Suffolk*	13	T27
Ysbyty Ifan *Aber/Conw*	8	R16
Ysbyty Ystwyth *Card*	9	ST1
Ystalyfera *Neath P Talb*	9	U16
Ystradgynlais *Powys*	9	U16

Z

Zennor *Cornw'l*	2	X12